Creative Small Groups

Ready-To-Use Lessons For Grades K-5

Written By

Karen Gannon Griffith

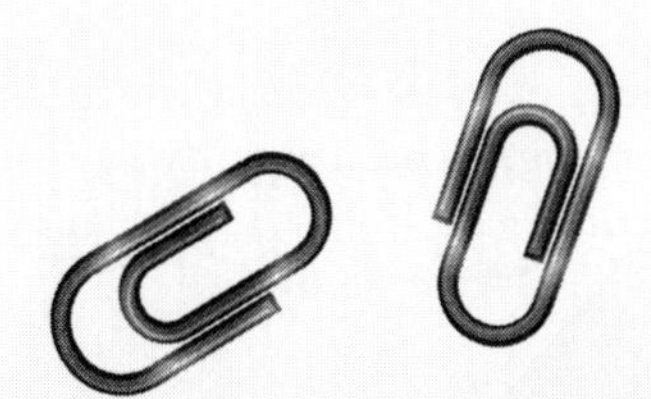

Karen Gannon Griffith, Ed.S.

Karen Griffith has been an educator since 1977. She began teaching fifth grade following graduation from Samford University in Alabama. After earning a master's degree in special education from the University of Tennessee, she began teaching children with behavior disorders. She earned additional degrees in school counseling at Georgia State University and began work as a school counselor in 1986. She considers counseling to be the best job in the school and is passionate about her work. She is actively involved in professional organizations and is a frequent presenter at professional conferences and staff-development workshops.

Dedication

I am always grateful for the people in my life:

My parents Truett and Margaret Gannon, my husband Mike, and my brother Kenny, for providing a loving home base and the belief in me that makes anything seem possible.

My sons Nathan and Patrick and my daughter-in-law Evelyn, who tease me and laugh with me and always make me prove everything I claim.

My colleagues Kelly Cowart, Laura Marantz, Bonnie O'Neil, and John Poidevant, who are always there to encourage and support me and are forever nudging me to try something more.

Thank you.

CREATIVE SMALL GROUPS: READY-TO-USE LESSONS FOR GRADES K-5

Graphic Design: Cameon Funk   Children's Illustrations: Harry Norcross

10-DIGIT ISBN: 1-57543-158-0   13-DIGIT ISBN: 978-1-57543-158-1

Published by mar*co products, inc.
1443 Old York Road
Warminster, PA 18974
1-800-448-2197
www.marcoproducts.com

PRINTED IN THE U.S.A.

Table Of Contents

Introduction

I love small groups. I believe they are the most effective way for a counselor to facilitate change for a student and the best way to establish a meaningful bond with the children who need us most. A small group is an opportunity for the counselor and students to get to know each other in a personal way. Each student discovers an adult in the school who genuinely cares about helping with whatever change the student needs or wants to make. The counselor discovers who the student could become. These discoveries create a sense of normalcy for children whose individual needs, situations, or problems create a sense of being isolated and different from their peers. Learning that others are experiencing similar circumstances can result in a virtual sigh of relief that perhaps one's problems are not so unusual after all. Once a problem seems less daunting, learning can begin. In small groups, significant lessons can be introduced, discussed, and implemented. New skills can be acquired and practiced.

If you want your groups to be meaningful and effective, it's important to know *why* you're doing what you choose to do with each group. If you're facilitating a group on grief or loss, for example, know the phases of grieving and plan a session for each one. Classroom time is precious, and you must be prepared to define and defend your reasons for taking students out of class. Know what you're doing and why and explain your plans and your motivation to the students, their teachers and parents, and the school administrators.

Early in my career, I had many days of panic and frustration when I realized I had another small group meeting in just 15 minutes. What could I do in group sessions? Did I have what I needed to conduct the group? Would the meeting make a difference? This book represents lessons I have put together over 20 years as a school counselor and the organizational system that enables me to teach any of the lessons at a moment's notice.

GRIFFITH'S RULE:

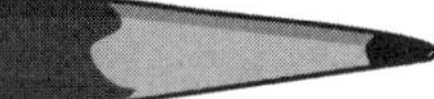

The more you do ahead of time, the less you have to do in the moment.

It's all about being prepared. A little preparation can make a significant difference in your school year. It helps you stay sane, increases your effectiveness, and makes you look like a genius. How can you be prepared? You must know what you need, have it, and know where find it. Collections can be accumulated over time. Begin by collecting games, books, and lessons that relate to one topic. Gather art supplies, specialty items, puppets, stuffed animals, and whatever else you need to support those activities. Then find a way to organize it all. It doesn't do much good to have what you need if you can't find it when you need it.

Group Materials In Boxes

My group materials are stored in boxes approximately 16" x 12" x 8". I have one box for each group, clearly labeled by topic. The title and page number of the lessons in this book are noted on cardstock for quick reference and stored in the box. In this book, you'll find a master list of supplies necessary for each of the lessons described. I keep those supplies in each group's box. When a group is going to meet, all I have to do is grab the appropriate box and my *Creative Small Groups* lesson book. I know I'll have all the materials I need to present any lesson or activity I select. No more moments of panic or frustration.

I keep art supplies like crayons, drawing paper, colored construction paper, magazine scraps, tissue paper scraps, and wiggle eyes for all my groups and store them in a general area where they're easily accessible at all times.

Organize Reproducible Pages In A Master Notebook

Another organizational tool I use is a master notebook with reproducible pages. I place a master copy of any reproducible page needed for any group in a protective sleeve and store it in one large 3-ring binder. Labeled dividers separate easily accessible student pages. During the summer or at the beginning of the school year, I spend quality time with the copy machine and ensure that I have at least 12 copies of each reproducible page. I keep those copies in folders added to the appropriate boxes.

Organize Children's Books In Magazine Boxes

Try storing children's books in magazine boxes, labeled by topic. You can have a box of books on divorce, another box for books on loss, and still another for books on friendship. As your collection grows, buy more boxes and make your labels more specific. Initially, for example, I had one box for friendship books. Now I have several boxes, all related to friendship, including:

Friendship—Getting Along
Friendship—Making New Friends
Friendship—Choosing Wisely
Friendship—Special Problems

Each box contains books related only to that topic. When a problem arises at school, it's easy to find the box containing appropriate books. This is helpful when meeting with individuals as well as with small groups.

Color-Code Questions For Games

Facilitate group discussions with games based on colors. Create sets of color-coded questions or prompts by writing questions or sentence starters on colored index cards. Create a set of questions for each topic you plan to introduce to a group and store the questions in the appropriate box. Use one of your games to see which color card the group member must respond. For example, play a game of pick-up sticks, following the standard rules with one added dimension. A student who successfully picks up a green stick must draw a green card and answer the question on it. Dice with different colors, rather than dots, on each side would also work.

Informing Parents

Parents must be informed of a student's group participation, even if school district policy doesn't require you to inform them. Before enrolling any student in a group, send a parental permission slip home (page 351). When the group has come to an end, the summary sheet (page 352) gives parents an important accounting of what took place during each session.

Assessments

Assessments may be a necessary evil, but they don't have to be difficult. It's possible—and to me, preferable—to use existing data. For groups on improving school behavior, I use discipline referrals and simple teacher reports. Attendance records can indicate a student's attitude toward school. Attitudinal surveys from teachers, group participants, and parents can also be used to show group results. I compare report card grades from one quarter to the next for students in study skills groups. In fact, since group member referrals are supposed to be based on something interfering with academic success, improved report card grades could be used to demonstrate effectiveness of any group. We don't have to claim a specific causal relationship. We just need to show that we helped remove barriers to school success.

You can satisfy accountability by using the ASCA Standards found at the beginning of each group topic. The standards listed are included in the group lessons. For an overall view of ASCA Standards as they relate to the groups as a whole, see the Appendix (pages 342-350).

When you know what a group needs to accomplish and are prepared to present lessons and activities to address those needs, your groups will be more successful. You and the students will enjoy them more. The desired skills and attitudes will be more easily taught and acquired. The impact of group experience will be more evident. Try it! Your own attitude toward group will change and, consequently, your groups will be more effective. You have my word.

Instructions For Using The CD

The CD found on the inside back cover provides ADOBE® PDF files of each group's reproducible pages.

For some of the pages, both color and and black and white versions of the reproducible have been provided. If you use the color version, you may need to slightly modify the instructions provided in the lesson. For example: The kids may not need to color the activity sheet (which may shorten the lesson) or copies should be made on white paper/cardstock rather than the suggested color.

System requirements to open PDF (.pdf) files:

Adobe Reader® 5.0 or newer (compatible with Windows 2000® or newer or Mac OS 9.0® or newer).

These files offer the user color and black and white versions of the reproducible pages found in the book. For example: *094_creativegroups.pdf* is the same as page 94 in the book.

These files cannot be modified/edited.

SMALL-GROUP LESSONS

Anger Management

I have found groups that try to help students manage their anger to be some of the most challenging to facilitate. In the past, I've focused on presenting strategies for responding when angry, rather than helping students understand their own emotions. I've recently tried to focus more on awareness and understanding, and the groups seem to operate more smoothly. Students are given lots of opportunities to talk about their anger, with an emphasis on understanding, expressing, and managing it in healthier ways.

I believe anger is a secondary emotion, and that students having difficulty with angry outbursts are usually dealing with other primary factors. The small group is only one of the ways I work to establish and maintain a close connection to these students throughout the school year. I periodically invite them to lunch with the counselor and sometimes give them the option of bringing a friend. I often choose group members to be my helpers when I present guidance lessons in their classrooms. I believe that only through the ongoing relationship and multiple interventions can change occur.

The lessons in these groups address the following issues:

Grades K/1
Understanding anger
Expressing anger
Escalating anger hurts others
Cooling off

Grades 2/3
Understanding anger
Expressing anger
Escalating anger hurts others
Revenge
Controlling anger
Cooling off

Grades 4/5
Understanding anger
Expressing anger
Escalating anger hurts others
Words and thoughts that fuel anger
Cooling off
Making decisions about angry reactions

SMALL-GROUP LESSONS

Anger Management

GRADES K/1

GRADES 2/3

GRADES 4/5

ASCA STANDARDS, COMPETENCIES, AND INDICATORS FOR SMALL-GROUP LESSONS ON ANGER-MANAGEMENT

Participation in these group activities will address the following ASCA standards, competencies, and indicators:

Domain	**A/ACADEMIC DEVELOPMENT**
A/A:2.3	Use communication skills to know when and how to ask for help when needed
A/A:3.1	Take responsibility for their actions
A/A:3.5	Share knowledge
A/B:1.2	Learn and apply critical thinking skills

Domain	**C/CAREER DEVELOPMENT**
C/A:1.4	Learn how to interact and work cooperatively in teams
C/A:1.5	Learn to make decisions
C/A:2.1	Acquire employability skills such as working on a team, problem-solving and organizational skills
C/C:2.2	Learn how to use conflict management skills with peers and adults
C/C:2.3	Learn to work cooperatively with others as a team member

Domain	**PS/PERSONAL/SOCIAL DEVELOPMENT**
PS/A:1.1	Develop a positive attitude toward self as a unique and worthy person
PS/A:1.2	Identify values, attitudes and beliefs
PS/A:1.5	Identify and express feelings
PS/A:1.6	Distinguish between appropriate and inappropriate behaviors
PS/A:1.7	Recognize personal boundaries, rights and privacy needs
PS/A:1.8	Understand the need for self-control and how to practice it
PS/A:1.9	Demonstrate cooperative behavior in groups
PS/A:2.1	Recognize that everyone has rights and responsibilities
PS/A:2.2	Respect alternative points of view
PS/A:2.3	Recognize, accept, respect and appreciate individual differences
PS/A:2.4	Recognize, accept and appreciate ethnic and cultural diversity
PS/A:2.5	Recognize and respect differences in various family configurations
PS/A:2.6	Use effective communication skills
PS/A:2.7	Know that communication involves speaking, listening, and nonverbal behavior
PS/B:1.1	Use a decision-making and problem-solving model
PS/B:1.2	Understand consequences of decisions and choices
PS/B:1.3	Identify alternative solutions to a problem
PS/B:1.4	Develop effective coping skills for dealing with problems
PS/B:1.5	Demonstrate when, where, and how to seek help for solving problems and making decisions
PS/B:1.6	Know how to apply conflict resolution skills
PS/B:1.9	Identify long- and short-term goals
PS/B:1.10	Identify alternative ways of achieving goals
PS/C:1.3	Learn the difference between appropriate and inappropriate physical contact
PS/C:1.4	Demonstrate the ability to assert boundaries, rights, and personal privacy
PS/C:1.5	Differentiate between situations requiring peer support and situations requiring adult professional help
PS/C:1.6	Identify resource people in the school and community, and know how to seek their help
PS/C:1.9	Learn how to cope with peer pressure
PS/C:1.10	Learn techniques for managing stress and conflict
PS/C:1.11	Learn coping skills for managing life events

Master Supply List For Small Group On Anger

Collect these supplies prior to presenting the group.
Place all special supplies in the same box as the lessons copied on cardstock.

GENERAL SUPPLIES:

- ☐ Chart paper and marker
- ☐ Stapler and staples
- ☐ Scissors
- ☐ Pencils
- ☐ Pens

ART SUPPLIES:

- ☐ Crayons or markers
- ☐ Light-colored construction paper
- ☐ Drawing paper or sketch book
- ☐ Glue/Glue sticks
- ☐ Clay
- ☐ Pipe cleaners
- ☐ Beads

MISCELLANEOUS SUPPLIES:

- ☐ Optional: Collection of stuffed animals or puppets
- ☐ Bags or boxes
- ☐ Inexpensive timers
- ☐ Resealable plastic bags
- ☐ Balloons
- ☐ 2 pitchers
- ☐ Food coloring
- ☐ Eye dropper
- ☐ Oil
- ☐ Small plastic bottles with lids
- ☐ Liquid soap
- ☐ Trash can
- ☐ Index cards
- ☐ Small round balloons
- ☐ Several scoops and funnels
- ☐ Flour
- ☐ Short story or student book that includes problems

COPY ON WHITE CARDSTOCK: *Note*: Heavyweight copy paper may be substituted for cardstock.

- ☐ *Anger-Management Small-Group Lessons,* as a quick reference to each lesson's page number (page 14)
- ☐ *Animal Cards:* several sets cut apart (pages 41-44)
- ☐ *Hall Passes:* one for each student, cut apart (page 46)
- ☐ *Egg-Ons:* one egg for each student, cut out (page 48)
- ☐ *Faulty Belief Cards:* one set, cut apart (page 53)
- ☐ *Faulty Belief Statement Cards:* one set, cut apart (page 54)

COPY ON WHITE COPY PAPER:

- ☐ *Animal Cards:* several sets, cut apart (pages 41-44)
- ☐ *Rules For Getting Your Anger Out: Primary:* one for each student and the leader (page 45)
- ☐ *Rules For Getting Your Anger Out:* one for each student and the leader (page 47)
- ☐ *I Can Control Myself:* one for each student (page 49)
- ☐ *Heat Up Or Cool Down:* one for each student (page 50)
- ☐ *Hot Thoughts That Turn Up The Heat Inside:* one for each student (page 51)
- ☐ *Beliefs That Fuel Anger:* one for the leader (page 52)
- ☐ *Accordion Book:* one or more book for each student (pages 55)

COPY ON COLORED COPY PAPER:

- ☐ *Flip Book Pattern:* one for each student—each page reproduced on different-colored paper, cut out (pages 56-58)

Understanding My Anger

Materials:

For The Leader:
- ☐ Stuffed animals or puppets
  or
  Animal Cards: several sets reproduced on white cardstock and cut apart (pages 41-44)
- ☐ Scissors

Activity:

- ▶ Ask each student to select one stuffed animal/puppet from your collection or an *Animal Card* that reminds him/her of his/her anger. For example:
  - An elephant might represent anger that stomps around and yells, smashing anything nearby.
  - A goat or ram could show anger by butting its head against everything in its path.
- ▶ Have each student describe why he/she chose a particular animal. The following questions may help you elicit appropriate responses. Emphasize any positives or negatives associated with a specific animal and anger.
  - How is your anger like something this animal does?
  - Which of your angry actions or attitudes might make others think of this animal?
  - What might happen when this animal is angry?
  - What usually happens when you act like this animal?
  - What other animal would you rather be like when you're angry?

Understanding My Anger

Materials:

For The Leader:

- ☐ Stuffed animals or puppets from Lesson #1
  or
  Animal Cards from Lesson #1
- ☐ Chart paper and marker or chalkboard and chalk
- ☐ *Animal Cards:* several sets reproduced on white copy paper and cut apart (pages 41-44)
- ☐ Scissors

For Each Student:

- ☐ 9" x 6" piece of light-colored construction paper (standard construction paper, cut in half)
- ☐ Glue stick
- ☐ Crayons or markers

Activity:

- ▶ Ask the students to select the *Animal Card*, stuffed animal, or puppet chosen in Lesson #1 to personify their anger.

- ▶ Then have the students select a different *Animal Card*, stuffed animal, or puppet. This animal should represent the part of each student that demonstrates anger control. Something about this animal should be similar to what might help the student control angry thoughts, words, and actions. For example: A turtle retreating inside its shell could represent the student moving away or withdrawing from people or situations that evoke anger.

- ▶ Allow each student time to explain his/her selection. Encourage the students to identify specific animal characteristics that help control anger. On the chart paper/chalkboard, summarize the responses that relate to anger control.

- ▶ Brainstorm other ideas for controlling anger. Add them to the list.

- ▶ Allow each student to select two of the *Animal Cards* reproduced on white copy paper—one that represents anger and one that represents anger control. These selections may be the same or different from the students' previous selections.

- ▶ Give each student a piece of construction paper, a glue stick, and crayons or markers. Tell the students to color their cards, then glue the cards to opposite sides of the construction paper. Tell the students this paper can be a reminder of these lessons.

Expressing My Anger

Materials:

For The Leader:

- ☐ *Animal Cards* from Lesson #1
- ☐ *Rules For Getting Your Anger Out*: *Primary* reproduced on white copy paper (page 45)

For Each Student:

- ☐ *Rules For Getting Your Anger Out*: *Primary* reproduced on white copy paper (page 45)

Activity:

- ▶ Using the *Animal Cards*, review the problem-causing angry behaviors identified in the previous lesson.

- ▶ Ask the students to brainstorm things they can do to show they are angry without getting into trouble. (stomp feet, scream into pillow, describe feelings, clench fists or tighten muscles, grunt, walk away, etc.)

- ▶ Give each student a copy of *Rules For Getting Your Anger Out: Primary.* Review the rules with the students and compare them with the answers the students gave while brainstorming.

- ▶ Talk about when and where each of these behaviors might be an acceptable way to show anger.

- ▶ Explain that anger usually generates a lot of energy that needs to be released in a safe way. Brainstorm ideas for getting rid of that energy, having the students think about where and when each action might be allowed.

    - Exercising, running, playing basketball, going for a walk
    - Drawing angry pictures (Discuss what to do with these pictures.)
    - Working with clay
    - Blowing up balloons
    - Talking with a friend

- ▶ Challenge the students to practice a safe method of releasing anger during the next week.

Hurting Others/Escalating Anger—The Meanies

Materials:

For The Leader:

- ☐ Chart paper and marker or chalkboard and chalk

For Each Student:

- ☐ Drawing paper
- ☐ Crayons or markers

Activity:

- ▶ Tell the students that everyone has moments or days when bad feelings well up inside. When we're grumpy or tired or sick or just feel bad inside, we sometimes take our bad feelings out on someone else. These Meanies can hurt other people's feelings.

- ▶ Ask the students how we can stop the Meanies from hurting people around us. Write their ideas on chart paper/chalkboard. The students might suggest:

    - Talk with someone about the feelings we have inside.
    - Pay attention to our bodies' warning that we're about to have strong feelings.
    - Use words to express feelings.

- ▶ Remind the students that nothing is worse than hurting inside and being unable to talk about those feelings.

- ▶ Give each student a piece of drawing paper and crayons or markers.

- ▶ Ask the students to draw their Meanies.

- ▶ When the students have finished drawing their Meanies, have them draw a large box around the picture, then add vertical lines in front of it, creating the look of a cage. Around the cage, have them write two things they will do to keep their Meanies caged.

Cooling Off

Materials:

For The Leader:

- ☐ *Hall Passes* reproduced on cardstock and cut out—one copy for each student (page 46)
- ☐ Scissors

For Each Student:

- ☐ Bag or box
- ☐ Crayons or markers
- ☐ Box of 8 crayons
- ☐ Inexpensive timer
- ☐ Drawing paper or sketchbook
- ☐ Balloons
- ☐ Clay in a resealable plastic bag

Activity:

- ▶ Each student will create his/her personal Cool Kit—a bag or box containing items that can be kept in the classroom and used whenever the student feels angry. Talk with the teacher about what the kits will contain and how and when they may be used.
- ▶ Review the methods discussed for releasing anger energy. Decide which methods might be useful in the classroom.
- ▶ Give each student a bag or box large enough to contain the items.
- ▶ Explain that this will be the student's Cool Kit and how it will be used. Tell the students they will fill their Cool Kit with things that can help them release anger energy in a safe way that keeps them out of trouble. They and their teacher will decide where in the classroom to keep the Cool Kits and how to use them. They may want to decide on a silent signal.
- ▶ Let the students decorate their bag or box. Label each one with the student's name and Cool Kit.
- ▶ As the items are placed in each student's Cool Kit, review previous lessons about how to use each item to control anger. You might want to include:
  - "emergency hall passes" which allow the student to walk to a specific place.
  - a small sketch book or book of drawing paper and a box of 8 crayons.
  - clay in a resealable bag.
  - small balloons.
  - a timer—to limit time the student may spend with the Cool Kit.
- ▶ Let the students return to the classroom with their Cool Kits.

Understanding My Anger

Materials:

For The Leader:

- ☐ *Animal Cards:* several sets reproduced on white cardstock and cut apart (pages 41-44).
- ☐ Scissors
- ☐ Chart paper and marker or chalkboard and chalk

Activity:

- ▶ Ask each student to select an *Animal Card* that represents his/her anger. For example, a chimpanzee or gorilla might jump around, yell, and beat its chest. An angry dog might growl, show its teeth, bark, and even bite.

- ▶ Have each student describe why he/she chose a particular animal. The following questions may help you elicit appropriate responses. Emphasize any positives or negatives associated with a specific animal and anger.

  - How is your anger like something this animal does?
  - Which of your angry actions or attitudes might make others think of this animal?
  - What might happen when this animal is angry?
  - What usually happens when you act like this animal?
  - What other animal would you prefer to be like when you are angry?

- ▶ On the chart paper/chalkboard, list all the behaviors and actions the students mention. Review the list after everyone has had a turn to add to it. Use the following questions to discuss which behaviors might cause the most or fewest problems.

  - Which behavior is hardest for you to control?
  - Which behavior gets you into the most trouble?
  - Does anyone else in your family behave this way when angry? What usually happens? How do you feel when your family member does this?

- ▶ Remind the students that they'll work as a group to learn how to control angry behaviors.

Understanding My Anger

Materials:

For The Leader:

- ☐ *Animal Cards* from Lesson #1
- ☐ Chart paper and marker or chalkboard and chalk
- ☐ *Animal Cards:* several sets reproduced on white copy paper and cut apart (page 41-44)
- ☐ Scissors

For Each Student:

- ☐ 9" x 6" piece of light-colored construction paper
- ☐ Glue stick
- ☐ Crayons or markers

Activity:

- ▶ Ask each student to select the *Animal Card* chosen in Lesson #1 to personify his/her anger.
- ▶ Then have each student select a different *Animal Card*. The animal on this card should represent the part of the student that demonstrates anger control. Something about that animal should help the student control angry thoughts, words, and actions.
- ▶ Allow each student time to describe why he/she chose a specific animal. Encourage the students to identify the animals' traits or characteristics that represent a controlled response to anger.
- ▶ Summarize the students' responses on the chart paper/chalkboard.
- ▶ Brainstorm other ideas for maintaining control. Add them to the list.
- ▶ Allow each student to select two of the *Animal Cards* reproduced on white copy paper—one that represents anger and one that represents anger control.
- ▶ Give each student a piece of construction paper, a glue stick, and crayons or markers. Have the students color their cards, then glue the cards to opposite sides of the construction paper. Tell the students these cards can be a reminder of these lessons.

Expressing My Anger

Materials:

For The Leader:

- ☐ *Animal Cards* from Lesson #1
- ☐ *Rules For Getting Your Anger Out* reproduced on white copy paper (page 47)
- ☐ Pipe cleaner
- ☐ 10 colored beads

For Each Student:

- ☐ *Rules For Getting Your Anger Out* reproduced on white copy paper (page 47)
- ☐ Pipe cleaner
- ☐ 10 colored beads

Activity:

- ▶ Using the *Animal Cards*, review the problem-causing angry behaviors already identified.
- ▶ Explain that anger energy must be released in a safe way.
- ▶ Ask the students to brainstorm ways they can safely release their energy to let people know they are angry without getting into trouble. Talk about when and where each of these behaviors might be an acceptable way to show anger.
- ▶ Give each student a copy of *Rules For Getting Your Anger Out.* Discuss each rule. Talk about what might happen if anger energy is not released in an appropriate way.
- ▶ Tell the students that counting to 10 when angry is a way to delay responding. Most students count too fast, so they don't wait long enough before responding. A bead counter can help them learn to count more slowly.
- ▶ Give each student one pipe cleaner and 10 colored beads. Tell the group you're going to show them how to count to 10 more slowly. Using a pipe cleaner and 10 beads, demonstrate each of the following directions as you give them.
    - Fold over about one inch of the end of the pipe cleaner, twisting it around itself to create a loop.
    - Slide the beads onto the pipe cleaner.
    - Fold over about one inch at the other end of the pipe cleaner, creating another loop. These loops keep the beads on the pipe cleaner.

- Tell the students that as they count to 10, they should slide one bead from one end of the pipe cleaner to the other for each number said aloud. Sliding the bead forces the student to pause between numbers.

- Allow time for the students to practice counting to 10, using the beads.

- Encourage the students to use this trick the next time they feel angry.

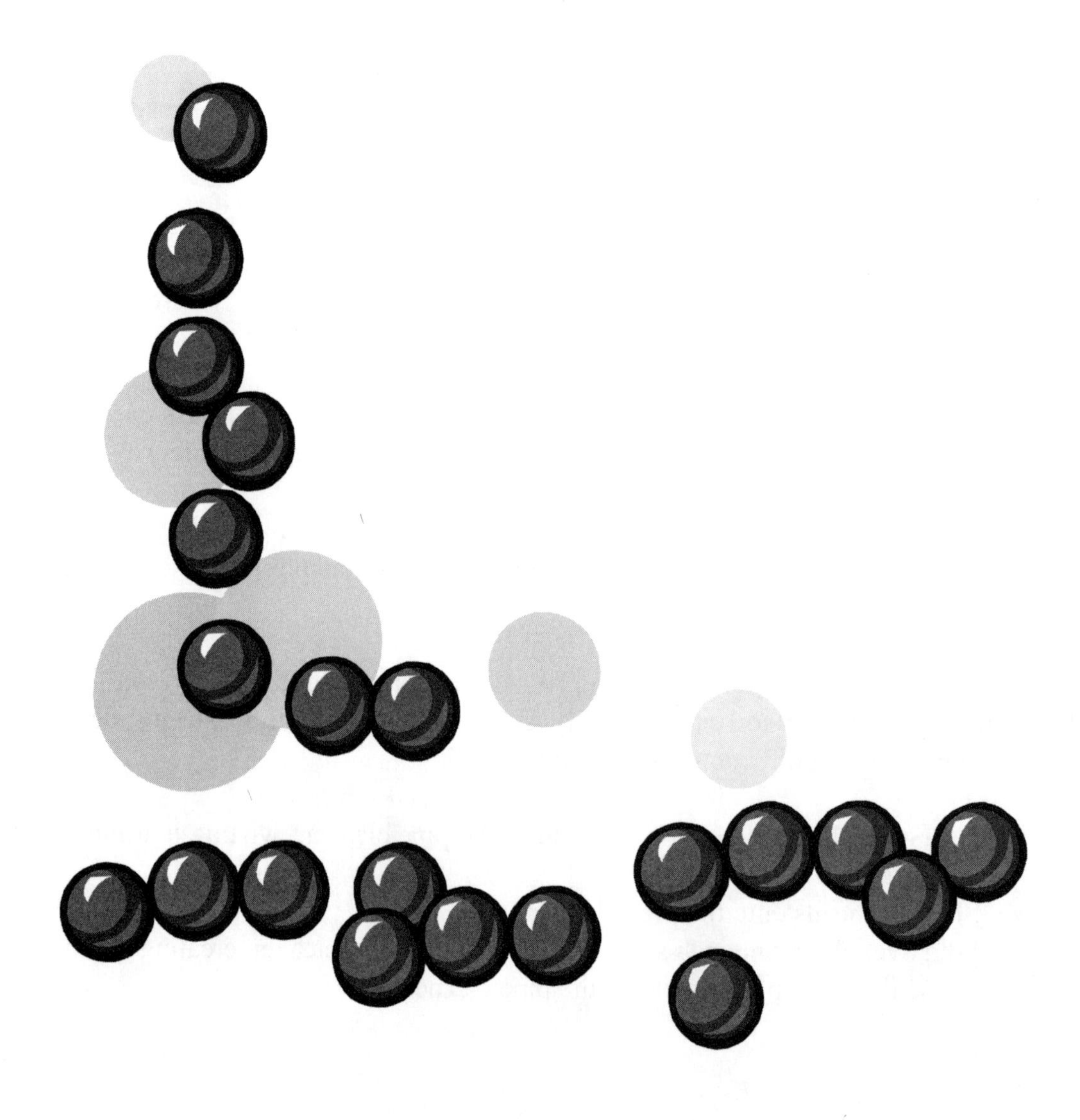

Hurting Others/Escalating Anger—Egg-Ons

Materials:

For The Leader:

- ☐ Chart paper and marker or chalkboard and chalk
- ☐ *Egg-Ons* reproduced on white cardstock and cut out—one egg for each student (page 48)
- ☐ Scissors

For Each Student:

- ☐ Pencil or pen

Activity:

- ▶ Explain that Egg-Ons are words or actions that escalate angry behaviors. An Egg-On can be in our own thoughts, words, and deeds; come from the person with whom we're angry; or come from bystanders watching an angry episode.

- ▶ Provide a few examples:

    - Jim says, "Oh, yeah?" after Joe threatens to beat him up.
    - John bumps into Zach on the way to lunch. Zach thinks, "He did that on purpose. He's always hitting me."
    - Melinda laughs when you mispronounce a word while reading aloud. You call Melinda a name.
    - Sabrina tells Alicia that Laura is telling everyone what Alicia wrote in her diary.

- ▶ Have the students contribute more examples. Create a T-chart and write a few of these examples on the left side of the chart paper/chalkboard.

- ▶ Working together, brainstorm words (or thoughts) that would counter each Egg-On and write those ideas on the right side of the chart paper/chalkboard. Come up with at least one idea for each scenario listed.

- ▶ Give each student a cut-out egg and a pen or pencil. Have the students select one of the Egg-Ons from the list and write it on one side of the egg.

- ▶ On the reverse side of the egg, have the students write a thought or comment that will not escalate their angry feelings or behaviors or those of others.

Hint: Keep a master list of the Egg-Ons the students report. You can use them to create your own set of Egg-On cards that present students with possible real-life situations. Write one scenario on each paper egg, then color or decorate the egg. Save the eggs as a card game in which students read the situation, then describe a better response. An alternative is to write the scenarios on slips of paper and place each paper inside a plastic egg.

Thinking About Revenge

Materials:

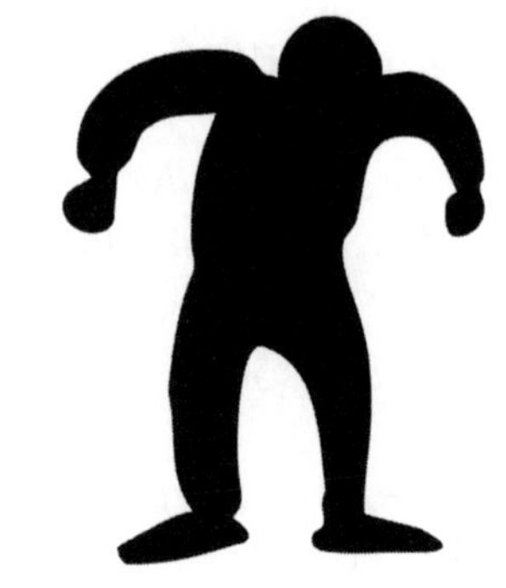

For The Leader:

- ☐ 2 Pitchers—1 empty, 1 filled with water
- ☐ Food coloring
- ☐ Eye dropper
- ☐ Oil (Place a small amount in bottom of the empty pitcher prior to group. The oil keeps the food coloring from dispersing too quickly in the water.)

Activity:

- ▶ Explain that we often think about how we'd like to get back at those we believe have wronged us.

- ▶ Discuss the following points with the group.

    - Thinking about getting even keeps us angry. We cannot let go of anger as long as we think about revenge.
    - Thoughts of revenge hurt only ourselves. The other person isn't even aware of them.
    - As long as we're stuck in our anger, we can't play and have fun.

- ▶ Provide the following examples of possible *revenge* words or thoughts:

    - It's not fair! I'll make her sorry.
    - He can't get away with that! I'll get back at him.
    - I'll show them! Just you wait and see.
    - If he hurts me, I have the right to hurt him back.

- ▶ Have the students suggest additional *revenge* words. Tell them it's important to learn to talk about anger and their angry thoughts. Ask:

    - How does thinking about hurting someone make you feel better about yourself?
    - What can you think instead?

- Demonstrate how thinking of revenge or wanting to get even keeps anger in us.

  - Pour about half the water from the full pitcher into the empty pitcher, explaining that this clear water represents each of us when we are calm and thinking clearly.

  - Explain that the food coloring will represent thoughts of revenge and what those thoughts do to us. Add one drop of food coloring to the water. At first, the food coloring will float on top, but soon it will spread through the water in a ribbon.

  - Ask how we can return the water to the way it was before food coloring was added to it. As each suggestion is made, add more clear water. While the color may lighten, it will not return to clear. Emphasize that the only way to return to clear, calm thinking is to completely get rid of the thoughts of revenge and start with fresh water.

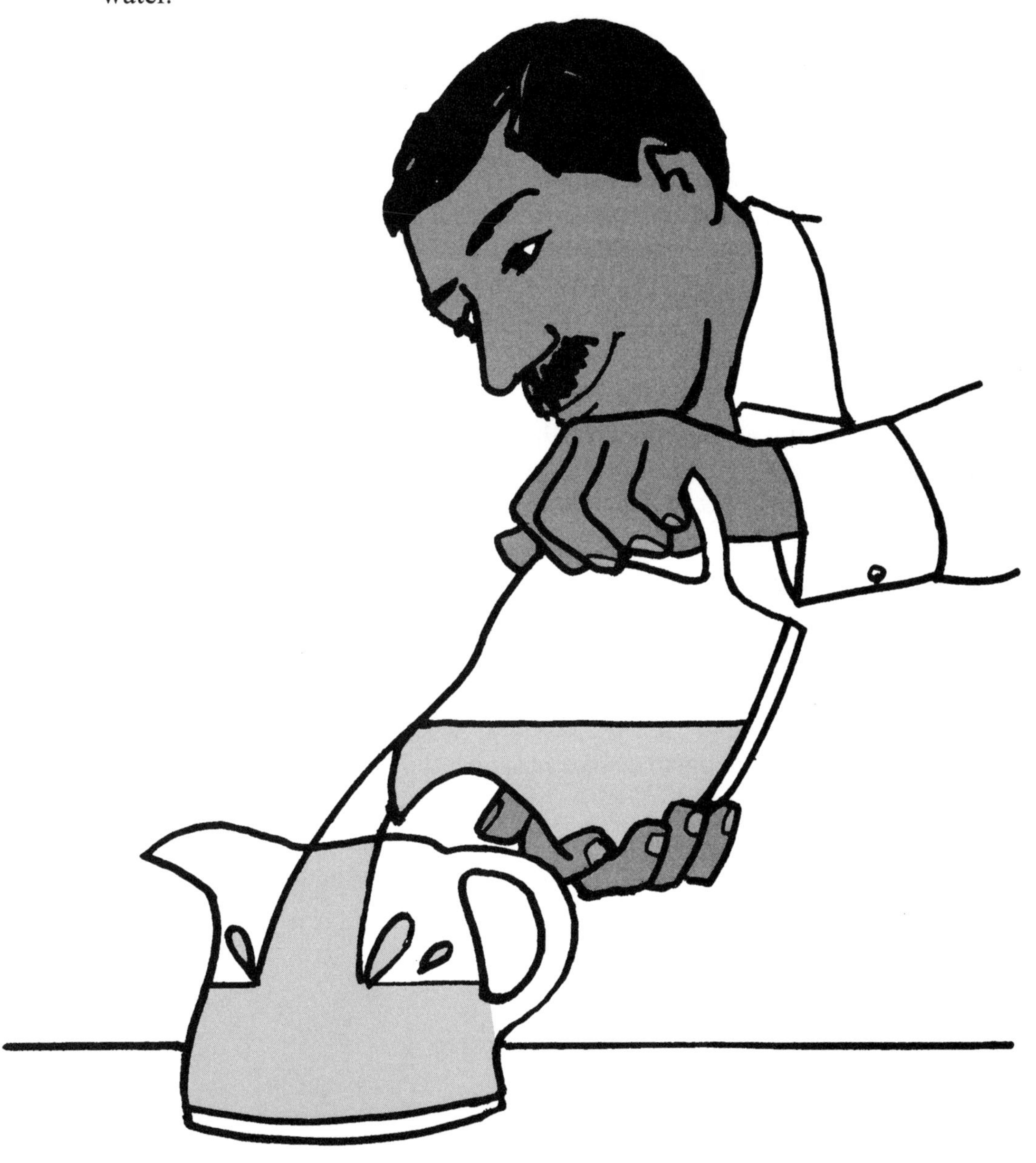

Controlling Anger/Controlling Myself

Materials:

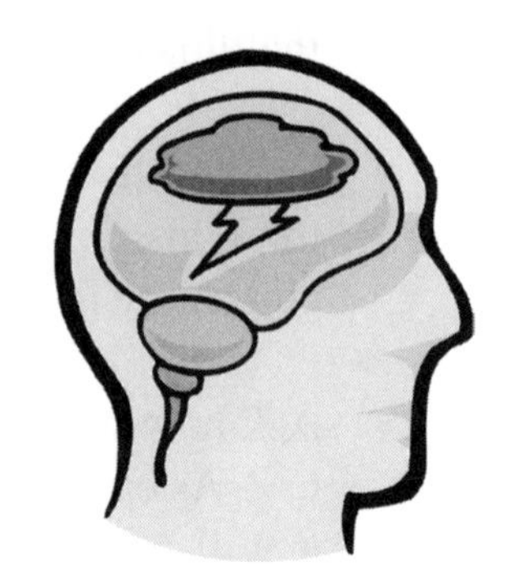

For Each Student:

- ☐ *I Can Control Myself* reproduced on white copy paper (page 49)
- ☐ Pencil

Activity:

- ▶ Ask the students to describe their personal "inside part" that quells their angry words or behaviors. Explain, if necessary, that you're referring to what stops them from hurting others when they're angry. (They may call it a *conscience.*) If the students can remember to pay attention, this inside part will help them think before they act. Examples could be:

    - brain—clear thinking, perspective
    - stomach—nervous, funny feelings
    - heart—caring, love, empathy
    - lungs—calming breaths

- ▶ Clarify the concept by asking:

    - What part of your body might help you control your anger?
    - What might that body part say to you when you're angry? What kinds of words might it use?

- ▶ Give each student a copy of the *I Can Control Myself* worksheet and a pencil.

- ▶ Ask the students to draw the inside part on the body shape and write a word describing how it helps them stay in control. For example, draw a brain and write "think" on the drawing.

- ▶ Have the students add thought bubbles in which they write what their body might say to remind them not to be hurtful.

- ▶ Have the students take the worksheet with them as a reminder of ways to control their hurtful/angry behaviors.

Cool Off And Chill Out

Materials:

For Each Student:
- ☐ Drawing paper
- ☐ Crayons or markers

Activity:

- Discuss the idea of "hot thoughts" that fuel anger. These thoughts may make angry feelings erupt quickly, even with trivial triggers, or keep anger simmering long after the episode ends.
- Ask the students the most outlandish or ridiculous place they can think of to cool down their hot thoughts. Acting silly will enhance creativity. Use the following examples, if necessary:
    - Letting them slide down the bathtub drain after a bath.
    - Sending them to the North Pole.
    - Blowing them into a balloon and sending them into space.
- Explain that releasing anger can be easier if the students can imagine doing what they've suggested the next time they're angry.
- Give each student a piece of drawing paper and crayons or markers.
- Have the students draw the chill-out place for their hot thoughts. When everyone has finished, have the students share their drawings with the group.

Understanding My Anger

Materials:

For The Leader:

- ☐ *Animal Cards:* several sets reproduced on white cardstock and cut apart (pages 41-44)
- ☐ Scissors
- ☐ Chart paper and marker

Activity:

- ▶ Ask each student to select one *Animal Card* that represents his/her anger. For example, a shark might glide silently, then suddenly bite. A skunk may spray "anger" all over everyone, not just the intended target, causing a stink that lingers.

- ▶ Have each student describe why he/she chose a particular animal. If necessary, use the questions below to help students with their descriptions. Emphasize any positives or negatives associated with that animal and anger.

    - What might happen when this animal is angry? What might make this animal angry?
    - How is your anger like something this animal does? Which of your angry actions or attitudes might make others think of this animal?
    - What kinds of things tend to make you angry? What usually happens when you act like this animal?

- ▶ Create two two-column charts on the chart paper. Write all the reasons and behaviors the students mention as being part of their own anger or the animals' anger.

    - Chart 1, column 1: Reasons Animals Get Angry
    - Chart 1, column 2: Angry Animal Behaviors
    - Chart 2, column 1: Reasons People Get Angry
    - Chart 2, column 2: Angry People Behaviors

- ▶ Review the list after everyone has had a turn to speak. Then ask:

    - What are some common reasons why animals and people get angry?
    - Which reasons do you agree with most/least?
    - What behavior is hardest for you to control?
    - Which behavior gets you into the most trouble?
    - Does anyone else in your family behave this way when angry? What usually happens? How do you feel when he/she does this?

- ▶ Remind the students that you'll be working as a group to learn to control these behaviors.

- ▶ Save the two charts for the next session.

Understanding My Anger

Materials:

For The Leader:
- ☐ *Animal Cards* from Lesson #1
- ☐ Charts from the Lesson #1
- ☐ Chart paper and marker

For Each Student:
- ☐ Drawing paper
- ☐ Crayons or markers

Activity:

- Ask each student to find the *Animal Card* chosen in the previous session to personify his/her anger.
- Review the charts created in the previous session.
- Have each student select an animal that might represent control over his/her anger. For example: A turtle retreating inside its shell could represent the student moving away or withdrawing from people or situations that evoke anger. Present this concept by asking:
    - What stops you from acting in a hurtful way or saying hurtful words when you're angry?
    - What about the animal you chose is similar to something that might help you control your angry thoughts, words, and actions?
- Allow each student time to describe why he/she chose a particular animal.. Encourage the students to identify specific animal traits or characteristics that represent a controlled response to anger. Write those traits and characteristics on the chart paper.
- Brainstorm other ideas for maintaining control. Add them to the list.
- Give each student a piece of drawing paper and crayons or markers. Ask the students to draw their two animals—one representing anger and another representing controlled anger. The students should draw both animals on the same side of the paper, perhaps with a line drawn in the center of the paper, between the two animals.
- Ask the students to identify specific animal behaviors that relate to them personally. The students' responses should be based on the reasons they selected the animals. Allow time for them to share their drawings with the group.

Expressing My Anger—Chill Me Out

Materials:

For The Leader:

- ☐ *Rules For Getting Your Anger Out* reproduced on white copy paper (page 47)
- ☐ Small clear plastic soda bottle with lid

For Each Student:

- ☐ *Rules For Getting Your Anger Out* reproduced on white copy paper (page 47)
- ☐ Small plastic bottle with a lid

Have Available For The Group:

- ☐ Water
- ☐ Liquid soap
- ☐ Food coloring—different colors
- ☐ Glue

Preparation:

Using the directions found below, make a Churning Feelings Bottle for demonstration purposes.

Activity:

- ▶ Review the inappropriate angry behaviors identified in the previous session and discuss the problems these behaviors might cause. Display the bottle you made earlier. Shake it vigorously to show how anger can churn up inside us. Set the bottle aside.
- ▶ Ask the students to brainstorm how they can let people know they're angry without getting into trouble. Then discuss when and where each of these behaviors might be acceptable.
- ▶ Explain that anger energy must be released in a safe way. Then brainstorm ideas for getting rid of anger energy. Be sure to consider where and when each behavior might be allowed.
- ▶ Give each student a copy of *Rules For Getting Your Anger Out.* Review the handout with the students. Then discuss what might happen if students don't release anger energy in an appropriate way.
- ▶ Allow the students to make their own Churning Feelings Bottles. Give each student a small clear plastic soda bottle with a lid. Tell the students to fill their bottle with water, liquid soap, and a few drops of food coloring, then to apply glue to the lip of the bottle and screw on the lid.
- ▶ Tell the students to take their Churning Feelings Bottle with them as a reminder of the way angry feelings bubble up, then disperse over time.

Hurting Others/Escalating Anger—The Comeback

Materials:

For Each Student:

- ☐ *Heat Up Or Cool Down* reproduced on white copy paper (page 50)
- ☐ Pencil

Activity:

▶ Explain that another problem often occurs when students use negative words with angry or aggressive people. Provide the following examples, then ask the students for additional suggestions.

- Shut up!
- You just try. I dare you.
- Oh, yeah? Show me.
- Who do you think you are?
- Try and make me.
- You and who else?
- Using curse words
- Name-calling

▶ Tell the students that sarcastic comments create more anger. *Sarcasm* is saying one thing but meaning another and using a tone of voice that doesn't match what's being said. Sarcasm is often accompanied by anger and a sneer. Provide the following examples. Ask the students to add their own.

- Oh, sure! You're *way* smarter than me.
- Of *course,* you'll get to go to recess.

▶ Continue the lesson by saying that anger is fueled by behaviors such as:

- rolling eyes
- sneering
- standing with hands on hips
- clenching fists
- stepping close to the other person, chest first
- making a face

- Discuss why these behaviors sustain or strengthen anger. Help the students see that responding to anger with anger only causes more problems. The person trying to make them lose their cool wins the confrontation.

- Give each student a copy of *Heat Up Or Cool Down* and a pencil. With the students, read aloud the first statement in the left column. Ask the students to imagine themselves in a situation where they would say the words "Shut up." Have a few students give examples. Then ask the students what they could say or do instead of saying "Shut up." Have the students write their ideas in the column to the right of the words "Shut up." Choose a few students to share their ideas. Instruct the students to complete the rest of the worksheet in the same manner. Then have several students share their ideas with the group.

- Ask the students to add other cool-down statements to their worksheet.

Hot Thoughts And Cool Downs

Materials:

For The Leader:

- ☐ *Beliefs That Fuel Anger* reproduced on white copy paper (page 52)
- ☐ *Faulty Belief Cards* reproduced on cardstock and cut apart (page 53)
- ☐ *Faulty Belief Statement Cards* reproduced on cardstock and cut apart (page 54).
- ☐ Scissors

For Each Student:

- ☐ *Hot Thoughts That Turn Up The Heat Inside* reproduced on white copy paper (page 51)

Activity:

- Tell the students that hot thoughts are things we think and say out loud that keep us angry. They turn up the heat inside. (See *Beliefs That Fuel Anger* page 52.)
- After providing the following examples, have the students identify their own hot thoughts.
    - She's mean.
    - I hate him.
    - He's a jerk!
    - It's not fair.
    - He did that on purpose.
    - She doesn't care about me.
    - The teacher hates me.
    - I'll never be able to fix it.
- Use the *Faulty Belief Cards* and *Beliefs That Fuel Anger* to discuss various underlying reasons for hot thoughts—blaming, making mountains out of molehills, accepting only one point of view, etc. Begin with the card labeled *Hot Thoughts.* When you finish discussing each *Faulty Belief Card* concept, place the card face-up on the table.
- Place the *Faulty Belief Statement Cards* face-down on the table. Have each student draw a statement card and tell what type of hot thought it is. He/she should then place the *Faulty Belief Statement Card* with the matching *Faulty Belief Card.* (*Note:* Some *Faulty Belief Statement Cards* may fit into more than one category.)
- Give each student a take-home copy of *Hot Thoughts That Turn Up The Heat Inside.*

Cool Off And Chill Out

Materials:

For The Leader:
- ☐ Trash can

For Each Student:
- ☐ Index card
- ☐ Pencil
- ☐ Small round balloon

Have Available For The Group:
- ☐ Several scoops and funnels
- ☐ Flour

Activity:

- ▶ Explain that it's helpful to have a specific way to express thoughts and feelings. One way is to let bad feelings go by writing them down and tossing the paper into the trash.
- ▶ Give each student an index card and a pencil. Ask the students to think of a time they were angry recently and write it on the index card. Allow the students to tell the group what they wrote.
- ▶ Have each student tear his/her card into tiny pieces and put them into the trash can. Emphasize that the angry feelings go into the trash. Let the students know that as they are throwing their pieces of anger into the trash, they can say something like, "I can use this Cool Tool and Chill Out my anger. I'm throwing my anger away."
- ▶ Continue by telling the students that it's also important to release anger energy. Going for a walk or jog or shooting hoops can provide that release. However, it's not usually possible to do those things in the classroom. This take-home activity provides students with a way to express anger without being hurtful.
- ▶ Set the funnels, scoops, and flour on the table.
- ▶ Give each student an uninflated balloon. Then, using the scoops and funnels, have each student fill his/her balloon with flour. The balloon will not inflate, but will stretch with the flour. When no more flour can be added, help the students tie their balloons.
- ▶ Explain that this balloon can be a stress reliever. Students who start to feel angry can try squeezing the balloon to get rid of some of their anger energy. (*Note:* Rules must be established if students are to be allowed to use these balloons in their classroom.)

I Can Decide

Materials:

For The Leader:

- ☐ Short story or student book that includes problems

For Each Student:

- ☐ *Accordion Book* reproduced on white copy paper (page 55)
- ☐ Pencil or pen
- ☐ Glue stick
- ☐ Scissors

Activity:

- ▶ Tell the students that the longer they hold onto angry or vengeful thoughts, the more likely they are to act on them. Explain that acting on those thoughts will get them into more serious trouble.

- ▶ Discuss what might happen if students act on their anger or desire for revenge. Ask:

  - What will *getting even* do for you?
  - How does that help you? How does that get you what you want?

- ▶ Continue by asking how students can feel good about themselves without getting even. (Being successful is the best payback. Your success can show others how much self-control you have.)

- ▶ Discuss how one decision can change the day for everyone. Select a short story or student book that includes problems. Retell the story briefly, changing the poor decisions or actions, as well the outcome, into something more positive.

- ▶ Give each student a copy of the *Accordion Book.* Instruct the students to cut out, glue, and fold the template to make an accordion book. Have each student complete his/her book based on what will happen if he/she decides *not* to act on angry or vengeful thoughts. For example:

  - Page 1 I did not hit back.
  - Page 2 I went to recess instead of to the office.
  - Page 3 I played soccer with my friends.
  - Page 4 I made a goal.
  - Page 5 My teacher sent a positive note to my parents.
  - Page 6 I got to choose what we had for dinner.

Ending The Group

Materials:

For The Leader:

- ☐ List of topics discussed or activities completed. The list might include:
  - expressing anger appropriately and inappropriately.
  - how to control anger.
  - avoiding things that hurt others.
  - learning not to fuel anger.
- ☐ *Flip Book Pattern:* each page reproduced on different-colored copy paper and cut out (pages 56-58)
- ☐ Scissors

Have Available For The Group:

- ☐ Stapler and staples

Activity:

- ▶ Briefly review the general topics that were discussed during group sessions.
- ▶ Give each student a set of *flip book* pages. Tell the students to write their names in the top rectangle on the first page. Review each page, discussing the ideas students remember regarding that anger-management topic. Then instruct the students to write on each page the best-remembered or favorite strategy from the lesson related to the topic. The students' ideas are written above the title so they're visible only when the pages above are lifted.
- ▶ Staple the completed pages together to create a *flip book* in which the top page is shortest and the final page is longest. The specific topic is written at the bottom of each page, so it is visible at all times.
- ▶ Congratulate the students on what they've learned. Tell them the *flip book* can serve as another reminder of the new skills and tools they now have.
- ▶ Tell the students you know they will continue to manage their anger in healthy ways.

ANIMAL CARDS

Copy each page on cardstock, then cut the cards apart. Use with *Understanding My Anger* lessons.

ANIMAL CARDS

Copy each page on cardstock, then cut the cards apart. Use with *Understanding My Anger* lessons.

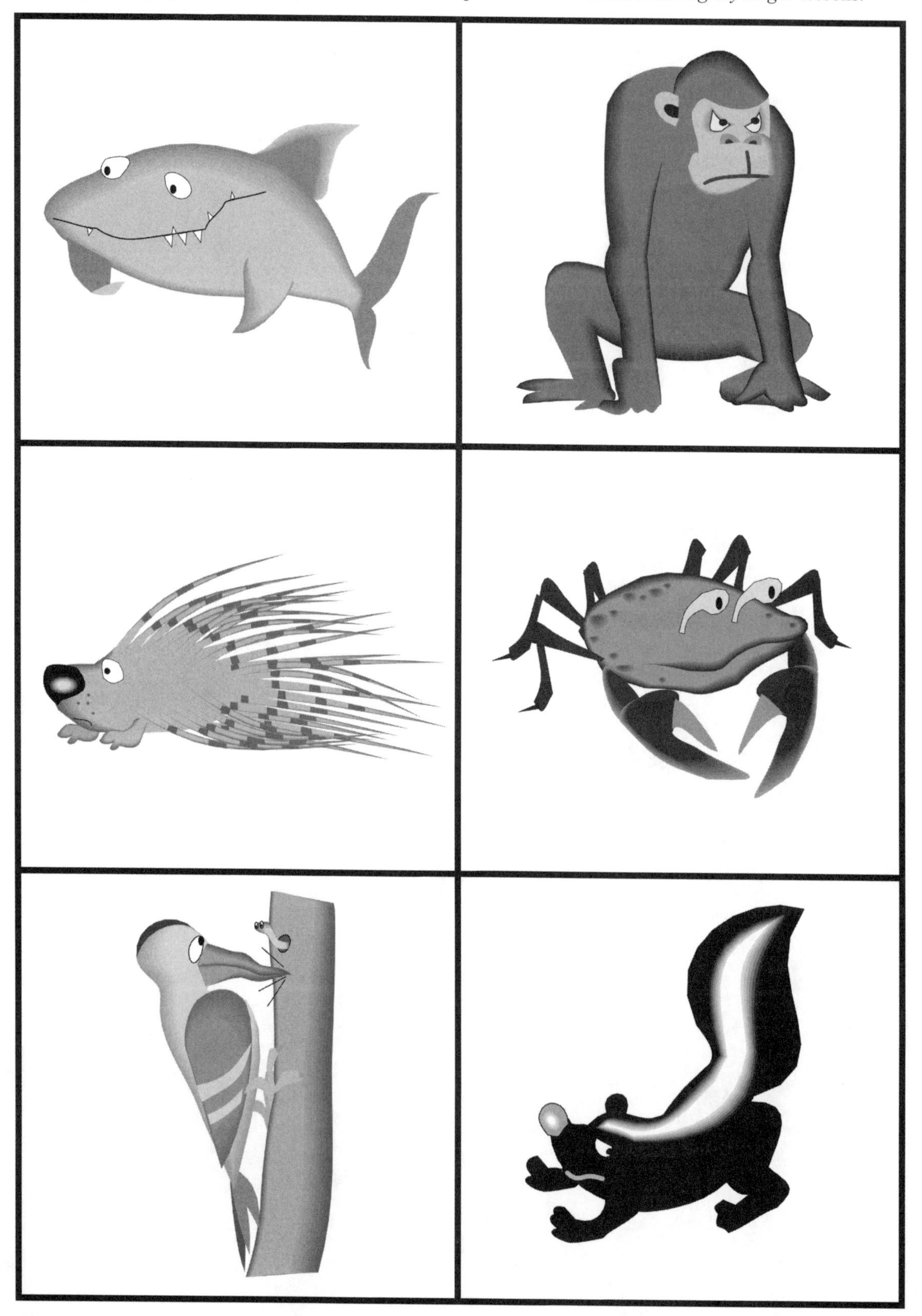

ANIMAL CARDS

Copy each page on cardstock, then cut the cards apart. Use with *Understanding My Anger* lessons.

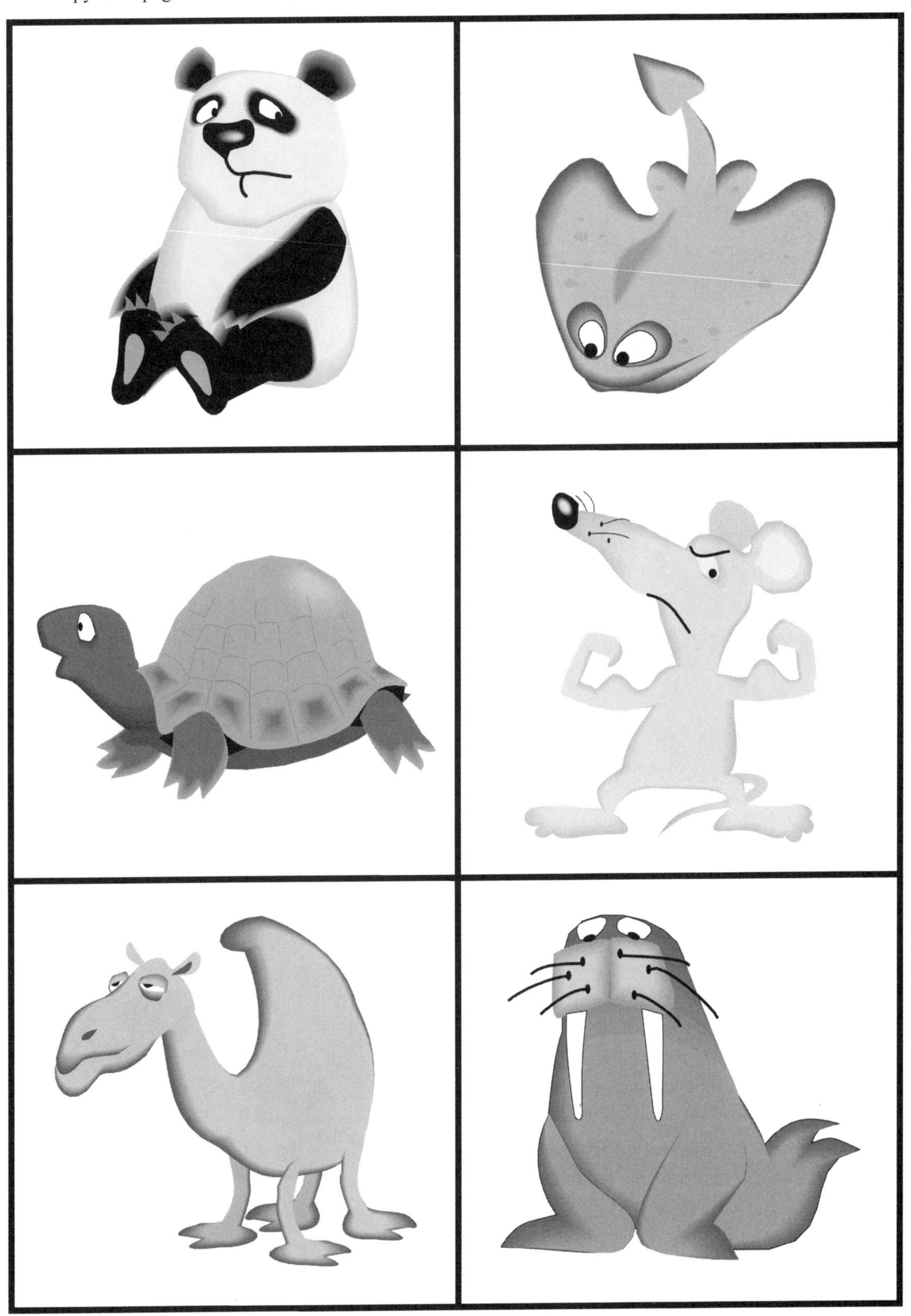

ANIMAL CARDS

Copy each page on cardstock, then cut the cards apart. Use with *Understanding My Anger* lessons.

RULES FOR GETTING YOUR ANGER OUT

BREATHE!

Blow your anger out.

AND THINK:

Make a healthy choice.

DO NOT HURT

anything or anyone with your hands, feet, or voice.

SAY:

"I feel **ANGRY.**
I want you to____."

WALK AWAY.

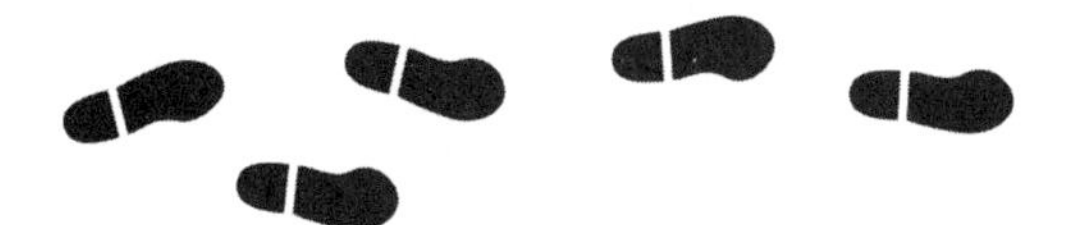

HALL PASSES

Hall Pass

This ticket allows ______________________________

to walk to the gym. Student is to return directly to class from the gym.

Time left class: ____________ Time left gym: ____________

Date: ____________________ Teachers' Initials: _____ _____

Hall Pass

This ticket allows ______________________________

to walk to the art room. Student is to return directly to class from the art room.

Time left class: ____________ Time left art room: ____________

Date: ____________________ Teachers' Initials: _____ _____

Hall Pass

This ticket allows ______________________________

to walk to the counselor's office. Student is to return directly to class from the counselor's office.

Time left class: ____________ Time left office: ____________

Date: ____________________ Teachers' Initials: _____ _____

RULES FOR GETTING YOUR ANGER OUT

Check your tummy, jaws, and fists.
Are you getting angry?

Breathe!
Blow your anger out.

Stop and think:
Make a healthy choice.

People are not to be hurt
with your hands, feet, or voice.

Things may not be hurt with your hands or feet.

Use firm words, not your fists.

Say "I feel angry. I want you to ____."

Take a time-out if you need it
to get your control back.

Go to a safe place and talk to yourself.

Pat yourself on the back.

EGG-ONS

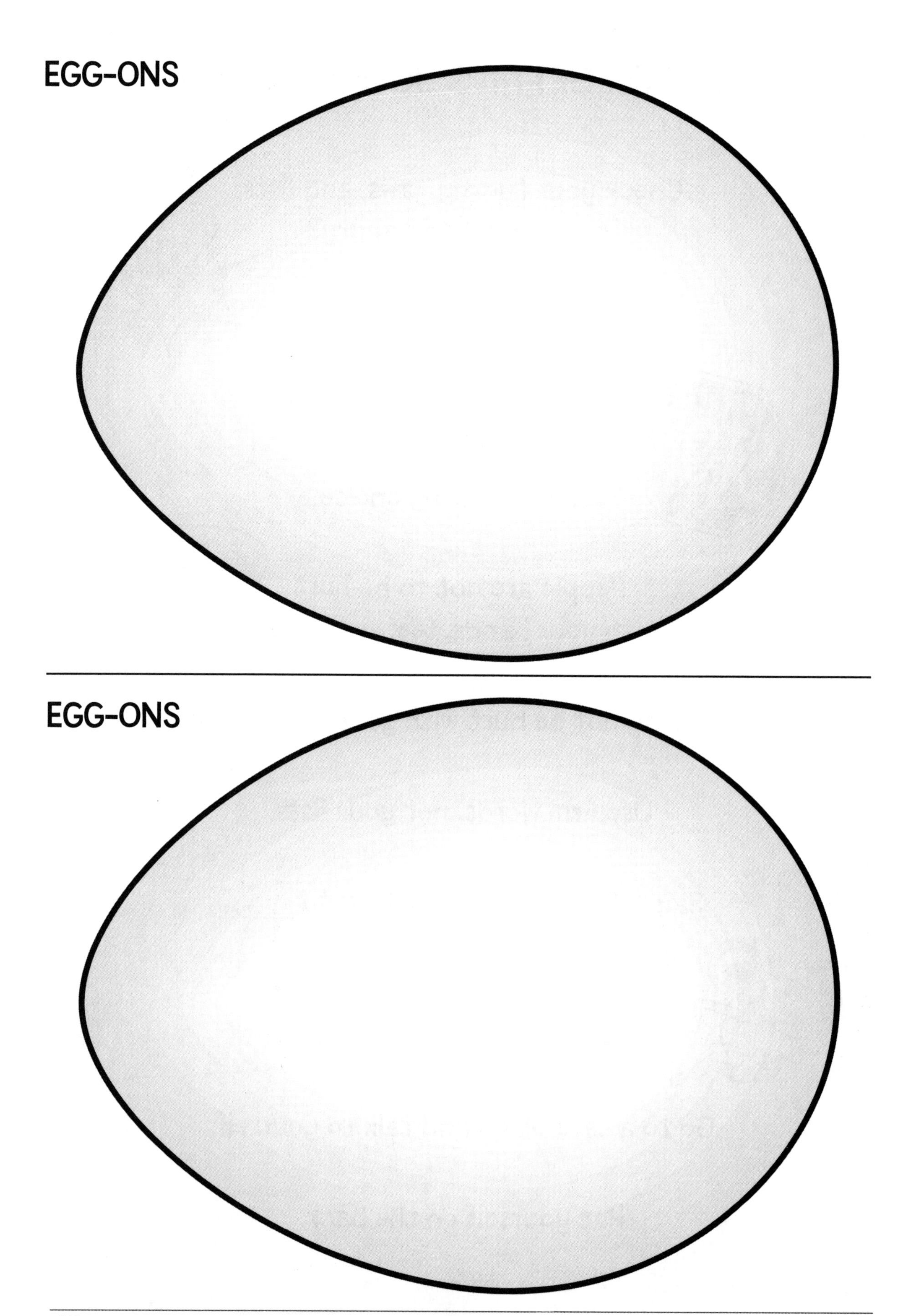

EGG-ONS

I Can
Control
Myself

Heat Up or Cool Down

What could you do or say instead?

These are things people might say or do that create more anger.	These are things people might say or do that create more feelings of calm.
Shut up!	
Roll your eyes.	
Just try me!	
Oh, yeah? Make me!	
You're just a crybaby!	
Make a fist and pretend to use it.	
I dare you to try!	
Use curse words.	
Kick your desk.	
I'm telling!	

HOT THOUGHTS

THAT TURN UP THE HEAT INSIDE

Name-calling or labeling someone in a negative way.
You jerk! You are crazy.

Making judgments and "should" statements that create a sense of injustice.
He should not try to boss me. If he does, it's OK for me to get angry.

Blaming others instead of looking at one's own part in what went wrong.

Assuming that everyone is out to get you.
Thinking that the other person meant to harm you. She did that on purpose.

Making mountains out of molehills.
Blowing things out of proportion.
Does it really matter? Can you can forget or ignore it?

Seeing things from only one point of view.
I was right and that's all there is to it. There's no way they could be right.

Revenge thoughts.
Getting upset and wanting to hurt others who are different or weak.
I hate having people like her in my class.
If she doesn't like what I do, she can go back where she came from.

Posturing or acting tough and superior to others to cover up bad feelings inside.

BELIEFS THAT FUEL ANGER

Name-Calling:

Calling people names doesn't solve problems. Name-calling only keeps people angry at each other. Instead of calling names, try to figure out what to do.

Seeing Things Only From Your Point Of View:

Insisting that people see things the way you do is another way of staying upset. Insisting your way is the only way is a control issue. Becoming angry because other people do things differently is a waste of energy. Judging others and worrying about what they do use up time you could spend being happy.

Not Taking Responsibility For Your Part Of The Situation: (Blaming)

Blaming others is a defense against feeling bad inside. People who cannot take responsibility for their behavior turn the energy toward someone else.

Mountains Out Of Molehills:

Making small things seem catastrophic is another way of turning up the heat inside. Blowing up over small things can be a learned response to stress. Making mountains out of molehills can also be a way of trying to get attention.

Assuming Others Are Out To Get You: (Everybody's Against Me)

Making assumptions about other people's negative motivations is another way of staying angry. Students sometimes base actions on assumptions they believe to be true. Teach them to distinguish between facts and assumptions. Advise them that a reality check is in order when they're in doubt about someone's motivations. A reality check involves asking for an opinion of a bad situation. When it doubt, check it out!

FAULTY BELIEF CARDS

Hot Thoughts	Blaming— Not Taking Responsibility
Only One Point Of View	Making Mountains Out Of Molehills
Everybody's Against Me	Name-Calling
Revenge Thoughts	Posturing

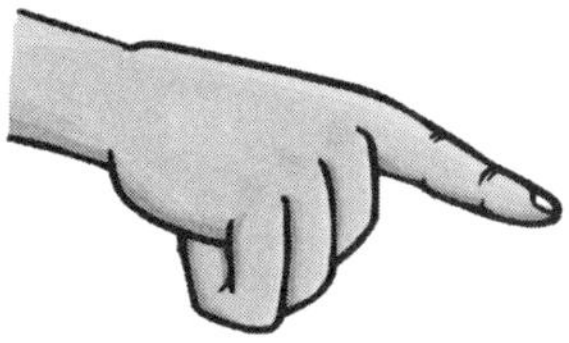

FAULTY BELIEF STATEMENT CARDS

You're a jerk.	My way or the highway!
It's not my fault. He made me do it.	He took my pencil. He has to buy me a new one.
Everyone always picks on me.	I don't care what you say. I know I'm right.
He bumped into me in line. He should lose recess.	I'm always last in line. The teacher hates me.
Crybaby… crybaby… crybaby!	You're just a tattletale.
You did that on purpose.	I want to do it my way.
Her desk is too close to mine.	You started it.
I wouldn't push you if you stayed on your side of the room.	I could tell you were talking about me.
You're the only one who could have taken it.	I'm always blamed for what goes wrong.
She shouldn't even be here. She should go back where she came from.	If someone hits me, I can hit back.
Margo is standing with her hands on her hips frowning, staring into Kelly's face.	Ralph shakes his fists in Miguel's face.

ACCORDION BOOK TEMPLATE

Provide at least one copy to each student. One copy will create a six-page accordion book. Adding strips will provide additional pages. Cut out the strips and glue the small tab to the back of the next strip. Fold the book at the lines to create an accordion book.

GLUE THIS TAB BEHIND NEXT STRIP.

GLUE THIS TAB BEHIND NEXT STRIP. IF LAST PAGE OF BOOK, REMOVE THIS TAB.

FLIP BOOK PATTERN

Copy one set on colored paper for each student. Cut apart each page. You may copy each set on a different color and distribute the pages so students receive a different color for each page. Their books will be unique and colorful.

My Flip Book

What My Anger Looks Like

Things I Cannot Do In Anger

Expressing Anger In A Healthy Way

Stopping My Anger From Getting Bigger

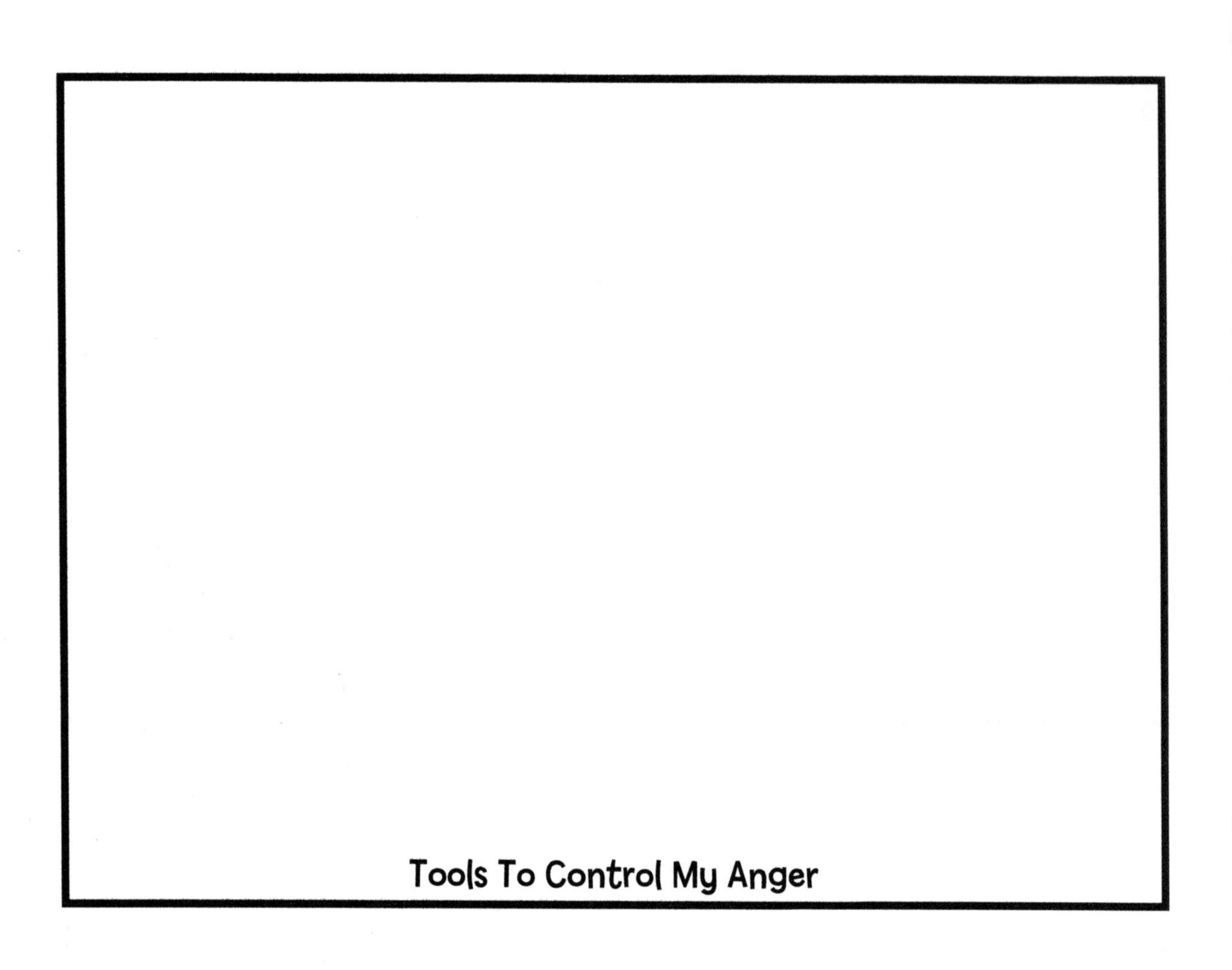
Tools To Control My Anger

SMALL-GROUP LESSONS

Behavior

Students may be referred because of aggression, passivity, inappropriate language, anxiety, and a host of other behaviors. Students may be grouped with others who behave the same way, and sometimes there's a mixture of behaviors. No matter what the configuration, behavior groups are extremely challenging for the counselor. Too many passive or shy students will challenge the counselor to elicit contributions, while too many over-active students can be difficult to settle down. Regardless of participants' ages or group composition, the counselor should have a reason for choosing any activity.

The following goals should be addressed for each grade level:

Grades K/1
Identifying trouble-causing behaviors and their consequences
The need for rules
Sharing
Words and phrases that calm inappropriate behaviors

Grades 2/3
Identifying positive behaviors
The need for rules
Behavior-related feelings
Problem-solving situations

Grades 4/5
Positive behaviors from students' perspectives
Positive behaviors from adults' perspectives
Behavior-related feelings
Actions that trigger negative behaviors
Problem-solving situations

SMALL-GROUP LESSONS

Behavior

GRADES K/1

GRADES 2/3

GRADES 4/5

ASCA STANDARDS, COMPETENCIES, AND INDICATORS FOR SMALL-GROUP LESSONS ON BEHAVIOR

Participation in these group activities will address the following ASCA standards, competencies, and indicators:

Domain	**A/ACADEMIC DEVELOPMENT**
A/A:1.5	Identify attitudes and behaviors which lead to successful learning
A/A:3.1	Take responsibility for their actions
A/A:3.1	Demonstrate the ability to work independently, as well as the ability to work cooperatively with other students
A/A:3.5	Share knowledge
A/B:1.2	Learn and apply critical-thinking skills
A/B:2.5	Use problem-solving and decision-making skills to assess progress toward educational goals
A/B:2.6	Understand the relationship between classroom performance and success in school
C/A:1.3	Develop an awareness of personal abilities, skills, interests, and motivations
C/A:1.4	Learn how to interact and work cooperatively in teams
C/A:1.5	Learn to make decisions

Domain	**C/CAREER DEVELOPMENT**
C/A:1.6	Learn how to set goals
C/A:2.1	Acquire employability skills such as working on a team, problem-solving and organizational skills
C/C:2.1	Demonstrate how interests, abilities, and achievement relate to achieving personal, social, educational and career goals.
C/C:2.2	Learn how to use conflict management skills with peers and adults
C/C:2.3	Learn to work cooperatively with others as a team member

Domain	**PS/PERSONAL/SOCIAL DEVELOPMENT**
PS/A:1.1	Develop a positive attitude toward self as a unique and worthy person
PS/A:1.2	Identify values, attitudes and beliefs
PS/A:1.3	Learn the goal setting process
PS/A:1.5	Identify and express feelings
PS/A:1.6	Distinguish between appropriate and inappropriate behaviors
PS/A:1.7	Recognize personal boundaries, rights and privacy needs
PS/A:1.8	Understand the need for self-control and how to practice it
PS/A:1.9	Demonstrate cooperative behavior in groups
PS/A:1.10	Identify personal strengths and assets
PS/A:2.1	Recognize that everyone has rights and responsibilities
PS/A:2.2	Respect alternative points of view
PS/A:2.3	Recognize, accept, respect and appreciate individual differences
PS/A:2.4	Recognize, accept and appreciate ethnic and cultural diversity
PS/A:2.5	Recognize and respect differences in various family configurations
PS/A:2.6	Use effective communication skills
PS/A:2.7	Know that communication involves speaking, listening, and nonverbal behavior
PS/B:1.1	Use a decision-making and problem-solving model
PS/B:1.2	Understand consequences of decisions and choices
PS/B:1.3	Identify alternative solutions to a problem
PS/B:1.4	Develop effective coping skills for dealing with problems
PS/B:1.5	Demonstrate when, where, and how to seek help for solving problems and making decisions
PS/B:1.6	Know how to apply conflict resolution skills
PS/B:1.9	Identify long- and short-term goals
PS/B:1.10	Identify alternative ways of achieving goals
PS/C:1.3	Learn the difference between appropriate and inappropriate physical contact
PS/C:1.4	Demonstrate the ability to assert boundaries, rights, and personal privacy
PS/C:1.5	Differentiate between situations requiring peer support and situations requiring adult professional help
PS/C:1.6	Identify resource people in the school and community, and know how to seek their help
PS/C:1.9	Learn how to cope with peer pressure
PS/C:1.10	Learn techniques for managing stress and conflict
PS/C:1.11	Learn coping skills for managing life events

Master Supply List
For Small Group On Behavior

Collect these supplies prior to presenting the group.
Place all special supplies in the same box as the lessons copied on cardstock.

GENERAL SUPPLIES:

- ☐ Chart paper and marker
- ☐ Scissors
- ☐ Pencils
- ☐ Unlined paper

ART SUPPLIES:

- ☐ Crayons or markers
- ☐ String or yarn
- ☐ Glue
- ☐ Glue sticks
- ☐ Wiggly eyes
- ☐ Construction paper (light blue, red, brown, black, green, gray, and other colors)
- ☐ Poster board
- ☐ Unlined paper
- ☐ Black marker
- ☐ Ribbon
- ☐ Optional: Heavy wrapping paper
- ☐ Optional: Cardboard
- ☐ Drawing paper
- ☐ Optional: Gold glitter
- ☐ White cardstock
- ☐ Wooden craft spoons (ice cream spoons)
- ☐ Paint and paintbrushes
- ☐ Wiggly eyes
- ☐ Black pipe cleaners
- ☐ Black fine-tip markers
- ☐ Various decorative art/craft supplies

MISCELLANEOUS SUPPLIES:

- ☐ Simple commercial board game suitable for participants' age
- ☐ Paper lunch bags
- ☐ Photograph or drawing of a classroom
- ☐ Inexpensive prizes

COPY ON WHITE CARDSTOCK: *Note*: Heavyweight copy paper may be substituted for cardstock.

- ☐ *Behavior Small-Group Lessons* as a quick reference to each lesson's page number (page 60)
- ☐ *Feelings Faces Cards:* one set cut apart (page 91)
- ☐ *Tools Of Emotion Cards:* one set for each student, cut apart (page 92)
- ☐ *Role-Play Cards:* one set reproduced on white cardstock (page 100)

COPY ON COLORED CARDSTOCK:

- ☐ *Keys To Good Behavior:* several keys for each student, cut out (page 85)

ONE COPY FOR EACH STUDENT ON WHITE COPY PAPER:

- ☐ *Wanted* (page 86)
- ☐ *Face Shapes* (page 87)
- ☐ *Magic Words* (page 88)
- ☐ *The Perfect Student* (page 89)
- ☐ *The Gift Of Good Behavior* (page 90)
- ☐ *A Perfect School* (page 95)
- ☐ *Student Interview Questions* (page 96)
- ☐ *Adult Interview Questions* (page 97)
- ☐ *Kettle* (page 99)
- ☐ *You Can't Get My Goat* (page 101)
- ☐ *Fence Pickets* (page 102)
- ☐ *The Better Bees* (page 103)

ONE COPY FOR EACH STUDENT ON COLORED COPY PAPER:

- ☐ *Sun:* on yellow paper (page 93)
- ☐ *Rays:* on yellow paper (page 94)
- ☐ *Gold Coins:* on gold paper (page 98)

Keys To Good Behavior

Materials:

For The Leader:
- ☐ Chart paper and marker or chalkboard and chalk
- ☐ *Keys To Good Behavior:* several keys for each student reproduced on colored cardstock and cut out (page 85)
- ☐ Scissors
- ☐ String or yarn—one short length per student

For Each Student:
- ☐ Pencil

Activity:

- ▶ Introduce the lesson by asking:
    - What behaviors get you into trouble with the teacher?
    - What usually happens when someone gets into trouble in class?
- ▶ Ask the following questions. List these positive behaviors on the chart paper/chalkboard.
    - What do you think teachers want students to do in class?
    - Without saying names, think about your classmates who are really good students. What are some things a good student does?
- ▶ Show the students the key cutouts. Ask them what keys do (open doors, start engines, unlock things). Explain that these keys can help them get started as good students or open the door to school success.
- ▶ Give each student several key shapes and a pencil.
- ▶ From the positive behaviors list, have the students select positive classroom behaviors they can practice, then write one behavior on each key. Students who are unable to write may draw pictures depicting the positive behaviors.
- ▶ String each student's collection of key shapes together and allow the students to take the key chains with them as a reminder of positive behaviors.

Who Needs Rules?

Materials:

For The Leader:

- ☐ Simple commercial board game suitable for participants' age

Activity:

- ▶ Ask:

  - What are some of the rules in your class? In our school?
  - Why do you think we have these rules?
  - What would school be like if we didn't have rules?

- ▶ Invite the students to join you in a game without rules. Everyone (including you) may play any way he/she wishes. Initially, students will want to follow the rules, especially if they're familiar with the game. Keep reminding them that this game has no rules. You may do outlandish things during the game. Play until someone gets frustrated.

- ▶ Ask:

  - How did you like playing the game that way?
  - What funny or silly things happened?
  - What upset you?
  - How do rules help us be fair?

- ▶ If time permits, play the game again. This time, follow the normal rules. Discuss the difference between the two experiences.

Wanted Poster

Materials:

For The Leader:

- ☐ Optional: Instant camera and film or digital camera
- ☐ Optional: Color printer
- ☐ Optional: Glue

For Each Student:

- ☐ *Wanted!* reproduced on white copy paper (page 86)
- ☐ Crayons or markers

Activity:

▶ Introduce the lesson by asking:

- What would your "best self" be like?
- What do you wish you were like in the classroom?

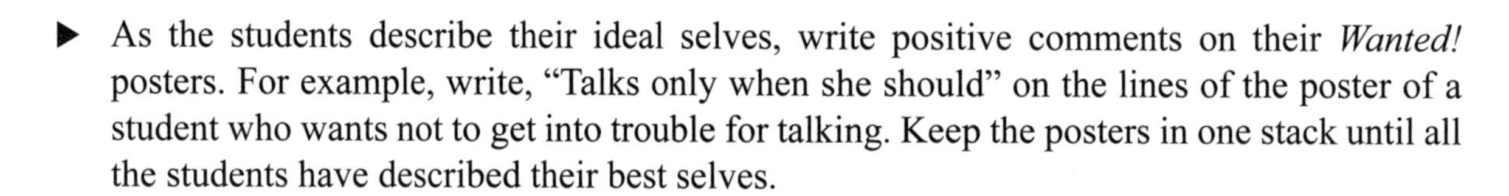

▶ As the students describe their ideal selves, write positive comments on their *Wanted!* posters. For example, write, "Talks only when she should" on the lines of the poster of a student who wants not to get into trouble for talking. Keep the posters in one stack until all the students have described their best selves.

▶ Give each student his/her *Wanted!* poster and crayons or markers. Have the students draw a self- portrait on the poster. (If you have a camera, you may take a picture of each group member to glue in the square.)

▶ Allow the group members to take their posters back to class as a reminder of how they want to behave.

Puppet Plays

Materials:

For The Leader Or The Students:
- ☐ Paper lunch bags
- ☐ Crayons or markers
- ☐ Optional: Various art/craft supplies

Preparation:

Make the paper-bag puppets. Depending on the students' skills and the time available, you may make the puppets, partially make the puppets and let the students add details, or allow the students to make the puppets themselves. To make the puppets:

- fold the bag flat. Draw or create a face on the bottom of the bag.
- the mouth should line up with the bottom edge, which folds over and lies on the body of the bag.
- the upper lip is on the bottom of the bag. The lower lip is on the body of the bag.
- other details may be added if desired.

Activity:

- ▶ Give each student one paper bag puppet or have the students complete or make the puppets. Have the students place their hands inside the bag. They can manipulate the fold to open and close the mouth.

- ▶ Use the puppets to act out polite conversations that fit each scene in the following role-plays. Change any names that are the same as participants' names.

    - Jerry is standing in the recess line behind Sam when Carrie cuts in front of him. Jerry steps out of line and smacks Carrie for getting in front of Sam.
    - When it's time to go home, Randy can't find his book bag. He starts to throw and kick things.
    - Melissa and Kim argue about whose shoes are nicer. Kim calls Melissa a name.
    - Barb bumps into Patty in the lunch line. Patty shoves Barb into Karen. Karen falls down.
    - Chris raises his hand several times to answer, but the teacher never calls on him. He gets angry and yells that the teacher is mean and he hates her.

- ▶ Complete as many scenarios as time permits. Students may add their own scenarios. You or the students may write, "I can use polite words" on the back of the puppets. Remind the students to practice polite conversation and to notice when others use polite conversation. Allow the students to take the puppets with them.

Classroom Sharing

Materials:

For The Leader:
- ☐ Photograph or drawing of a classroom

For Each Student:
- ☐ *Face Shapes* reproduced on white copy paper (page 87)

Have Available For The Group:
- ☐ Various colors of construction paper
- ☐ Various craft supplies
- ☐ Crayons or markers
- ☐ Scissors
- ☐ Glue sticks

Activity:

- ▶ Show the students the classroom picture.
- ▶ Ask:
    - What in the picture shows sharing?
    - What must you share in your classroom?
    - How do classmates work together?
    - What would make the classroom better?
- ▶ Give each student a copy of *Face Shapes*. Tell the students they're going to make self-portraits. Instruct them to cut out the face shape, glue it to a piece of construction paper, then add details (yarn for hair, wiggly eyes, etc.). In order to make it necessary for the students to share with each other, provide limited art supplies. As the students work, acknowledge those who are sharing well. Your attention to positive sharing will encourage this behavior.
- ▶ Conclude the lesson with a discussion of how sharing made completing the self-portraits possible.
- ▶ Ask for examples of how sharing could make the classroom a better place.

Magic Words

Materials:

For Each Student:

- ☐ *Magic Words* reproduced on white copy paper (page 88)
- ☐ Scissors
- ☐ Glue stick
- ☐ Pencil
- ☐ Crayons or markers

Activity:

- ▶ Discuss magic words that help us get along with each other and usually create pleasant feelings. (please, excuse me, you're welcome, thank you, I'm sorry, etc.)

- ▶ Give each student a copy of *Magic Words*, scissors, a glue stick, a pencil, and crayons or markers. Tell the students to cut the paper along the heavy black lines

- ▶ Tell the students to color the title page. Then discuss each magic word mentioned earlier and determine when during the school day the word would be helpful and/or useful. Have the students write one word on each page and draw an illustration for each word.

- ▶ Glue and fold the accordion book:

    - Glue the small second strip to the back of the third block of the strip with the title page on it. Do not glue it behind the title block.
    - You should now have one long strip with Magic Words in the first block.
    - Fold the strips at each line to make an accordion or fan shape. Fold the strip first one way, then the other. Be sure the title shows when the folds are completed.

- ▶ Tell the students to take their books back to class. They (or their teachers) may make tally marks each time each magic word is used in the classroom.

A Perfect Student

Materials:

For The Leader:

- ☐ Poster board with outline drawing of a boy or girl
- ☐ Black marker

For Each Student:

- ☐ *The Perfect Student* reproduced on white copy paper (page 89)
- ☐ Pencil

Activity:

▶ Ask the students:

- How do you think teachers want students to behave in school?
- How do you think parents want their children to behave in school?
- Which of your classmates is a really good student? How does this student behave in class? Be specific.
- Why do you think these positive behaviors are good for the school? For teachers? For students?

▶ As the positive behaviors are identified, write them on and around the outline on the poster board. For example, you could write "listens to the teacher" near the ears or "walks in line" on the feet.

▶ Give each student a copy of *The Perfect Student* and a pencil. Allow time for the students to create their own perfect student by writing on and around the outline the positive behaviors they consider most important.

Who Needs Rules?

Materials:

For The Leader:

☐ Optional: Inexpensive prizes

Preparation:

Think of some short, silly contests to present to the students. Collect any needed materials. Contests could be:

- Guess how many beans are in a jar.
- Everyone tries to draw a horse.
- List words that rhyme with *play.*
- The number of jumping jacks completed in a minute.

Activity:

▶ Ask the students:

- What are some of the rules in your class? In our school?
- Why do you think we have these rules?
- What would school be like if we didn't have rules?

▶ Explain that you'll be conducting a contest that has no rules and that you will determine the winner.

▶ Conduct several contests. Do things that go against the participants' assumption that common rules apply. For example, ask the students to guess how many beans are in a jar. Declare the student with the worst guess the winner. If you are using prizes, give that student a prize.

▶ After completing the contests, ask:

- What was it like to participate in these contests?
- What funny or silly things happened?
- What upset you?
- How do rules help us be fair?

▶ Remind the students that rules help ensure order, safety, and fairness. Ask them to notice between now and the next meeting how rules benefit them.

Good Gifts

Materials:

For The Leader:
- ☐ Chart paper and marker or chalkboard and chalk

For Each Student:
- ☐ *The Gift Of Good Behavior* reproduced on white copy paper (page 90)

or

Make several one-dimensional gift packages for each student using:
- ☐ Construction paper or heavy wrapping paper and cardboard
- ☐ Glue
- ☐ Ribbon
- ☐ Scissors
- ☐ Gift tags

Preparation:

If you are not using *The Gift Of Good Behavior* activity sheet, make several one-dimensional gift packages for each student:

- Cut several rectangles from construction paper or heavy wrapping paper. You may need to glue the wrapping paper rectangles to cardboard rectangles to make them sturdier.
- Glue ribbon or strips of construction paper across the rectangle to make it look like a package. Or make a bow from ribbon and glue it to the package. A flat bow will work best.
- Attach a tag to each package.

Optional: Have the students make gift packages at the beginning of the session.

Activity:

▶ Give each student a copy of *The Gift Of Good Behavior,* a pre-made gift package, or have the students make gift packages.

▶ Explain that behavior can be a gift you give to others at home and at school. You may decide to be patient and quiet while Mom shops for groceries, giving her your gift of good behavior. You may give your teacher the gift of listening quietly to her instructions.

- Generate a list of positive behaviors the children can give teachers, classmates, friends, and/or family. Write these on chart paper/chalkboard.
- Ask the students to select which listed behaviors they're willing to "give" someone. Then have the group members write one behavior on each package.
- Each package should include a "To: ____" tag identifying to whom this gift of good behavior will be given.
- If the *The Gift Of Good Behavior* activity sheet was used, tell the students to cut out each package.
- Encourage the students to give their gifts to those whose names are written on the tag.

Feelings Influence Behavior

Materials:

For The Leader:

- ☐ *Feelings Faces Cards* reproduced on white cardstock and cut apart (page 91)
- ☐ Scissors

For Each Student:

- ☐ *Tools Of Emotion Cards* reproduced on white cardstock and cut apart (page 92).

Activity:

- ▶ Give each student a set of *Tools Of Emotions Cards*.
- ▶ Ask the students to use their *Tools Of Emotions* to demonstrate how they show their feelings (stamp feet when angry, stick out bottom lip when pouting, smile when happy, etc.).
- ▶ Discuss how different events can evoke different feelings.
- ▶ Place the *Feeling Faces Cards* face-down in the center of the table.
- ▶ Have each student draw a *Feeling Faces Card*, suggest an event that might evoke that feeling, and show which *Tools Of Emotions* could be used to show that feeling.
- ▶ Discuss the possible results of using the selected tools for showing the specified emotion.
- ▶ When appropriate, suggest more effective or healthier ways to show the emotion.
- ▶ Continue the activity until all group members have an opportunity to participate.

Problems and Solutions

Materials:

For Each Student:
- ☐ Drawing paper
- ☐ Crayons or markers
- ☐ Pencil

Activity:

- ▶ Give each student a piece of drawing paper, a pencil, and crayons or markers.
- ▶ Tell the students to fold the drawing paper in half, lengthwise, then unfold it. On the left side of the fold line, they should illustrate a particular problem that might occur in the classroom. No one should see anyone else's drawing until every drawing is complete.
- ▶ Allow each group member to show and describe the problem he/she illustrated.
- ▶ Discuss and brainstorm possible solutions to each situation presented.
- ▶ Tell the students to illustrate, on the right side of their paper, a solution developed in the brainstorming session.
- ▶ Encourage each student to explain why he/she selected that particular solution.

Gonna' Shine!

Materials:

For The Leader:

- ☐ Chart paper and marker or chalkboard and chalk

For Each Student:

- ☐ *Sun* reproduced on yellow copy paper (page 93)
- ☐ *Rays* reproduced on yellow copy paper (page 94)
- ☐ Large piece of light blue construction paper
- ☐ Glue stick
- ☐ Pencil
- ☐ Scissors
- ☐ Gold glitter (optional)

Activity:

- ▶ Encourage the students to name things about behavior that the group experience has taught them. List the students' responses on the chart paper/chalkboard.
- ▶ Give each student a copy of *Sun* and *Rays*, a piece of light blue construction paper, a pencil, scissors, a glue stick, and gold glitter (optional).
- ▶ Instruct the students to cut out the sun and rays, glue the rays in the center of the blue construction paper, then glue the sun in the center of the rays.
- ▶ Tell the students to write one idea about good behavior on each ray. They may select from the ideas listed on the chart paper/chalkboard or write their own.
- ▶ Ask the students to add "STUDENT'S NAME Is Gonna' Shine!" to the blue paper.
- ▶ If time permits, the students may add glitter outlines to the rays.
- ▶ Have each student share his/her completed sun with the group, telling what good behaviors he/she plans to use.

A Perfect School

Materials:

For The Leader:

- ☐ Poster board
- ☐ Red, brown, light blue, and gray construction paper
- ☐ Markers
- ☐ Scissors
- ☐ Chart paper and marker or chalkboard and chalk
- ☐ Glue

For Each Student:

- ☐ Optional: *A Perfect School* reproduced on white copy paper (page 95)
- ☐ Optional: Pencil

Preparation:

On poster board, create a simple line drawing of a school building. Cut out:

- enough red construction-paper rectangles (bricks) to cover the front of the building.
- one brown rectangle for a front door.
- light blue rectangles for windows.
- a gray triangle or strip for the roof.

Activity:

▶ Ask the following questions. List each identified behavior on the chart paper/chalkboard.

- How do you think teachers want students to behave in school?
- How do you think parents want their children to behave in school?
- Think of someone who is a really good student. How does this student behave in class? Be specific.
- Why do you think these positive behaviors are good for the school? For teachers? For students?

▶ Allow the students to create their perfect school by writing the positive behaviors on the cutout components. Depending on the students' sophistication, you may write the most basic behaviors on foundation bricks and write on the roof behaviors requiring greater commitment to learning. Then glue the cutout bricks, etc. to the outline of the school.

▶ Optional: Give each student a copy of *A Perfect School* and a pencil. Have the students copy the listed behaviors on their personal school building as a reminder of positive behaviors.

Interviews

Materials:

For Each Student:

- ☐ *Student Interview Questions* reproduced on white copy paper (page 96)
- ☐ *Adult Interview Questions* reproduced on white copy paper (page 97)
- ☐ Pencil

Preparation:

Determine which adults will be available to interview during the time allotted for the lesson.

Activity:

- ▶ Give each student a copy of the *Student Interview Questions* and a pencil.
- ▶ Have the students complete the activity sheet.
- ▶ Then ask:
  - What problem behaviors do you think occur most often in this school?
  - How would you describe the overall behavior of students in this school?
  - What do you think should happen when someone misbehaves in school?
  - How do you think the adults in this school would answer these questions?
- ▶ Divide the group into pairs. Give each student a copy of *Adult Interview Questions*.
- ▶ Review the expectations for the interviews:
  - Each pair of students will interview two adults in the school.
  - Determine who will interview whom and allow time for the interviews. (Fifteen minutes is usually ample time to complete the two interviews.)
- ▶ When the students have completed the interviews, compare the answers they heard. Compare these adult perspectives to the students' perspectives.
- ▶ Optional: Invite peer mediators, safety patrol members, or other positive role models to partner with students who cannot conduct interviews by themselves.

Behavior Fortune

Materials:

For The Leader:
- ☐ Chart paper and marker or chalkboard and chalk

For Each Student:
- ☐ *Gold Coins* reproduced on yellow copy paper (page 98)
- ☐ *Kettle* reproduced on white copy paper (page 99)
- ☐ Marker
- ☐ Scissors
- ☐ Glue/glue stick
- ☐ Optional: Glitter

Preparation:

Optional: To shorten the lesson, cut out the gold coins and sprinkle them with glitter.

Activity:

- ▶ Give each student a copy of *Gold Coins* and *Kettle*, scissors, glue, and a marker. Have the students cut out the gold coins. Optional: Give each student gold glitter. Have the students make a glue line around the edge of the coin, then sprinkle it with glitter.

- ▶ Explain that our behavior can be worth a great deal to those around us. When you decide to cooperate in the classroom, everyone accomplishes more and feels better. When you decide to be tolerant in gym class of someone you dislike, everyone can participate in the activity/game.

- ▶ On the chart paper/chalkboard, list positive behaviors valuable to teachers, classmates, friends, and/or family.

- ▶ Ask the students to select the behaviors they are willing to try and write one of the chosen behaviors on each of their gold coins.

- ▶ Tell the students to glue their coins of good behavior at the top of their kettles.

What Will You Do?

Materials:

For The Leader:

- ☐ *Role-Play Cards* reproduced on white cardstock and cut apart (page 100)
- ☐ Scissors

Activity:

- ▶ Tell the students they'll perform role-plays demonstrating a poor behavior choice or a good behavior choice.
- ▶ Optional: Have the group generate a list of problem situations that often lead to misbehavior. Write each chosen idea on a blank *Role-Play Card.*
- ▶ Place the stack of *Role-Play Cards* in the center of the group. Ask one group member to select one card, read it aloud, and demonstrate a poor choice of how to handle the situation. Then have the same student demonstrate a better choice.
- ▶ Other group members may offer suggestions and role-play that same situation before the next group member selects a card.
- ▶ Give each student a chance to perform a role-play.

Feelings Influence Behavior

Materials:

For The Leader:
- ☐ *Feelings Faces Cards* reproduced on white cardstock and cut apart (page 91)
- ☐ Scissors

Activity:

- ▶ Discuss the relationship between *feelings* and *behavior.* (When we feel tired or frustrated, we may anger more easily and act out in unusual ways. If we're worried about an upcoming parent-teacher conference, we may act mean to a classmate who is a better student.)

- ▶ Place the *Feelings Faces Cards* face up where all the group members can easily see them.

- ▶ Identify events or situations in school that may evoke strong feelings.

    - An upcoming test
    - Parent-teacher conferences
    - A poor grade on a test
    - Being teased by a classmate
    - Losing a game/race in P.E.
    - Forgetting homework/project/etc.
    - A fight with a friend
    - Having to leave the classroom

- ▶ Ask the students to use the *Feelings Faces Cards* to identify how these events might make them feel.

- ▶ Discuss the behaviors/misbehaviors that might follow.

- ▶ Examine positive ways to handle feelings.

You Can't Get My Goat!

Materials:

For The Leader:

- ☐ Chart paper and marker or chalkboard and chalk

For Each Student:

- ☐ *You Can't Get My Goat!* reproduced on white copy paper (page 101)
- ☐ *Fence Pickets* reproduced on white copy paper (page 102)
- ☐ 12" x 18" piece of green construction paper
- ☐ Scissors
- ☐ Glue

Activity:

- ▶ Explain that *You can't get my goat* is an old-fashioned way of saying that someone who deliberately tries to aggravate or annoy another person won't elicit a strong reaction.

- ▶ Ask the students what classmates (or adults) do or say that can "get their goat." Examples might include: name-calling, talking about their mother, threatening, etc. Identify the feelings each statement or action might evoke.

- ▶ Brainstorm ideas for the students to use when something like this happens. Examples might include: pretending not to notice or hear, moving away from the annoying person, deep breathing, or positive self-talk. Write their suggestions on the chart paper/chalkboard.

- ▶ Give each student a copy of *You Can't Get My Goat!* and *Fence Pickets,* a piece of green construction paper, glue, and scissors. Have the students cut out the goat and glue it in the center of the green paper.

- ▶ Tell the students to cut out the fence pickets and write on each picket one idea that might help when someone tries to get their goat. Glue the pickets around the goat, emphasizing that these ideas will prevent others from "getting their goat."

- ▶ If time allows, practice role-playing one or two suggestions. To prevent hurt feelings, the leader should act as the irritant.

You'd Better Bee

Materials:

Have Available For The Group:

- ☐ Wooden craft spoons (ice cream spoons)
- ☐ Paint and paintbrushes
- ☐ Wiggly eyes
- ☐ Glue
- ☐ White cardstock
- ☐ Scissors
- ☐ Black pipe cleaner
- ☐ Black fine-tip markers
- ☐ Paper slightly larger than frame's center hole

For Each Student:

- ☐ Optional: *The Better Bees* reproduced on white copy paper (page 103)
- ☐ Optional: Pencil

Preparation:

Optional: Using the activity directions, make a sample to show the students.

Activity:

- ▶ Have the students sit around the table so they'll have easy access to the materials on it. If you made a sample, show it to the students.

- ▶ Tell the students they will be making a framed list of behavior rules or reminders. Each student will make one bee, one frame, and one list of rules or reminders. Give the following instructions:

    - **Bee:** Paint the bowl end of the craft spoon black. Paint yellow and black stripes on the handle. Use the handle of the paintbrush, dipped in paint, to create small pink cheeks and a white nose on the top/spoon end. Glue on wiggly eyes. Cut wing shapes from the white cardstock. Glue wings to the sides of the bee body. Glue short, curled pieces of black pipe cleaner to each side of the bee's head.

      Frame: Cut a frame from the white cardstock. Using a black fine-tip marker, draw dashes around the frame to show the bee's flight path. Write "You'd better" on the frame. Glue the finished bee to the frame to complete the phrase.

Rules: Give each student a paper rectangle slightly larger than the frame's center hole. On it, have the students write the rules or reminders they have learned in the group. Glue the completed list to the frame.

- Optional*:* If you're using *The Better Bees*, give each student a copy of the worksheet and a pencil. On the sheet, have the students write the rules/reminders they have learned in group sessions.

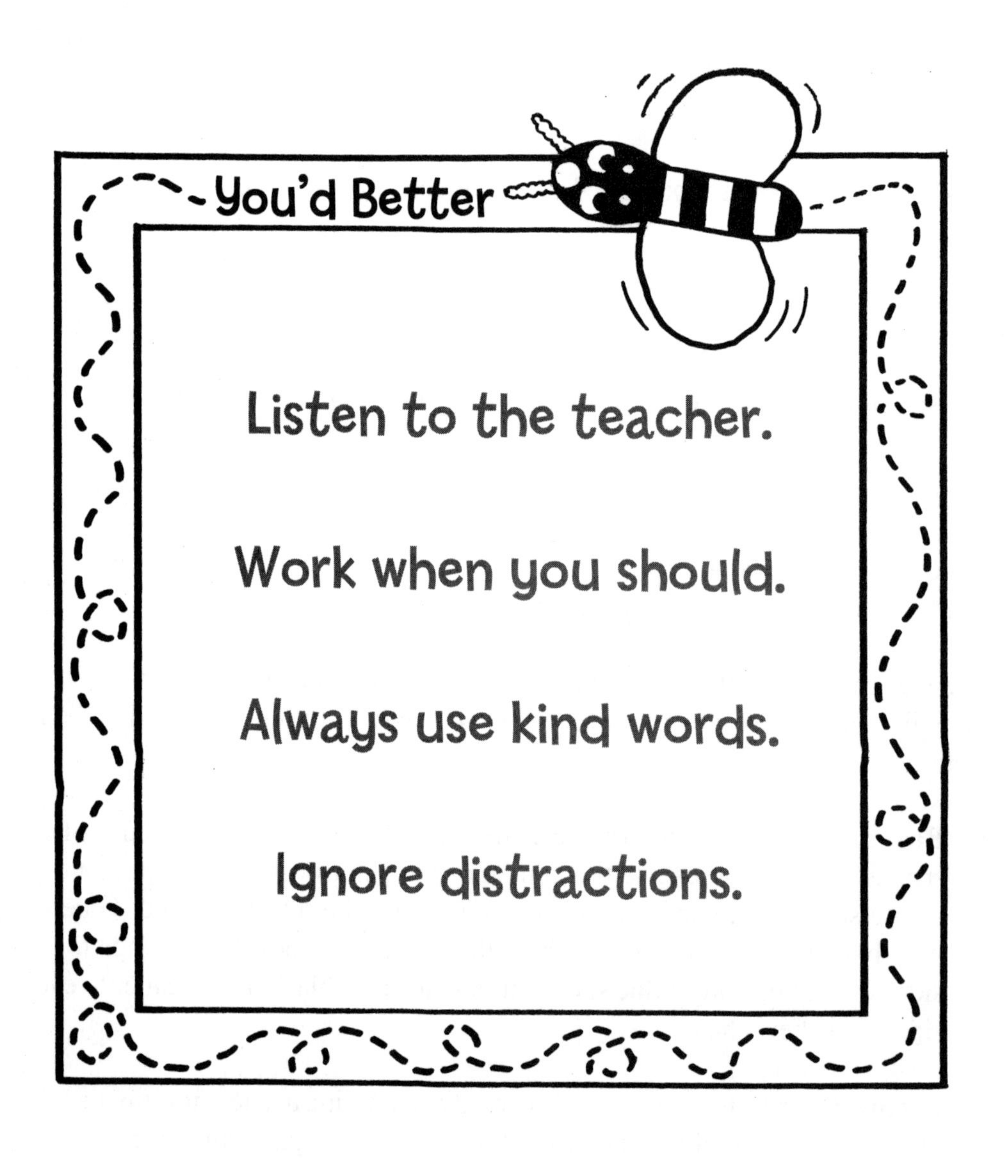

KEYS TO GOOD BEHAVIOR

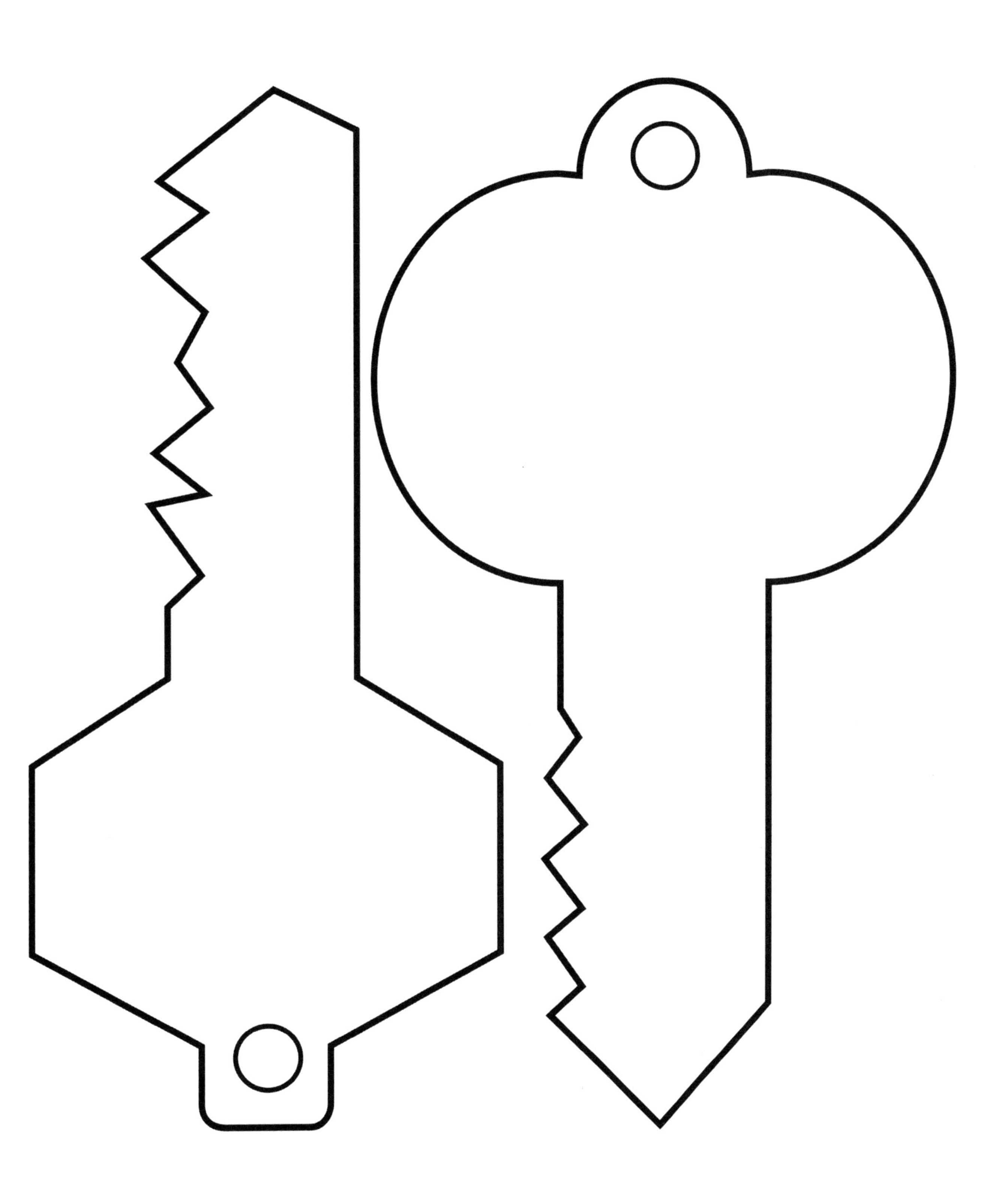

WANTED

MY BEST SELF

____

____

____

____

____

FACE SHAPES

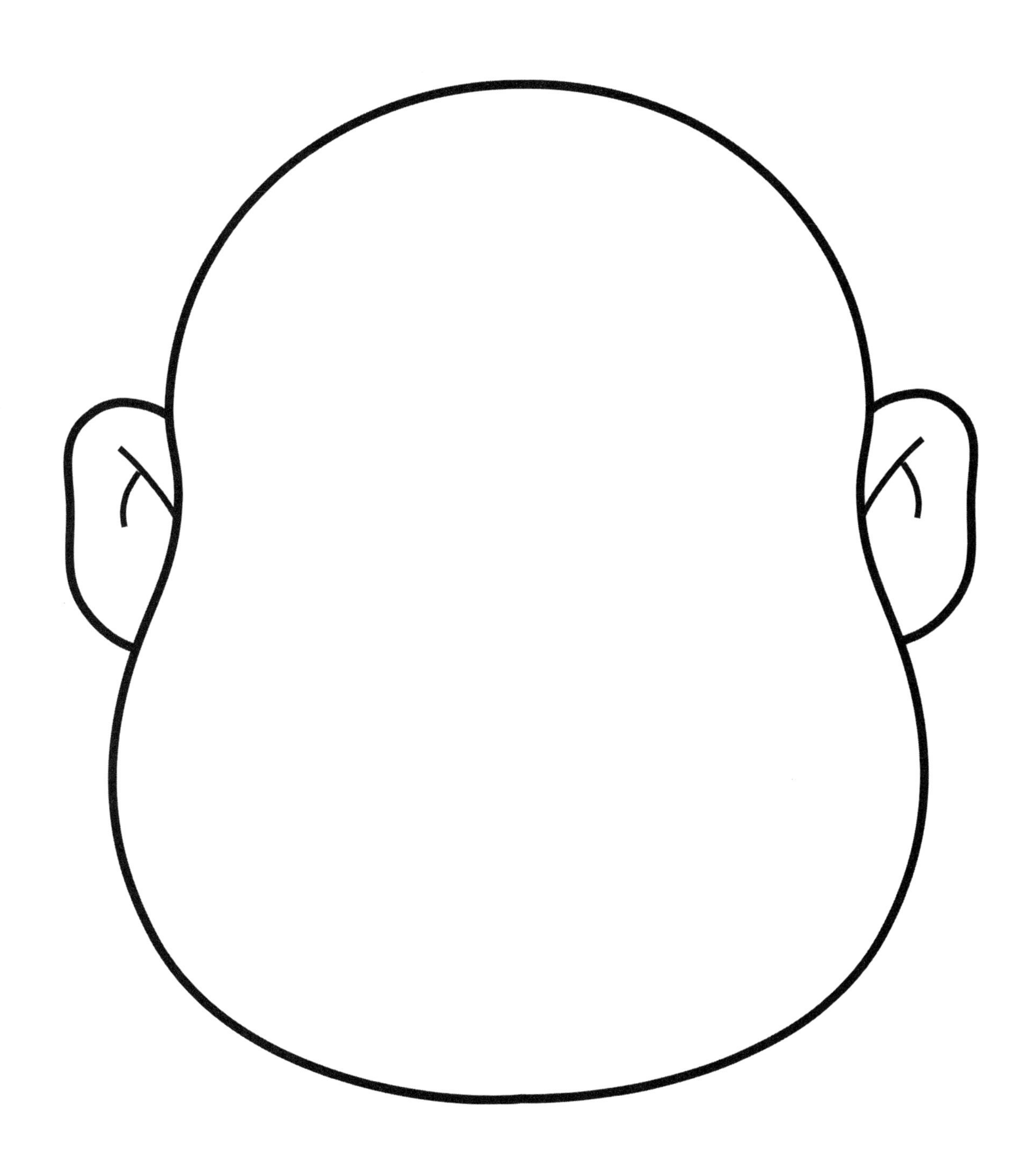

Cut along heavy dark lines. Do not cut the dotted lines.

GLUE THIS SECTION TO OTHER STRIP.

MAGIC
Words
by

The
Perfect
Student

THE GIFT OF GOOD BEHAVIOR

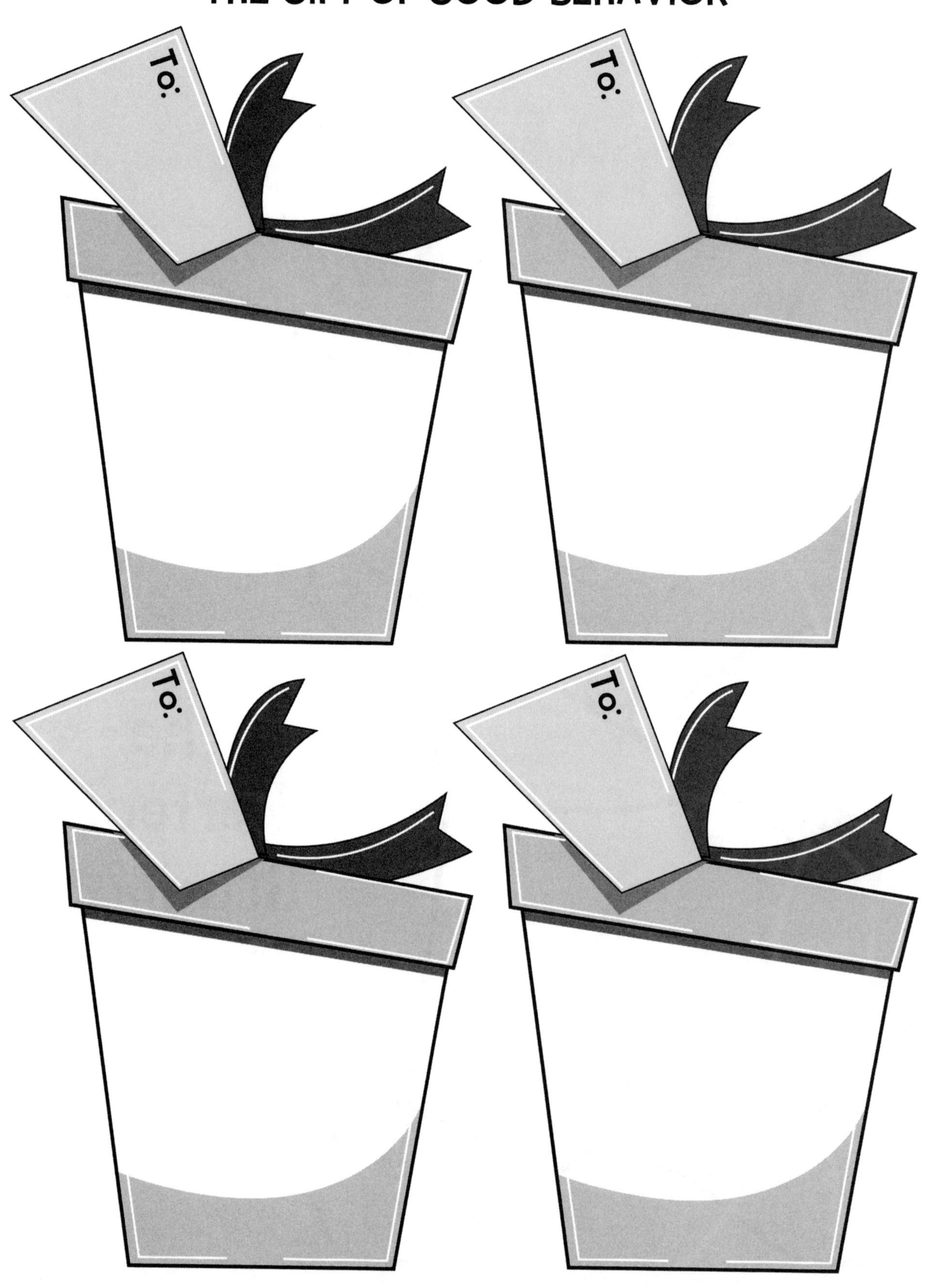

FEELINGS FACES CARDS

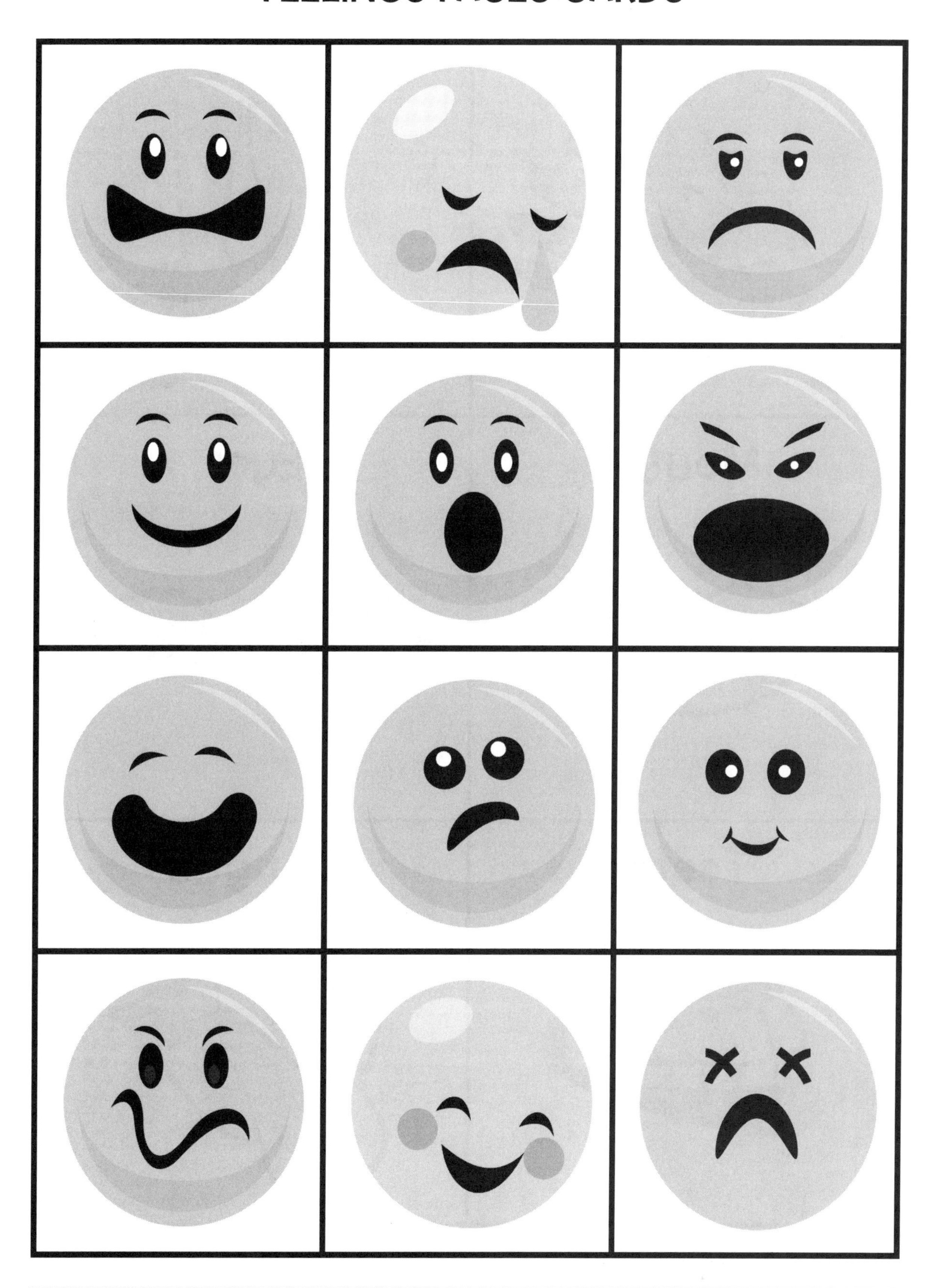

TOOLS OF EMOTIONS

Hand 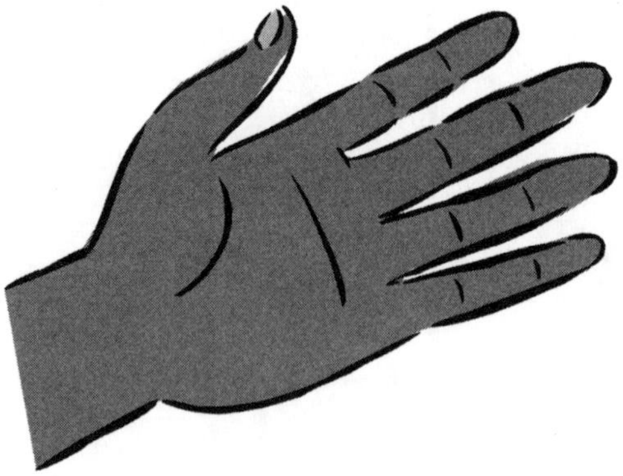	Foot 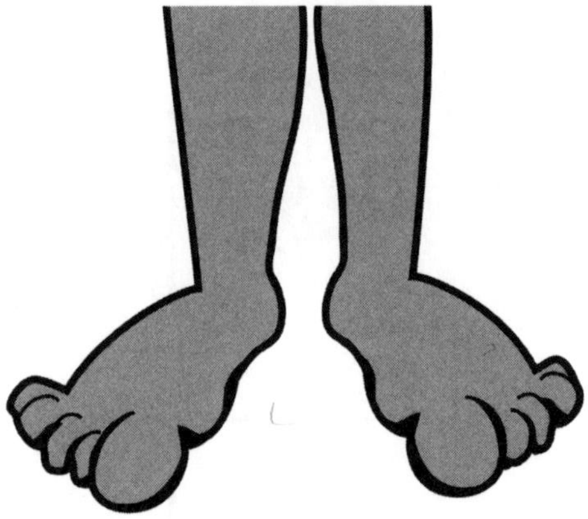
Mouth 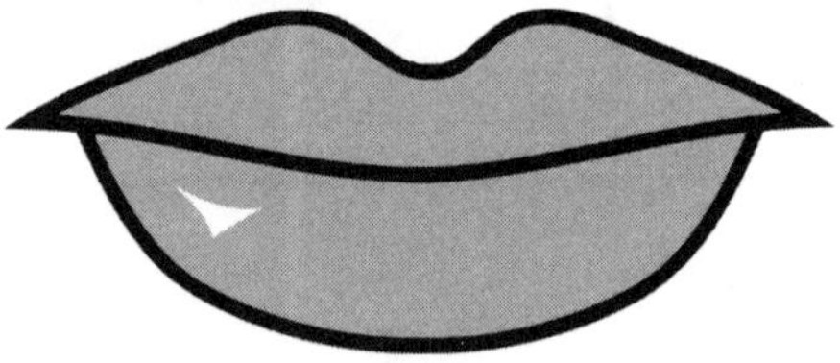	Eyes 
Teeth 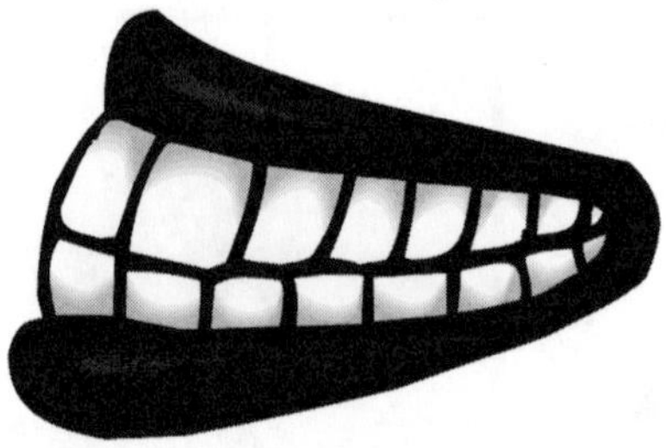	Tongue 

SUN

SUN

RAYS

A PERFECT SCHOOL

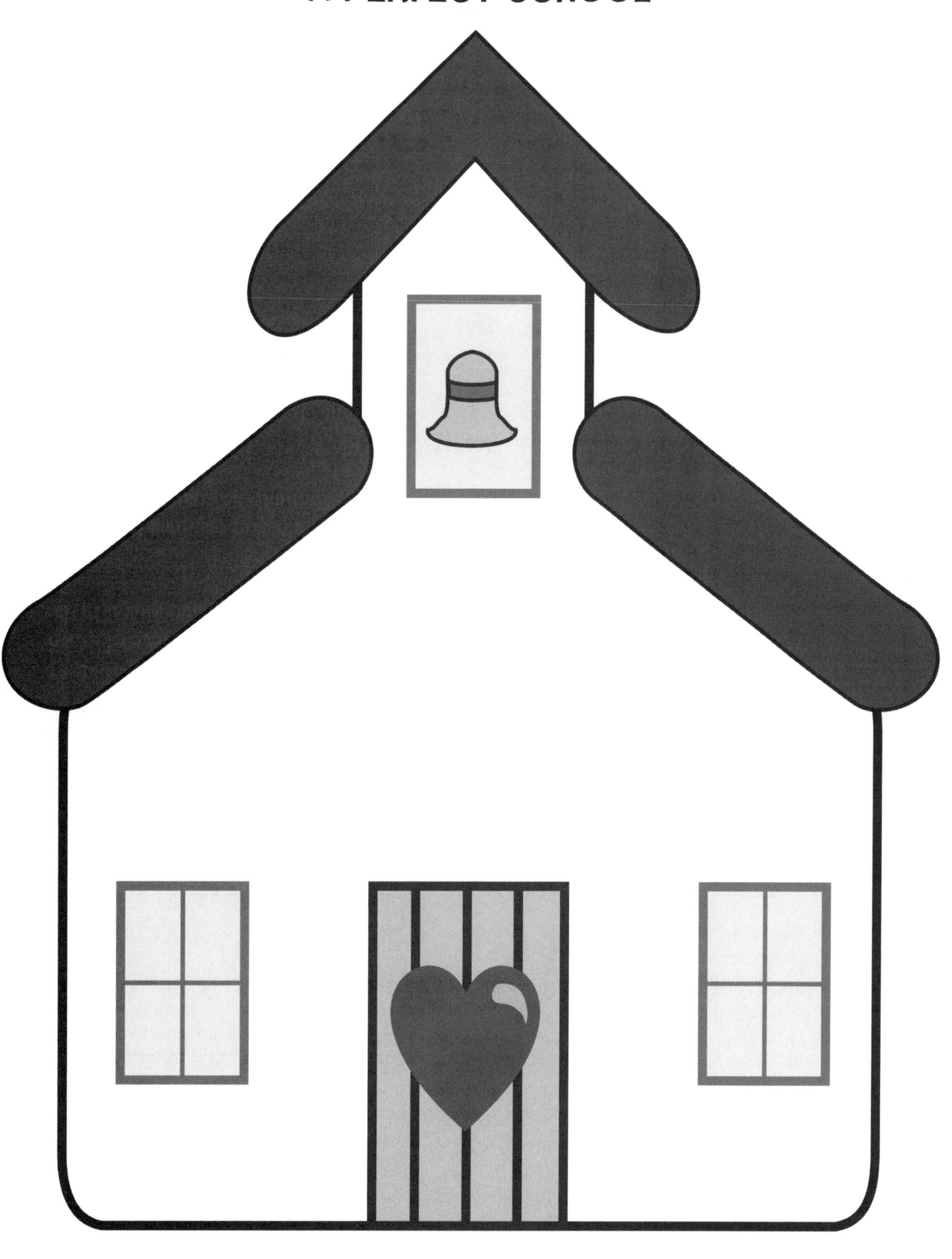

STUDENT INTERVIEW QUESTIONS

Student's Name: ______________________________

What problem behaviors do you think occur most often in this school?

____

____

____

How would you describe the overall behavior of students in this school?

____

____

____

What do you think should happen when someone misbehaves in school?

____

____

____

How do you think adults in this school would answer these questions?

____

____

____

ADULT INTERVIEW QUESTIONS

Date: ____________________

Students' Names: ______________________________

____

Person Interviewed: ______________________________

What problem behaviors do you think occur most often in this school?

____

____

____

How would you describe the overall behavior of students in this school?

____

____

____

What do you think should happen when someone misbehaves in school?

____

____

____

How do you think students in this school would answer these questions?

____

____

____

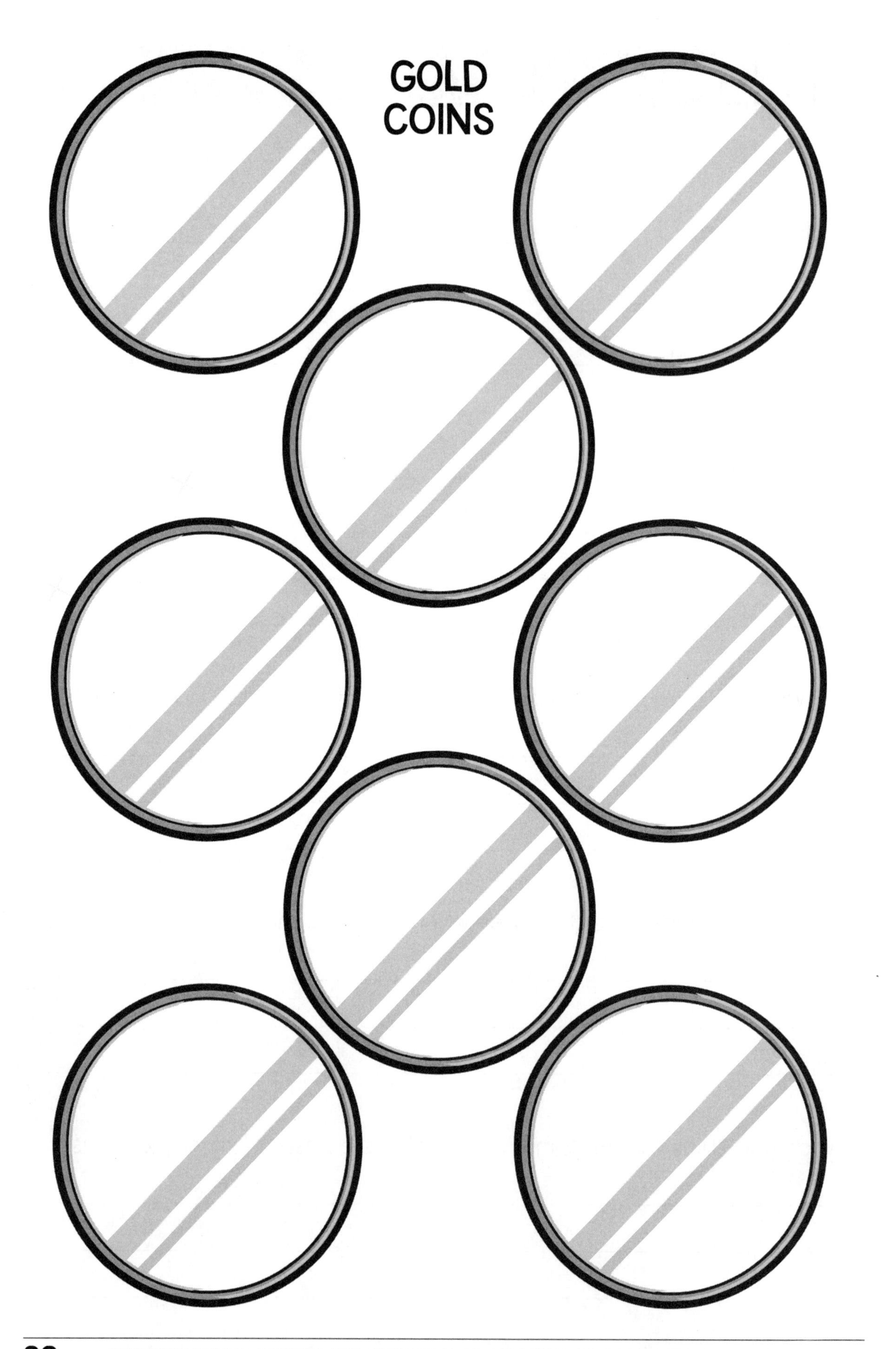
GOLD
COINS

KETTLE

ROLE-PLAY CARDS

Write additional relevant scenarios on the blank cards.

A classmate is calling you names.	A classmate gets in front of you in the lunch line.
You forgot to study for the test.	The teacher is collecting homework and you left yours at home.
A classmate won't let you play.	A friend says a classmate is talking about you.

YOU CAN'T GET MY GOAT

FENCE PICKETS

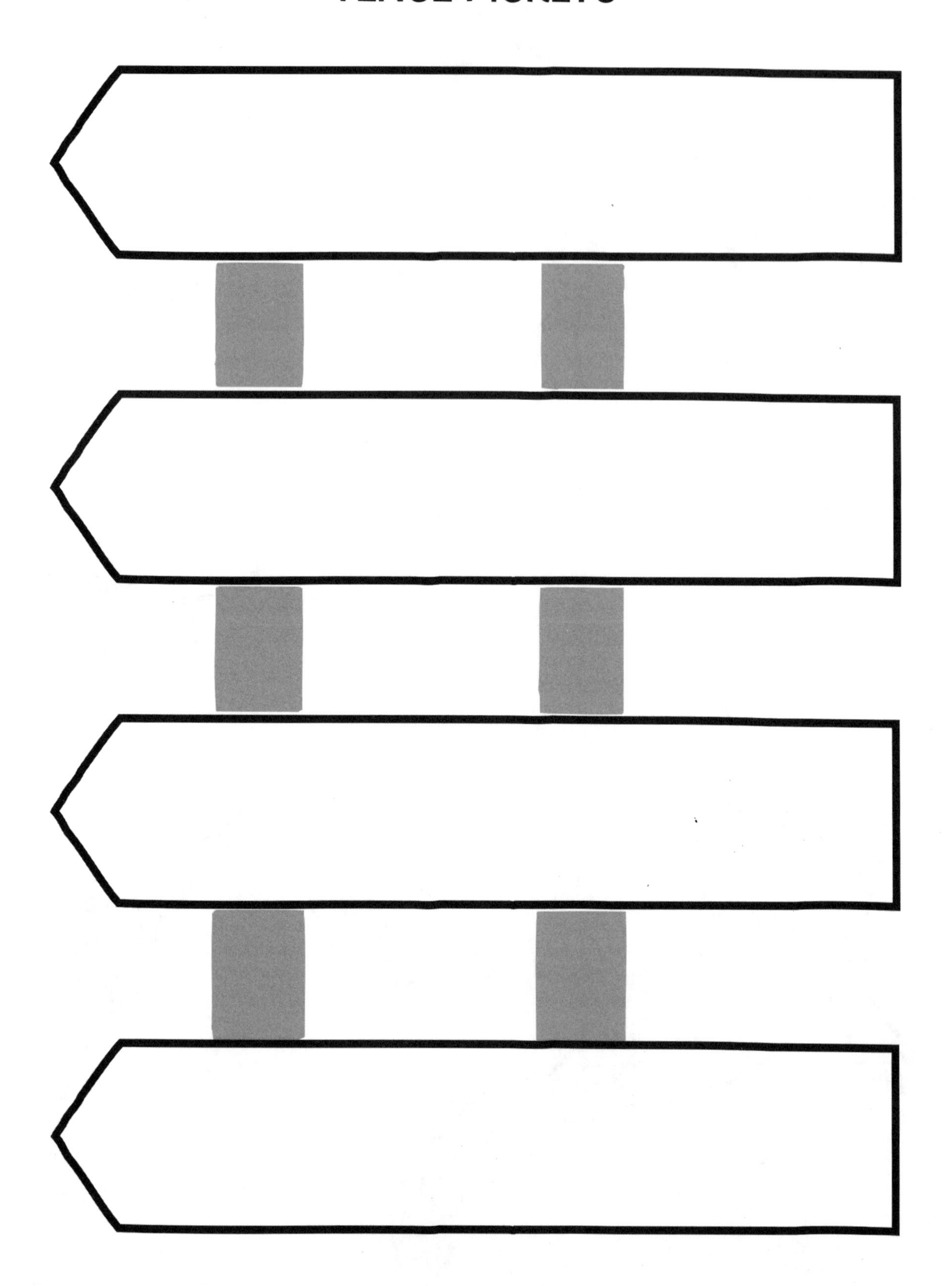

The Better Bees

SMALL-GROUP LESSONS

Cancer Support

This is a group for students with a family member who is dealing with cancer rather than a group for children who have cancer. This group can be an important and significant experience, but does require courage on the part of the counselor. Be sure you are emotionally ready to deal with the issues these children present. Take time to think of questions and concerns that might arise. For example, you need to know how to respond to differing spiritual belief systems children may present.

Group members have told me they worried that talking about their concerns would add to the family's stress. This group provides a safe environment in which students may discuss cancer and its impact, something they can rarely do anywhere else.

I typically offer the group for at least half the year and have conducted the group for an entire school year. Family members may drop in. Illness or death often makes it necessary for families to move. When these or other changes occur, be prepared to help remaining group members understand what has happened.

Once the administration is made aware of a cancer diagnosis, you can offer those children the opportunity to join an ongoing group. I prefer to keep group members within three years of the same age. I do not put siblings in the same group.

This group includes 12 lesson descriptions. Some lessons can be presented in one session, but several require multiple sessions. For example, students may write in their journals many times, and children's books that deal with cancer can be read during groups to facilitate discussion. Please note that Lesson #1 is important to use at a first meeting and should be used to begin every session.

The lessons deal with:

- discovering others with similar concerns.
- exploration of feelings, including opportunities to vent frustrations and anger.
- opportunity to discuss family changes which have occurred and might occur.
- looking at how life has changed—special events, holidays, responsibilities.
- misinformation and unrealistic fears.
- identification of support systems.

SMALL-GROUP LESSONS

Cancer Support

GRADES K-5

ASCA STANDARDS, COMPETENCIES, AND INDICATORS FOR SMALL-GROUP LESSONS ON CANCER SUPPORT

Participation in these group activities will address the following ASCA standards, competencies, and indicators:

Domain	**A/ACADEMIC DEVELOPMENT**
A/A:2.3	Use communication skills to know when and how to ask for help when needed
A/A:3.1	Take responsibility for their actions
A/A:3.1	Demonstrate the ability to work independently, as well as the ability to work cooperatively with other students
A/A:3.5	Share knowledge
A/C:1.1	Demonstrate the ability to balance school, studies, extracurricular activities, leisure time and family life

Domain	**C/CAREER DEVELOPMENT**
C/A:1.3	Develop an awareness of personal abilities, skills, interests, and motivations
C/A:1.4	Learn how to interact and work cooperatively in teams
C/A:1.5	Learn to make decisions
C/A:1.8	Pursue and develop competency in areas of interest
C/A:1.9	Develop hobbies and vocational interests
C/C:2.2	Learn how to use conflict management skills with peers and adults
C/C:2.3	Learn to work cooperatively with others as a team member

Domain	**PS/PERSONAL/SOCIAL DEVELOPMENT**
PS/A:1.1	Develop a positive attitude toward self as a unique and worthy person
PS/A:1.2	Identify values, attitudes and beliefs
PS/A:1.4	Understand change as a part of growth
PS/A:1.5	Identify and express feelings
PS/A:1.6	Distinguish between appropriate and inappropriate behaviors
PS/A:1.9	Demonstrate cooperative behavior in groups
PS/A:1.10	Identify personal strengths and assets
PS/A:1.11	Identify and discuss changing personal and social roles
PS/A:1.12	Identify and recognize changing family roles
PS/A:2.1	Recognize that everyone has rights and responsibilities
PS/A:2.2	Respect alternative points of view
PS/A:2.5	Recognize and respect differences in various family configurations
PS/A:2.6	Use effective communication skills
PS/A:2.7	Know that communication involves speaking, listening, and nonverbal behavior
PS/B:1.4	Develop effective coping skills for dealing with problems
PS/B:1.5	Demonstrate when, where, and how to seek help for solving problems and making decisions
PS/C:1.4	Demonstrate the ability to assert boundaries, rights, and personal privacy
PS/C:1.6	Identify resource people in the school and community, and know how to seek their help
PS/C:1.10	Learn techniques for managing stress and conflict
PS/C:1.11	Learn coping skills for managing life events

Master Supply List For Small Group On Cancer Support

Collect these supplies prior to presenting the group.
Place all special supplies in the same box as the lessons copied on cardstock.

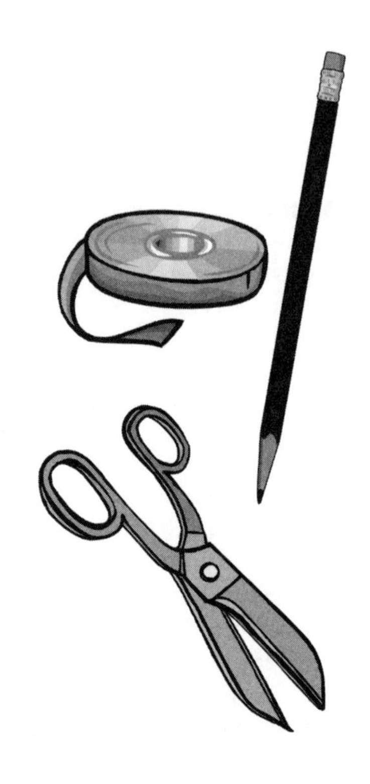

GENERAL SUPPLIES:
- ☐ Chart paper and marker
- ☐ Pencils
- ☐ Writing paper
- ☐ Scissors

ART SUPPLIES:
- ☐ Drawing paper
- ☐ Crayons or markers
- ☐ Black fine-tipped markers
- ☐ Glue/Glue sticks

MISCELLANEOUS SUPPLIES:
- ☐ Prepared journals or purchased diaries
- ☐ Tongue depressors
- ☐ Cotton balls
- ☐ Stationery
- ☐ Envelopes
- ☐ Optional: Sealed jar or locked box
- ☐ 2 die
- ☐ Gray construction paper

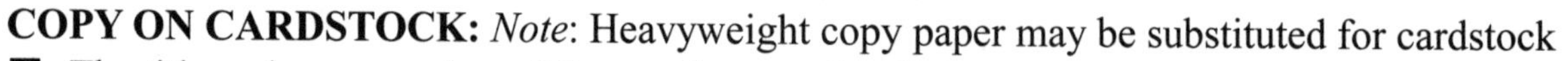

COPY ON CARDSTOCK: *Note*: Heavyweight copy paper may be substituted for cardstock
- ☐ The title and page number of *Cancer Support Small-Group Lessons* as a quick reference to each lesson's page number (page 106)
- ☐ *Sentence Stems:* one set reproduced on white cardstock and cut apart (pages 121-123)
- ☐ *Bricks:* several bricks for each student reproduced on different shades of red cardstock and cut apart (page 124)

First Discussion

Begin Every Session With This Discussion

Materials:

None required

Activity:

- Explain the purpose of the group—to provide support for those whose family members have cancer.

- Allow the students to identify the family member who has cancer and contribute anything they know about the cancer.

- Allow each student to respond to these questions:

  - What new things have happened in your family since last week?
  - How is your (PERSON WITH CANCER)? What treatments is he/she having?
  - What happened this past week that was difficult?
  - What good things happened this past week?

- Check on each student's school progress by asking:

  - How are you doing in school?
  - Are you having any problems with homework? Classwork?
  - What do you wish your teacher knew right now?

- Explain when the group will meet and how to reach the counselor, if needed, between sessions.

- In subsequent sessions, move to the planned activity following this opening discussion.

Journal Activities

Materials:

For Each Student:
- ☐ Prepared journal or purchased diary
- ☐ Pencil

Preparation:

▶ If you're making journals for the students, write the chosen topic at the top of each page. Include several blank pages. Colored paper or decorative paper can be a fun addition to the journals. Suggested journal topics are:

- Today in group, we ...
- Sometimes I feel ...
- About me and my family—autobiography, all about my family, what my family does together, all about my friends, my favorite things
- Reading log—place to list favorite books or books read in group

Additional suggestions can be found on page 111.

Activity:

▶ Give each student a journal and a pencil. Select the desired page or topic for the journal activity.

▶ Discuss the selected topic, then allow time for the students to write in their journals.

▶ Allow time for the students to share their journal entries with the group.

▶ Tell the students they may use blank journal pages to continue the journal when the group ends.

Discussion And Story Writing

Materials:

For Each Student:
- ☐ Paper
- ☐ Pencil

Activity: (This may be presented as a discussion or as a writing activity.)

- ▶ Using a go-around technique, ask the questions below.
- ▶ As a writing activity, give each student a piece of paper and a pencil. Use the following questions to encourage students to write a story about themselves. These stories can be wonderful additions to their diaries or journals.

    - What is the most important thing I should know about you?
    - How would you describe yourself to someone who doesn't know you at all?
    - What do you do best? Worst?
    - Who is in your family?
    - How would you describe each member of your family?
    - Where do you live?
    - What's great about where you live? What would you like to see changed?
    - What do you like about school? What do you wish was different?
    - What is your favorite thing about school?
    - If you were in charge of your school, how would you change things?
    - Describe your classmates.
    - What do you think should be done to stop teasing?
    - Who are your friends?
    - What do you and your friends do together?
    - How can your friends help you?

Then And Now

Materials:

For Each Student:
- ☐ Drawing paper
- ☐ Crayons or markers

Activity:

- ▶ Give each student a piece of drawing paper and crayons or markers.
- ▶ Instruct the students to fold the paper in half, then unfold it. On one side of the paper, the students should draw a picture of their family before cancer. On the other side of the paper, they should draw a picture of their family since the onset of cancer.
- ▶ Allow time for the students to complete their pictures. Offer encouragement as necessary.
- ▶ Allow time for the students to share and talk about the completed pictures.
- ▶ It's important to be prepared for the students' expression of angry and negative feelings during this activity. This process can elicit feelings they haven't yet expressed or even acknowledged.

Now And Later

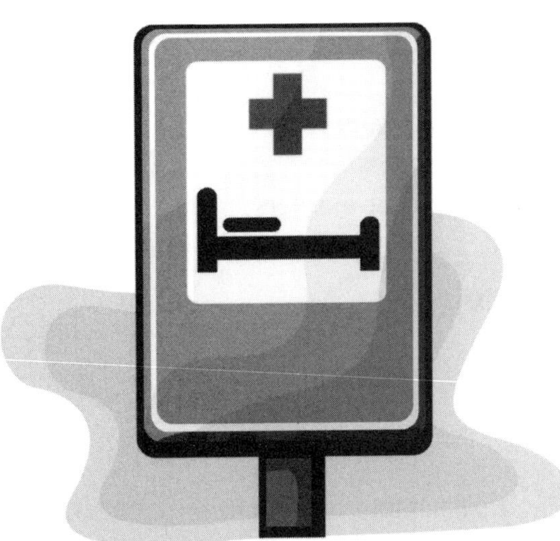

Materials:

For Each Student:
- ☐ Drawing paper
- ☐ Crayons or markers

Activity:

- ▶ Give each student a piece of drawing paper and crayons or markers.
- ▶ Instruct the students to fold the paper in half, unfold it, and draw a line on the crease. On one side of the paper, each student should draw a picture of how his/her family looks now. On the other side of the paper, each student should draw a picture of how his/her family will look five years from now.
- ▶ Allow time for the students to complete their pictures. Offer encouragement as necessary.
- ▶ Allow time for each student to share and talk about his/her completed picture.
- ▶ Discuss the students' expectations:
  - Are these possibilities realistic or unrealistic?
  - What will happen if your predictions come true? What if they don't?
- ▶ Be prepared to correct the students' faulty beliefs. For example, many children believe they, too, will contract cancer. Some believe everyone in their family will die and they'll have to live with strangers. Carefully and gently, balance reassurance, hope, and reality while allowing for all possibilities.

Yesterday And Today

Materials:

For Each Student:
- ☐ Drawing paper
- ☐ Crayons or markers

Activity:

- ▶ Give each student a piece of drawing paper and crayons or markers.

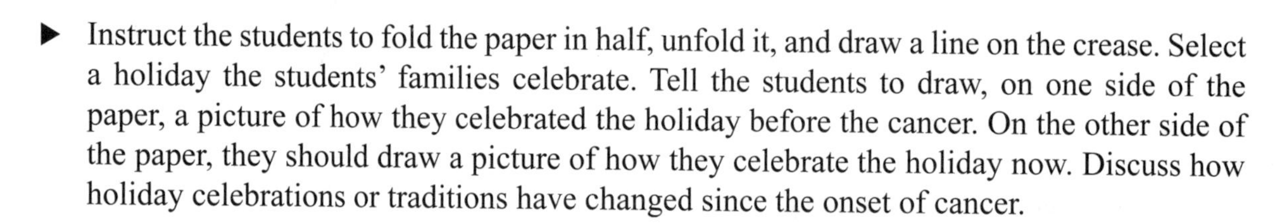

- ▶ Instruct the students to fold the paper in half, unfold it, and draw a line on the crease. Select a holiday the students' families celebrate. Tell the students to draw, on one side of the paper, a picture of how they celebrated the holiday before the cancer. On the other side of the paper, they should draw a picture of how they celebrate the holiday now. Discuss how holiday celebrations or traditions have changed since the onset of cancer.

- ▶ Allow time for the students to complete their pictures. Offer encouragement as necessary.

- ▶ Allow time for each student to share and talk about his/her completed picture.

- ▶ Discuss how family holiday celebrations have changed since the cancer has come into their lives. Include both positive and negative changes and the students' feelings about each.

What About My ______?

Materials:

For Each Student:
- ☐ Drawing paper
- ☐ Crayons or markers

Activity:

- ▶ Give each student a piece of drawing paper and crayons or markers.
- ▶ Instruct the students to draw a picture of a special event in their lives. You may designate a specific event such as a birthday or winning the soccer tournament. Or it may be a high school graduation or other future event.
- ▶ Discuss how/if the cancer has (or will) affect that event. While acknowledging the possibility of different outcomes, correct misinformation and calm unrealistic fears.

Chore Charts

Materials:

For The Leader:
- ☐ Chart paper and marker or chalkboard and chalk

For Each Student:
- ☐ Writing paper
- ☐ Pencil

Activity:

- Brainstorm a list of family chores or jobs the person with cancer did before getting sick. This list may be compiled by the group or by each student. Write the students' responses on the chart paper/chalkboard. The list might include:

    - laundry
    - cooking
    - paying bills
    - going to work
    - taking me to piano lessons
    - helping me with homework
    - coaching my soccer team

- Beside each chore listed, write the name of the person who now does that job.

- Give each student writing paper and a pencil. Have each student create a chart, listing his/her family members across the top columns. Under the name of each family member, the students should write that person's chores/jobs/responsibilities. Cooking dinner, doing laundry, and going to work might be listed under the *Dad* column. Getting well, going to chemo, and resting might be listed under the *Mom* column. (*Note*: If students are too young to write, the leader should make the chart.)

- Discuss how responsibilities and chores have changed since the onset of cancer.

Cancer Buddy

Materials:

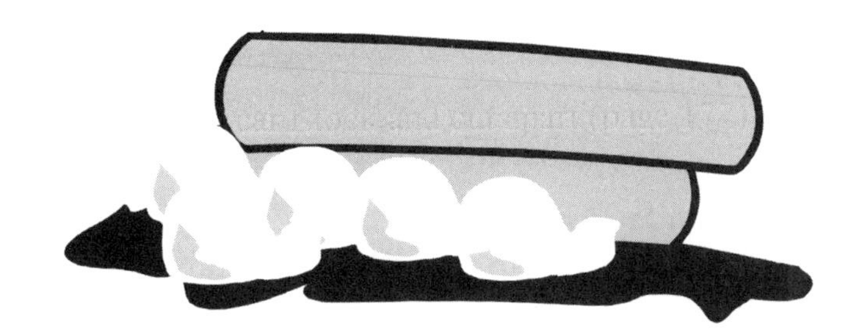

For Each Student:

- ☐ Tongue depressor
- ☐ Black marker
- ☐ Cotton ball
- ☐ Glue

Activity:

- ▶ Give each student a tongue depressor, a black marker, glue, and a cotton ball.

- ▶ Give the students the following instructions:

  - Using a marker, draw a face on the tongue depressor.
  - Put a small dot of glue on the top of the face.
  - Stretch the cotton ball to make hair.
  - Glue the cotton to the top of the tongue depressor.

- ▶ Tell the students this is their Cancer Buddy.

- ▶ Discuss the students' experiences in the hospital:

  - What did you see when you went to visit in the hospital?
  - What smells did you notice at the hospital?
  - What was positive about your visit? Negative?
  - What was something you didn't expect? Did expect?
  - Which people did you like? Dislike?
  - How did people treat you while you were at the hospital?

- ▶ Allow the students to take the Cancer Buddy with them for reassurance or comfort. Some children leave it with the patient.

- ▶ Optional: Give the students several tongue depressors. On each one, have them draw a face that represents a different feeling. The students may use these Cancer Buddies to show others how they're feeling or as a feelings check-in at the beginning of each group.

Write A Letter

Materials:

For The Leader:

- ☐ Optional: Sealed jar or locked box

For Each Student:

- ☐ Paper or stationary
- ☐ Pencil
- ☐ Envelopes

Activity:

▶ Writing letters can allow the students to express feelings or questions they may not have the opportunity or courage to present in person. The letters offer an opportunity for:

- venting or releasing fears and/or negative feelings.
- exploring questions or concerns.
- revealing innermost feelings.
- making a wish.

▶ The counselor must determine what happens to the letters. Appropriate letters may be distributed to the intended recipients. If the letters reflect wishes or feelings best not shared with the intended recipient, consider providing a special sealed jar or locked box in which they can be safely stored. This allows the student to let go of those feelings. Another option is to shred the letters, but only if the student agrees.

▶ Letter recipients might include:

- the person with cancer.
- the patient's doctor.
- a parent who doesn't have cancer.
- a grandparent.
- siblings.
- classmates.
- a teacher.
- friends.
- God.

Sentence Completion

Materials:

For The Leader:

- ☐ *Sentence Stems* reproduced on white cardstock and cut apart (pages 121-123)
- ☐ Scissors

  or
- ☐ Chart paper and marker or chalkboard and chalk
- ☐ Dice

Preparation:

Optional: If you are not using the cardstock *Sentence Stems,* write the numbered sentence stems on the chart paper/chalkboard.

Activity:

▶ Have each student roll the dice and use the number rolled to identify the sentence he/she will complete.

1. What makes me feel the most sad is…
2. If I tell the person who is sick anything, I say…
3. Since my ______________ got sick, my family doesn't…
4. My worst memory is…
5. If I could change things, I would…
6. One thing I would like to do with the person who is sick is…
7. When my ____________first got sick, I…
8. Since my family has been dealing with cancer, my friends…
9. When I am alone, I…
10. I am most afraid that…
11. When I am in school, I…
12. I wish my teachers would…

Identifying Support Systems

Materials:

For The Leader:

- ☐ *Bricks* reproduced on different shades of red cardstock and cut apart (page 124)
- ☐ Photograph of each group member

For Each Student:

- ☐ Fine-tip black marker
- ☐ 12" x 18" piece of gray construction paper
- ☐ Glue/Glue stick
- ☐ Journal from previous sessions

Preparation:

Prior to the lesson, ask each student to give a picture of him/herself to you.

Activity:

- ▶ Discuss support systems—why they're important, how they help, when to use them, etc.
- ▶ Give each student several paper bricks and a fine-tip black marker. Instruct the students to write on each brick the name of someone they consider part of their support system.
- ▶ It may help to guide the students in identifying supportive people. For example, ask them to name:
    - two or three schoolmates or staff members.
    - a neighbor.
    - two or three friends.
    - someone in the medical field.
    - someone who provides spiritual support.
- ▶ Give each student a piece of gray construction paper and glue. Instruct the students to glue their bricks onto the construction paper, creating a wall effect. Then give each student his/her picture. Tell the students to glue their pictures to the construction paper, at the top of the wall. Many students will post the completed paper where they'll see it every day.
- ▶ Review how the people listed on the students' bricks provide support.
- ▶ Designate a journal page and have the students write the names and contact numbers of individuals who serve as their support system. Encourage the students to work on adding to this list.

SENTENCE STEMS

1. What makes me feel the most sad is...
2. If I tell the person who is sick anything, I say...
3. Since my ____________ got sick, my family doesn't...
4. My worst memory is...

SENTENCE STEMS

5. If I could change things, I would...
6. One thing that I would like to do with the person who is sick is...
7. When my _______________ first got sick, I...
8. Since my family has been dealing with cancer, my friends...

SENTENCE STEMS

9. When I am alone, I...
10. I am most afraid that...
11. When I am in school, I...
12. I wish my teachers would...

BRICKS

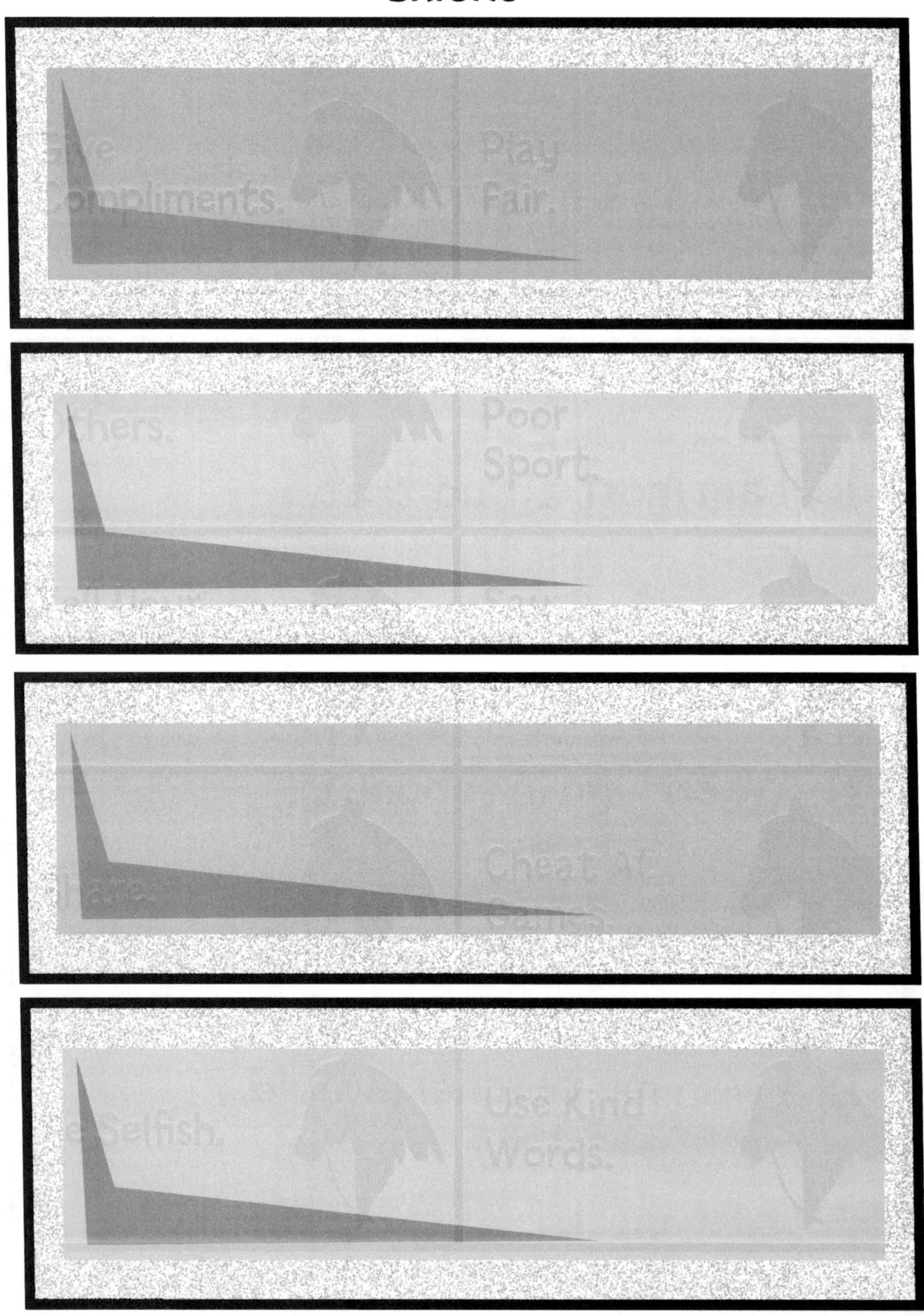
Compliments.
Play
Fair.
Poor
Sport.
Cheat At
Selfish.
Use Kind
Words.

Friendship

I believe children have unique friendship problems. Some children remain apart from classmates or use inappropriate and ineffective means to approach and acquire friends. Some children must learn how to choose friends wisely. Other students don't know how to keep the friends they have made. Some have frequent arguments and conflicts with friends. A child may have one of these friendship issues or any combination of these problems. Once group membership is established, you may choose lessons most appropriate for evident needs. Most of these lessons can be easily modified to address specific group needs simply by varying the discussion questions.

The goals for the various grade levels are identifying:

Grades K/1
Positive friendship traits
Words that help and hurt friendship
Differences between friendly and unfriendly behaviors
Things one would like to do with a friend

Grades 2/3
Behaviors that enhance and behaviors that block friendship
Things others do that bug you and things you do that bug others
People with admirable friendship traits

Grades 4/5
Solving problems in friendship situations
Ways to make new friends
Feelings associated with friendship

SMALL-GROUP LESSONS

Friendship

ASCA STANDARDS, COMPETENCIES, AND INDICATORS FOR SMALL-GROUP LESSONS ON FRIENDSHIP

Participation in these group activities will address the following ASCA standards, competencies, and indicators:

Domain	**A/ACADEMIC DEVELOPMENT**
A/A:1.5	Identify attitudes and behaviors which lead to successful learning
A/A:2.3	Use communication skills to know when and how to ask for help when needed
A/A:3.1	Take responsibility for their actions
A/A:3.1	Demonstrate the ability to work independently, as well as the ability to work cooperatively with other students
A/A:3.3	Develop a broad range of interests and abilities
A/A:3.5	Share knowledge
A/B:1.4	Seek information and support from faculty, staff, family, and peers
A/B:2.5	Use problem-solving and decision-making skills to assess progress toward educational goals

Domain	**C/CAREER DEVELOPMENT**
C/A:1.3	Develop an awareness of personal abilities, skills, interests, and motivations
C/A:1.4	Learn how to interact and work cooperatively in teams
C/A:1.5	Learn to make decisions
C/A:1.6	Learn how to set goals
C/A:1.8	Pursue and develop competency in areas of interest
C/A:1.10	Balance between work and leisure time
C/A:2.1	Acquire employability skills such as working on a team, problem-solving and organizational skills
C/A:2.5	Learn to respect individual uniqueness in the workplace
C/A:2.8	Understand the importance of responsibility, dependability, punctuality, integrity and effort in the workplace
C/C:1.3	Identify personal preferences and interests which influence career choices and success
C/C:2.1	Demonstrate how interests, abilities, and achievement relate to achieving personal, social, educational and career goals.
C/C:2.2	Learn how to use conflict management skills with peers and adults
C/C:2.3	Learn to work cooperatively with others as a team member

Domain	**PS/PERSONAL/SOCIAL DEVELOPMENT**
PS/A:1.1	Develop a positive attitude toward self as a unique and worthy person
PS/A:1.2	Identify values, attitudes and beliefs
PS/A:1.3	Learn the goal setting process
PS/A:1.4	Understand change as a part of growth
PS/A:1.5	Identify and express feelings
PS/A:1.6	Distinguish between appropriate and inappropriate behaviors
PS/A:1.7	Recognize personal boundaries, rights and privacy needs
PS/A:1.8	Understand the need for self-control and how to practice it
PS/A:1.9	Demonstrate cooperative behavior in groups
PS/A:1.10	Identify personal strengths and assets
PS/A:1.11	Identify and discuss changing personal and social roles
PS/A:2.1	Recognize that everyone has rights and responsibilities
PS/A:2.2	Respect alternative points of view
PS/A:2.3	Recognize, accept, respect and appreciate individual differences
PS/A:2.4	Recognize, accept and appreciate ethnic and cultural diversity
PS/A:2.5	Recognize and respect differences in various family configurations
PS/A:2.6	Use effective communication skills
PS/A:2.7	Know that communication involves speaking, listening, and nonverbal behavior
PS/A:2.8	Learn how to make and keep friends
PS/B:1.2	Understand consequences of decisions and choices
PS/B:1.3	Identify alternative solutions to a problem
PS/B:1.4	Develop effective coping skills for dealing with problems
PS/B:1.5	Demonstrate when, where, and how to seek help for solving problems and making decisions
PS/B:1.6	Know how to apply conflict resolution skills
PS/C:1.4	Demonstrate the ability to assert boundaries, rights, and personal privacy
PS/C:1.5	Differentiate between situations requiring peer support and situations requiring adult professional help
PS/C:1.6	Identify resource people in the school and community, and know how to seek their help
PS/C:1.11	Learn coping skills for managing life events

Master Supply List For Small Group On Friendship

Collect these supplies prior to presenting the group.
Place all special supplies in the same box as the lessons copied on cardstock.

GENERAL SUPPLIES:
- ☐ Chart paper and marker
- ☐ Scissors
- ☐ Pencils
- ☐ Hole punches

ART SUPPLIES:
- ☐ Crayons or markers
- ☐ Glue or glue sticks
- ☐ Construction paper (white)
- ☐ Cardstock (white, tan, yellow, gold, red, other colors)
- ☐ Large craft sticks
- ☐ Poster board (white, blue, green)
- ☐ Fabric pens
- ☐ Various art/craft supplies
- ☐ Black markers

MISCELLANEOUS SUPPLIES:
- ☐ Colorful small candy
- ☐ Serving spoon
- ☐ 2 Cans
- ☐ Straws
- ☐ Yarn
- ☐ Blunt-end needle
- ☐ Magazines
- ☐ Discarded ties
- ☐ Yarn or elastic
- ☐ Clear contact paper
- ☐ Old magazines, travel brochures, sports ads, etc depicting people involved in various activities
- ☐ String
- ☐ Optional: Small box about the size to hold a mug
- ☐ Optional: Various plastic "gems" or "jewels," rhinestones, glitter, etc.
- ☐ 9" x 12" pieces of yellow felt
- ☐ 4.5" x 6" pieces of green felt
- ☐ Color lined paper
- ☐ Hole reinforcements
- ☐ Raffia
- ☐ Large empty glue bottle or any container suitable for storing the cards
- ☐ Sharp knife

- ☐ Chips
- ☐ Small inexpensive prizes
- ☐ Small aluminum baking pan to store *Brownie Point Cards*
- ☐ Wire hangers or dowels
- ☐ Nylon thread or yarn
- ☐ Optional: Digital camera to take pictures of classmates and group members
- ☐ Toy microphone
- ☐ Optional: Stickers

COPY ON WHITE CARDSTOCK: *Note*: Heavyweight copy paper may be substituted for cardstock

- ☐ *Friendship Small-Group Lessons* as a quick reference to each lesson's page number (page 126)
- ☐ *Corralling Friendly Behavior Cards:* one set reproduced and cut apart (pages 156-157)
- ☐ *Fence Pickets:* several copies, cut out (page 163)
- ☐ *Fence Gate:* one copy, cut out (page 164)
- ☐ *Joining-In Role-Play Cards:* one set reproduced and cut apart (page 168)
- ☐ *Sticky Situation Cards:* one set reproduced and cut apart (page 175)
- ☐ *Friendship Discussion Cards:* one set reproduced and cut apart (page 177)

ONE COPY FOR EACH STUDENT ON WHITE CARDSTOCK:

- ☐ *Tie Shape*: cut out (page 160)
- ☐ *Treasure Chest Items* (page 166)
- ☐ *Flower Pattern* (page 167)

COPY ON COLORED CARDSTOCK:

- ☐ *Hobby Horse:* five copies on tan cardstock, cut out (page 158)
- ☐ *Star Shapes:* eight stars per student on yellow cardstock, cut out (page 159)
- ☐ *Bricks:* several copies on different shades of red cardstock, cut out (page 162)
- ☐ *I Treasure My Friends:* one for each student on gold cardstock (page 165)

COPY ON WHITE COPY PAPER:

- ☐ *Candy Game:* one for each student (page 151)
- ☐ *Best-Dressed Friend:* one for each student (pages 152-153)
- ☐ *Words That Help Or Hurt Friendships #1:* one for each student (page 154)
- ☐ *Words That Help Or Hurt Friendships #2:* one for each student (page 155)
- ☐ *Cartoon Conflicts:* several sets, cut apart (pages 169-174)
- ☐ *Brownie Points Cards:* several sets, cut apart (page 176)

COPY ON COLORED COPY PAPER:

- ☐ *Balloons:* five different-colored balloons for each student (page 161)

Friendship Candy Game

Begin Or End Every Group With This Game

Materials:

For The Leader:
- ☐ Colorful candy-coated chocolates or similar small candies
- ☐ Serving spoon

For Each Student:
- ☐ *Candy Game* reproduced on white copy paper (page 151)
- ☐ Crayons of colors that match the candies to be used

(***Note:*** Be sure the use of candy is appropriate for use in your school district and for each group member. If you cannot use candy, you may substitute something suitable such as pieces of colored paper punched out with a hole punch. Or omit the *Candy Game* from your lessons.)

Activity:

- ▶ Give each student one copy of the *Candy Game* and crayons that match the colors of the candies. Instruct the students to color each circle a different color. They may select which color to use for each circle and should not try to match anyone else's choices.
- ▶ When everyone has finished coloring the circles, give each student a spoonful of candy. Ask the students to line up the candy with the colored circles so all the red candies are with the red circle, the green candies are with the green circle, etc. If some circles don't match candy, you may give that student a candy of a different color. Have everyone count their candies. Give more to those who have fewer.
- ▶ Follow the worksheet instructions by giving each student the chance to respond to each statement. For example, the first statement asks students to tell one good way to have more friends for each piece of candy. A student who has four pieces of matching-colored candy for this first statement must tell four good ways to have more friends.
- ▶ It is usually best if the students eat the candy as they respond to the statements so all the candy is gone by the end of group.

Best-Dressed Friend

Materials:

For The Leader:

- ☐ Chart paper and marker or chalkboard and chalk

For Each Student:

- ☐ *Best-Dressed Friend* reproduced on white copy paper (pages 152-153)
- ☐ Scissors
- ☐ Glue stick
- ☐ Crayons

Activity:

- ▶ Ask the students to describe what characteristics they want a friend to have. As the characteristics are named, list them on the chart paper/chalkboard.
- ▶ Give each student a copy of *Best-Dressed Friend,* scissors, crayons, and a glue stick. Allow time for the students to cut out the clothes, which will be glued to the paper doll.
- ▶ Ask each student to choose one characteristic or trait that's important to him/her and write that word on one article of clothing. Continue until a trait is written on each article of clothing.
- ▶ Allow time for the students to color the clothing, being sure that the words remain legible.
- ▶ Tell the students to choose one outfit and glue the clothes and shoes to the paper doll.
- ▶ Discuss what it would be like to find a friend with these characteristics.
- ▶ Encourage the students to think of classmates who might possess these traits.
- ▶ Allow the students to take their completed paper dolls with them.

Words That Make Or Break Friendships

Materials:

For Each Student:

- *Words That Help Or Hurt Friendships #1* reproduced on white copy paper (page 154)
- *Words That Help Or Hurt Friendships #2* reproduced on white copy paper (page 155)
- Scissors
- Glue stick
- Construction paper
- Pencil

Activity:

- Give each student a copy of *Words That Help Or Hurt Friendships #1* and *Words That Help Or Hurt Friendships #2*, scissors, a glue stick, a piece of construction paper, and a pencil.
- Tell the students to cut out and glue the hearts and lightning bolts from *Words That Help Or Hurt Friendships #1* to the piece of construction paper, making sure not to glue the shapes to close to each other.
- Review *Words That Help Or Hurt Friendships #2* and discuss whether each word would help or hurt a friendship. Encourage the students to name other words and write them in the blank rectangles.
- After each word is discussed, have the students cut it out. Glue positive, helpful words/ phrases to the hearts and glue unhelpful words to the lightning bolts.
- If time allows, allow the students to role-play using the positive words.
- Students may take their completed activity sheet with them.

Corralling Friendly Behavior

Materials:

For The Leader:

- ☐ *Corralling Friendly Behavior Cards* reproduced on white cardstock and cut apart (pages 156-157)
- ☐ Scissors
- ☐ 2 Large pieces of poster board
- ☐ Markers in various colors

  or
- ☐ *Hobby Horse:* five copies reproduced on tan cardstock and cut out (page 158)
- ☐ Large craft sticks—one for each horse's head
- ☐ Glue
- ☐ Scissors
- ☐ 2 Cans

Lesson Preparation:

Option 1: Draw a corral or barn on each of the two pieces of poster board. Label one poster board "Friendly" and the other poster board "Unfriendly."

Option 2: Label one can "Friendly" and the other can "Unfriendly." On each craft stick, write one behavior from the *Corralling Friendly Behavior Cards*. Glue a *Hobby Horse* head to the top of each craft stick.

Activity:

- ▶ Have the students sit in a circle.
- ▶ Place the *Corralling Friendly Behavior Cards* and the corral posters (or the cans and the Hobby Horse craft sticks) in the center of the circle. One by one, allow group members to select a card/craft stick.
- ▶ Discuss the behavior described on the card/craft stick by asking:
  - What will happen if you do/say this to a friend?
  - What would you do if someone said/did this to you?
  - Is this friendly or unfriendly behavior?
- ▶ Have each student place his/her *Corralling Friendly Behavior Card* on the appropriate corral/barn poster or put the Hobby Horse craft stick in the appropriate can. When all the cards/craft sticks have been placed, explain that certain behaviors will gain friends, while other behaviors can ruin friendships.

Friendship Mobiles

Materials:

For The Leader:
- *Star Shapes:* eight stars per student, reproduced on yellow cardstock and cut out (page 159)
- Blunt-end needle with eye large enough for yarn to go through
- Yarn
- Hole punch
- Scissors

For Each Student:
- Scissors
- 4 Straws
- Glue stick
- 8 Lengths of yarn

Have Available For The Group:
- Magazines

Activity:

- Place the magazines and scissors in the center of a table. Tell the students to search for and cut out pictures of people doing things they would enjoy doing.
- Give each student eight stars, scissors, and a glue stick. Have the students glue the magazine pictures to the star shapes. A student who selects more than eight pictures may glue one picture to each side of the stars.
- Give each student four straws and eight lengths of yarn.
- Punch a hole in each star. Attach one end of the yarn to each star by threading the yarn through the hole and tying it. Attach the other end of the yarn to a straw. You may hole-punch the straw and thread the yarn or simply tie the yarn around the straw. Each completed straw should have one picture at each end. Each student should have eight stars with one or two pictures on each.
- Place the four straws together so they cross each other at the center, creating a star or asterisk. You can stitch these by passing the needle through the center and wrapping the yarn around several times. Leave extra yarn at the center for hanging the mobile.
- Discuss the things group members like to do and how to get friends to join them in each activity.
- Hang the mobiles around the room or let the students take them home.

Friendship Ties

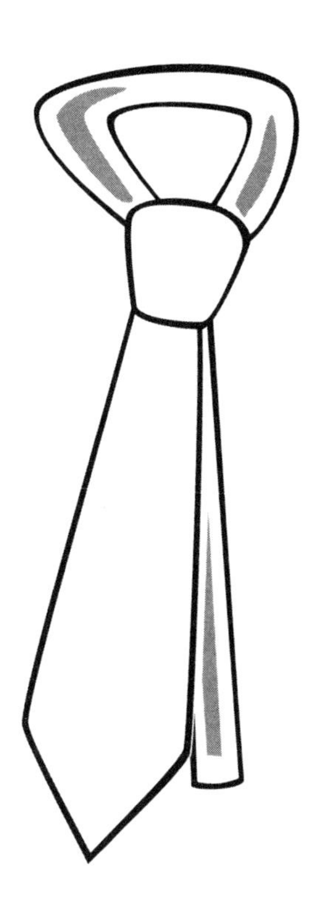

Materials:

For The Leader:
- ☐ Chart paper and marker or chalkboard and chalk
- ☐ Pencil or chalk
- ☐ Scissors
- ☐ Yarn, string, or elastic
- ☐ Hole punch

For Each Student:
- ☐ Discarded man's tie
- ☐ Fabric pen

  or
- ☐ *Tie Shape* reproduced on white cardstock and cut out (page 160)
- ☐ Crayons or markers

Have Available For The Group:
- ☐ Various art/craft supplies

Lesson Preparation:

If you're using real ties, cut 16" off each tie. Create the "knot" at the top to look like a normally tied man's tie. You may need to stitch or glue the knot to make it hold. Add string or yarn to the tie so it can be tied around the neck. Elastic works well, too. Make one tie per student. Be sure to choose light-colored ties so the writing will be visible.

If you're using the *Tie Shape,* cut out the shape and punch holes where indicated. String a piece of yarn or elastic through the holes so the *Tie Shape* can be tied around the neck.

Activity:

- ▶ Discuss a topic related to friendship—things to do with a friend, ways to make friends, positive friendship traits, etc.

- ▶ Brainstorm a list related to the topic and write the students' contributions on the chart paper/chalkboard. For example, you may end up with a list of positive friendship traits—kind, nice, funny, loyal, generous, etc.

- ▶ Give each student a man's tie and a fabric pen or a cutout *Tie Shape* and crayons or markers.

- Let each student choose the brainstormed words/phrases that are most meaningful to him/her. Write these in chalk or pencil on that student's tie. Using the fabric pens or crayons or markers, have the students trace the words written on the ties.
- Have the students decorate their ties with buttons, charms, beads, glitter, ribbons, etc.
- Let the students wear their ties home.

Things-To-Do Placemat

Materials:

For The Leader:
- ☐ Clear contact paper

For Each Student:
- ☐ 12" x 18" piece of construction paper or cardstock
- ☐ Scissors
- ☐ Glue stick
- ☐ Black marker

Have Available For The Group:
- ☐ Old magazines, travel brochures, sports ad, etc. depicting people involved in various activities

Activity:

- ▶ Discuss things the students might enjoy doing with a friend. Try to come up with activities that are reasonable and possible. Be sure to include activities that don't cost money or require transportation or special equipment. (Swimming, walking, hiking, team sports, games, watching the clouds float by, etc.)
- ▶ Ask:
  - What would be important when enjoying these activities with a friend?
  - How can you get a friend to do these things with you?
- ▶ Give each student a piece of construction paper/cardstock, scissors, a black marker, and a glue stick.
- ▶ Allow time for the students to search through the materials and cut out pictures depicting activities they would enjoy sharing with a friend.
- ▶ Have the students arrange and glue the pictures collage-style on the construction paper/cardstock.
- ▶ Ask the students to use a black marker to add a title to their placemat.
- ▶ Cover front and back of the completed collage with clear contact paper. Children may use this placemat to remind them of things they enjoy doing with friends.

Friend Wanted

Materials:

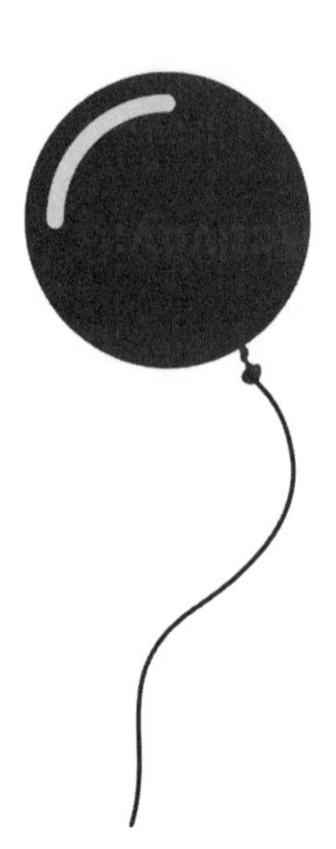

For The Leader:

- ☐ Chart paper and marker or chalkboard and chalk

For Each Student:

- ☐ 5 *Balloons* reproduced on different colors of copy paper (page 161)
- ☐ Black marker
- ☐ Large piece of white construction paper
- ☐ Scissors
- ☐ 5 Pieces of string or yarn
- ☐ Glue stick

Preparation:

Make a list of friendship words—*caring, cheerful, helpful, polite, fun-loving, good listener, patient, kind*, etc.— on the chart paper/chalkboard.

Activity:

- ▶ Review the list of friendship words. Let group members add words to the list. Discuss what each word means and why it might be a good quality for a friend to have.
- ▶ Give each student five different-colored *Balloons*, a large piece of construction paper, five pieces of string or yarn, a black marker, a glue stick, and scissors.
- ▶ Tell the students to select five words that describe qualities they want in a friend and write one word on each balloon.
- ▶ Have the students cut out and glue their balloons to the construction paper, add strings to the ends of the balloons with glue, and gather the strings at the bottom of the paper to create a balloon bouquet.
- ▶ Allow time for each group member to describe his/her perfect friend.
- ▶ End the session by asking each group member what he/she might have to do in order to have a perfect friend.

Bricks Or Gates

Materials:

For The Leader:

- ☐ Chart paper and marker or chalkboard and chalk
- ☐ *Bricks* reproduced on several shades of red cardstock and cut out (page 162)
- ☐ Glue stick
- ☐ Black marker
- ☐ *Fence Pickets:* several copies reproduced on white cardstock and cut out (page 163)
- ☐ *Fence Gate:* one copy reproduced on white cardstock and cut out (page 164)
- ☐ 2 Large pieces of blue or green poster board
- ☐ Scissors

Activity:

▶ With the students, brainstorm two lists of behaviors. Write the students' ideas on the chart paper/chalkboard in columns labeled:

- "Things kids do that make me WANT to be their friend"
- "Things kids do that make me NOT WANT to be their friend"

▶ Make a "wall" of friendship-blocking behaviors. On each brick, write one behavior listed in the second column. Glue the bricks to the poster board in a wall-like pattern. Label the poster "The Unfriendly Wall." The group may add decorations like weeds or other items to make the wall less appealing.

▶ Make a "fence" of friendship-promoting behaviors. On each fence picket, write one behavior listed in the first column. Glue the pickets to the other piece of poster board, leaving space in the middle for the gate.

▶ Discuss how these behaviors differ. Encourage the students to practice the positive behaviors. (*Note:* It's helpful to have each student choose one specific positive behavior to practice before the next group session.)

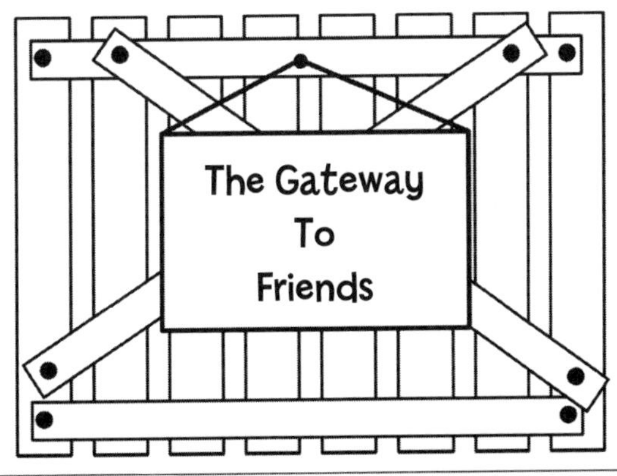

Treasured Friends

Materials:

For Each Student:

- ☐ *I Treasure My Friends* reproduced on gold cardstock (page 165)
  or
  Small box about the size to hold a mug
- ☐ *Treasure Chest Items* reproduced on white cardstock (page 166)
- ☐ Scissors
- ☐ Glue stick
- ☐ Crayons or markers
- ☐ Pencil

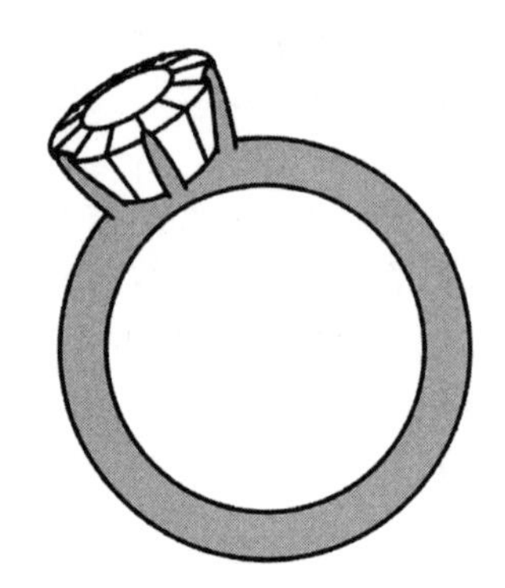

Have Available For The Group:

- ☐ Optional: Various plastic "gems" or "jewels," rhinestones, glitter, etc.

Activity:

- ▶ Give each student a copy of *Treasure Chest Items*, a pencil, scissors, and crayons or markers.
- ▶ Explain each item, allowing time for the students to write an ending to each sentence starter.
- ▶ Have the students share their completed sentences.
- ▶ Tell the students to cut the treasure chest items apart, then color and decorate each item without covering up the writing.
- ▶ Give each student a glue stick and a copy of *I Treasure My Friends* or a small box. Tell the students to glue the treasure chest items to the chest on the activity sheet or place them inside the box. If you're using plastic gems or rhinestones, have the students decorate their treasure chests by gluing them to the paper treasure chest or putting them in the box. If the students are using boxes, have them write *I Treasure My Friends* on the outside of the box.
- ▶ The completed sentences should be placed inside the box or glued around the paper treasure chest. Have the students take the treasure chests home as a reminder of qualities we value in friends.

Friendship Bugs

Materials:

For The Leader:
- ☐ Chart paper and marker or chalkboard and chalk

Have Available For The Group:
- ☐ Crayons or markers
- ☐ Scissors
- ☐ Drawing paper
- ☐ Glue sticks
- ☐ Various decorative art/craft supplies

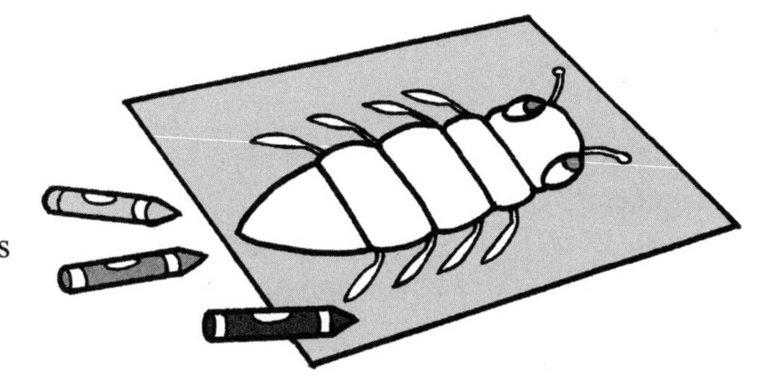

Activity:

- ▶ Place crayons or markers, scissors, drawing paper, glue sticks, and other art/craft supplies on a table.
- ▶ Tell the students they may use these supplies to create their own personal "bug." Encourage them to create several sections, like the segments on a worm or an insect's legs and wings.
- ▶ When the students have completed their bugs, brainstorm a list of things kids do that bug other people and may cause them to lose friends. Write these things on the chart paper/chalkboard. Possible behaviors include: *tattling, laughing at mistakes, teasing, name-calling, being a copycat, being bossy, hitting or poking, telling lies, being jealous of other friends, needing to be the center of attention, breaking promises.*
- ▶ Have the students write, on their bugs, five things that bug them most, then draw a star next to the thing that most upsets them. Discuss why the students chose specific behaviors and why those behaviors bug them.
- ▶ Have the students create another "bug" and write on it behaviors of theirs that bug others. Discuss why these behaviors might bother others.
- ▶ Students may take their bugs with them as reminders of things they should not do if they want to keep friends.

Flower Power Friends

Materials:

For Each Student:

- ☐ *Flower Pattern* reproduced on white cardstock (page 167)
- ☐ 2 Pieces of yellow felt (9" x 12")
- ☐ 4.5" x 6" piece of green felt
- ☐ Glue
- ☐ Scissors
- ☐ Several sheets of colored lined paper
- ☐ Marker

Have Available For The Group:

- ☐ Hole punches
- ☐ Hole reinforcements
- ☐ Raffia

Activity:

▶ Tell the students they're each going to create a flower-shaped book.

▶ Give each student a copy of the *Flower Pattern*, two 9" x 12" pieces of yellow felt, one 4.5" x 6" piece of green felt, glue, scissors, a marker, and several sheets of colored lined paper.

▶ Tell the students:

- To make the book's cover, place the flower pattern on top of the yellow felt. Using the marker, trace one flower on each piece of felt. Cut the flowers out to create the front and back of the book.
- Trace and cut out two green felt circles. Glue them to the centers of the yellow felt flowers.
- Stack the two felt flowers together and punch two holes in them, along the side where the book's binding will be.
- Make several pages by using the *Flower Pattern* to cut flower-shaped pages from the lined paper.
- Stack the paper flowers together and punch two holes in the same locations as on the felt flowers.
- Reinforce the holes.
- Sandwich the paper flowers between the felt flowers.
- Thread raffia through the holes and make a double knot.

- ▶ Have the students write a desirable friendship trait on each page of the book. Then ask:

  - Who do you know who possesses that trait?
  - Is this person your friend?
  - Would you like this person to be your friend?
  - What can you do to become this person's friend?

- ▶ Tell the students to look for people who demonstrate the traits written on the book's pages and record their names next to the appropriate traits.

- ▶ Tell the students to bring their Flower Power Books to the next group session.

Joining In

Materials:

For The Leader:

- ☐ *Joining-In Role-Play Cards* reproduced on white cardstock and cut apart (page 168)
- ☐ Scissors

For Each Student:

- ☐ Flower Power Books from the previous session

Activity:

- ▶ Have the students share with the group what they've written in their Flower Power Books.

- ▶ Discuss ways to join a group already engaged in play by asking:

  - What kinds of things do you see kids doing at recess?
  - Which games would be hard to join after they begin?
  - Which games would be easy to join?
  - What should you say if you want to join a group or a game that has already started?
  - What will you do if others don't want you to join?

- ▶ Give each student a *Joining-In Role-Play Card.* Have the students practice joining a group by acting out the situations on the cards.

- ▶ Ask each student to name one thing he/she learned during the group sessions. Acknowledge any growth in friendship skills that you have observed. Congratulate the students on working hard to improve their friendship skills.

Cartoon Quips

Materials:

For The Leader:

- ☐ *Cartoon Conflicts:* multiple copies reproduced on white copy paper (pages 169-174)

For Each Student:

- ☐ Pencil

Activity:

- ▶ Place copies of the *Cartoon Conflicts* in the center of a table.
- ▶ Give each student a pencil.
- ▶ Allow each group member to select one cartoon from the pile.
- ▶ Working independently, have each student:
  - develop a list of *feeling words* matching what is expressed by the individuals in the cartoon frame and write the words beside the cartoon.
  - write a possible negative exchange in the conversation bubble for each individual in the cartoon frame.
  - complete the *Positive Exchange* box by drawing the figures and writing a possible positive exchange in the conversation bubble for each individual in the cartoon frame.
- ▶ Allow time for the students to share their cartoons with the group.
- ▶ Encourage students to share their cartoons with their teachers and parents.

Sticky Situations

Materials:

For The Leader:

- ☐ *Sticky Situation Cards* reproduced on white cardstock and cut apart (page 175)
- ☐ Scissors
- ☐ Large empty glue bottle or any container suitable for storing the cards
- ☐ Sharp knife
- ☐ Chips
- ☐ Small inexpensive prizes

Preparation:

Clean the glue bottle. Using a sharp knife, cut off the top portion (about $^{1}/_{2}$"). Leave one side attached so it can flip open and shut.

Place the *Sticky Situation Cards* in the container.

Activity:

- ▶ Instruct each student to select a *Sticky Situation Card* from the container.
- ▶ Have the student read the situation and make suggestions for solving the dilemma described. When the person who has drawn the card runs out of ideas, others may contribute their ideas.
- ▶ Award chips for each good idea presented. Award prizes to each student who earns a predetermined number of chips.

Brownie Points

Materials:

For The Leader:

- *Brownie Points Cards:* several sets reproduced on white copy paper and cut apart (page 176)
- Scissors
- Small aluminum baking pan to store *Brownie Point Cards*
- Optional: Brownies to serve at the end of group

For Each Student:

- Piece of construction paper
- Glue stick
- Pencil

Have Available For The Group:

- Crayons or markers and other art/craft supplies

Preparation:

Place the *Brownie Points Cards* in the aluminum baking pan.

Optional: Make brownies prior to the lesson.

Activity:

- Place the crayons or markers and any other art supplies on a table where they're accessible to group members.
- Give each student a piece of construction paper, a pencil, and a glue stick.
- Have each student select one *Brownie Points Card,* read it silently, and write an ending to the sentence starter on the card.
- Have each student share his/her completed sentence.
- Repeat this process until the allotted time has elapsed.
- Allow the students to decorate their *Brownie Points Cards.*
- Have the students glue their completed *Brownie Points Cards* on construction paper.

Friendship Mobiles

Materials:

For The Leader:

- ☐ Large number of magazine pictures showing people doing things
- ☐ Hole punch
- ☐ Wire hangers or dowels
- ☐ Nylon thread or yarn
- ☐ Digital pictures of classmates and group members or copies of students' pictures from a school annual. If pictures are not available, children's names and drawings may be used.

For Each Student:

- ☐ Scissors
- ☐ Glue stick
- ☐ Piece of colored construction paper

Activity:

- ▶ Place the magazine pictures on a table where they're accessible to group members.
- ▶ Give each student scissors, a glue stick, and a piece of colored construction paper.
- ▶ Tell the students to cut out pictures of people doing something they'd enjoy doing and glue each picture to a piece of construction paper slightly larger than the picture.
- ▶ Provide group members with digital pictures of classmates or group members.
- ▶ Have the students cut out the faces of classmates/group members and glue them over the faces in the magazine pictures. Be sure each student includes his/her own face.
- ▶ Create a friendship mobile by punching a hole in each picture, adding thread or yarn, and hanging the picture from the hangers or dowels.
- ▶ Discuss the various activities group members selected and how they can get friends to share these things with them.
- ▶ Students may take their mobiles with them.

Friendship Discussion

Materials:

For The Leader:

- ☐ *Friendship Discussion Cards* reproduced on white cardstock and cut apart (page 177)
- ☐ Scissors
- ☐ Toy microphone
- ☐ Optional: Stickers

Activity:

- ▶ Place the *Friendship Discussion Cards* face-down in the center of the group.
- ▶ Give one student the microphone. The student chooses who gets to speak during his/her turn. Students may speak or offer an opinion only when they're holding the microphone or the person with the microphone holds it in front of them.
- ▶ The group member holding the microphone selects a card. Speaking into the microphone, he/she reads it to the group and adds his/her thoughts.
- ▶ Then the student holds the microphone in front of other students who want to share ideas.
- ▶ Pass the microphone to the next person and begin the next turn, following the same procedure.
- ▶ Optional: As an added incentive, give a sticker for each good suggestion.

Making New Friends

Materials:

For The Leader:
- ☐ Chart paper and marker or chalkboard and chalk

Activity:

- ▶ Discuss the group members' experiences trying to make new friends. Include times when they were successful in making a new friend and times when they weren't. Generate discussion by asking:

  - Describe a time you tried to make a new friend. What did you do? What happened?
  - What do you do when you want to get to know someone new?
  - What kinds of things can you say?
  - What things don't work?

- ▶ List the students' ideas on the chart paper/chalkboard.

- ▶ Divide the group into pairs. Have each pair of students role-play one of the ideas listed.

- ▶ After each role-play, ask the participating students:

  - Do you think this would work at recess? In class? With classmates?
  - What will be hard about trying this?
  - What will you do if it doesn't work?

- ▶ Ask each student to name the strategy he/she intends to try in the next week. Encourage the students and tell them to let you know how it's working. Congratulate them on their hard work on learning to make and keep friends.

Candy Game

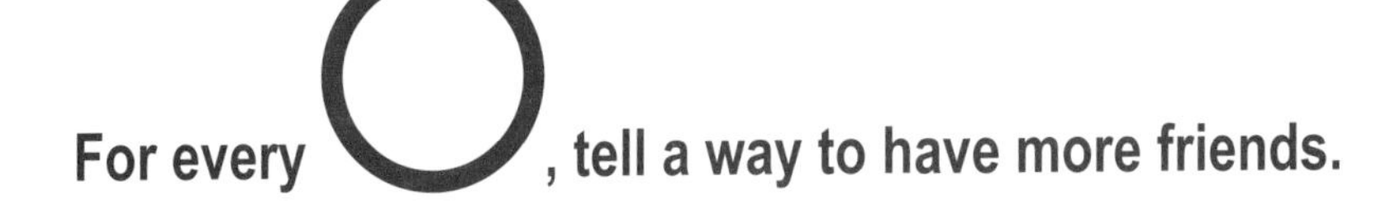

For every ◯, tell a way to have more friends.

For every ◯, tell something you can do with a friend.

For every ◯, tell a way to solve a conflict with a friend.

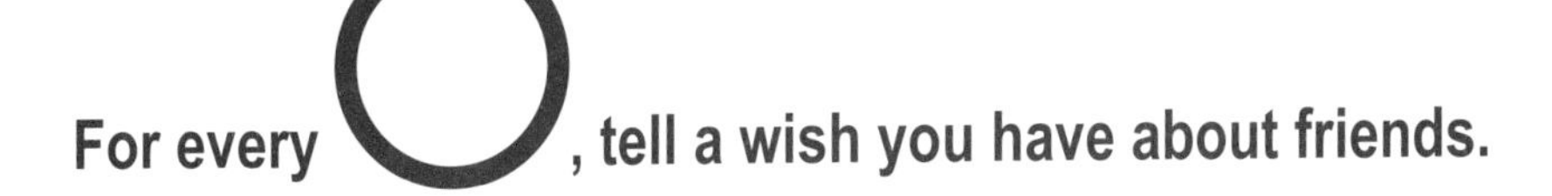

For every ◯, tell a wish you have about friends.

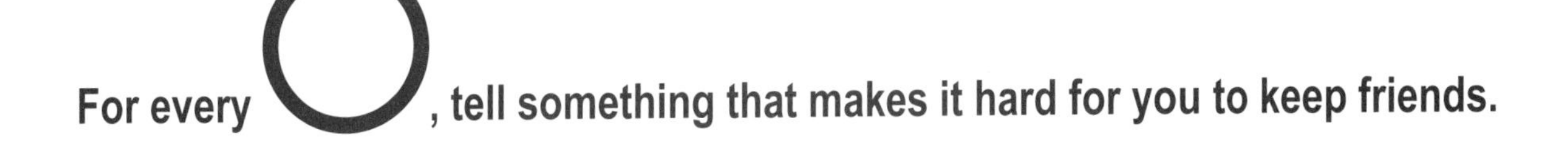

For every ◯, tell something that makes it hard for you to keep friends.

For every ◯, tell something you plan to do to make a new friend.

BEST-DRESSED FRIEND

BEST-DRESSED FRIEND

WORDS THAT HELP OR HURT FRIENDSHIPS #1

WORDS THAT HELP OR HURT FRIENDSHIPS #2

Cut the cards apart. Students may write their ideas on the blank cards.

Thank you.	I'm sorry.	
Give me that!	Excuse me.	
Me first!	Please.	
You're welcome.	It's mine!	
May I share your crayons?	Get out of my way!	
Nobody likes you!	May I play, too?	
Come sit with us.	No way! I don't want you on our team.	
I don't want to sit with you.	You'll be sorry.	
You stole my pencil!	Leave me alone!	
Let's play a game.	Can you help me find my book?	

CORRALLING FRIENDLY BEHAVIOR CARDS

Give Compliments.

Play Fair.

Help Others.

Be A Poor Sport.

Tell Your Friend's Secrets.

Say Mean Things.

Share.

Cheat At Games.

Be Selfish.

Use Kind Words.

Be A
Good Sport.

Act Like
A Bully.

Push And
Shove.

Be
Bossy.

Always
Insist On
Having
Your Way.

Take
Things
Without
Asking.

Play The
Game Others
Choose
Sometimes.

Eat
Lunch
Together.

Ignore Friends
When Others
Are Near.

Encourage
Friends To
Do Their Best.

HOBBY HORSES

Cut out 20 horse-head shapes. Glue the horse heads to large craft sticks. Write a different friendly or unfriendly behavior on each stick.

STAR SHAPES

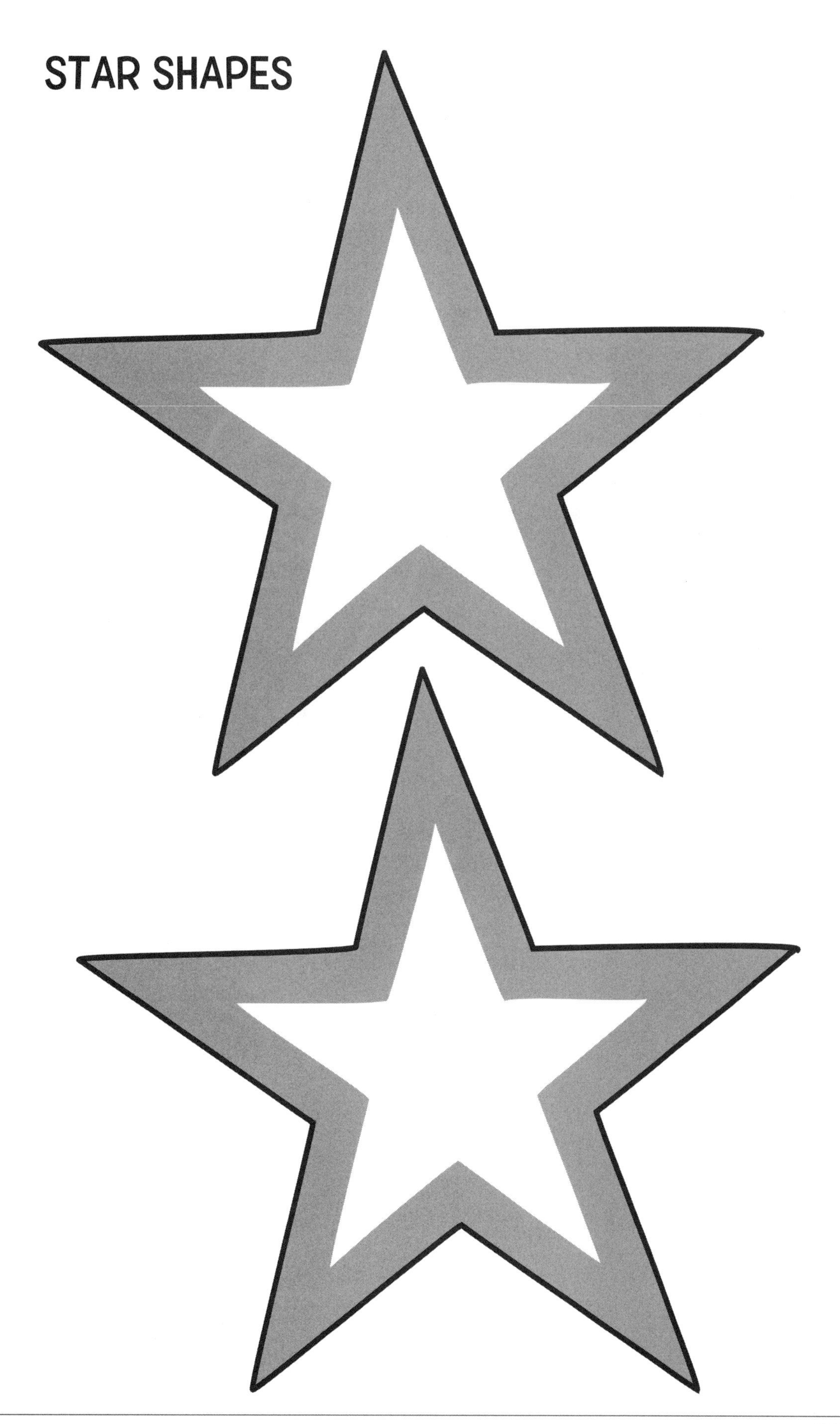

TIE SHAPE

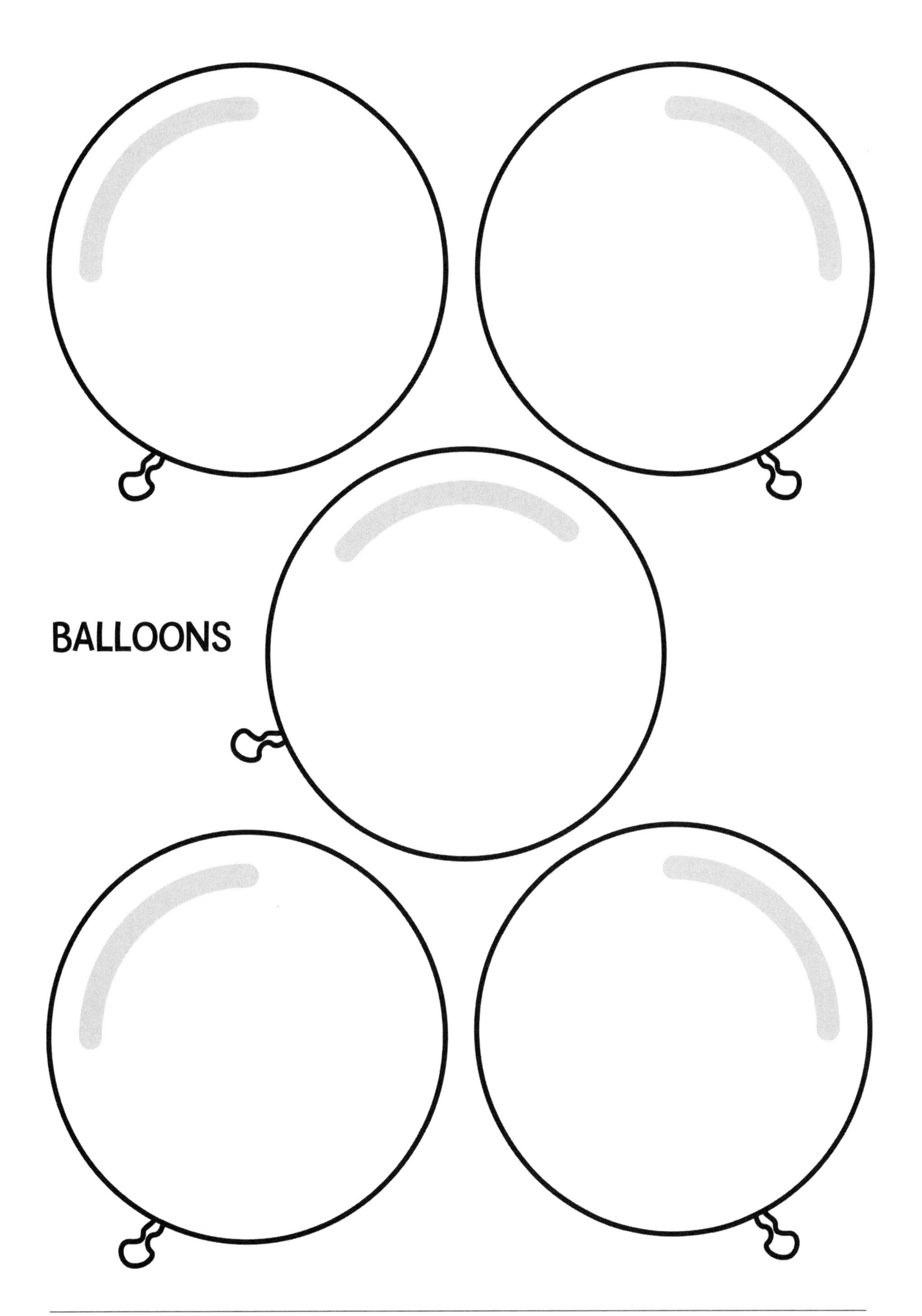
BALLOONS

BRICKS

FENCE PICKETS

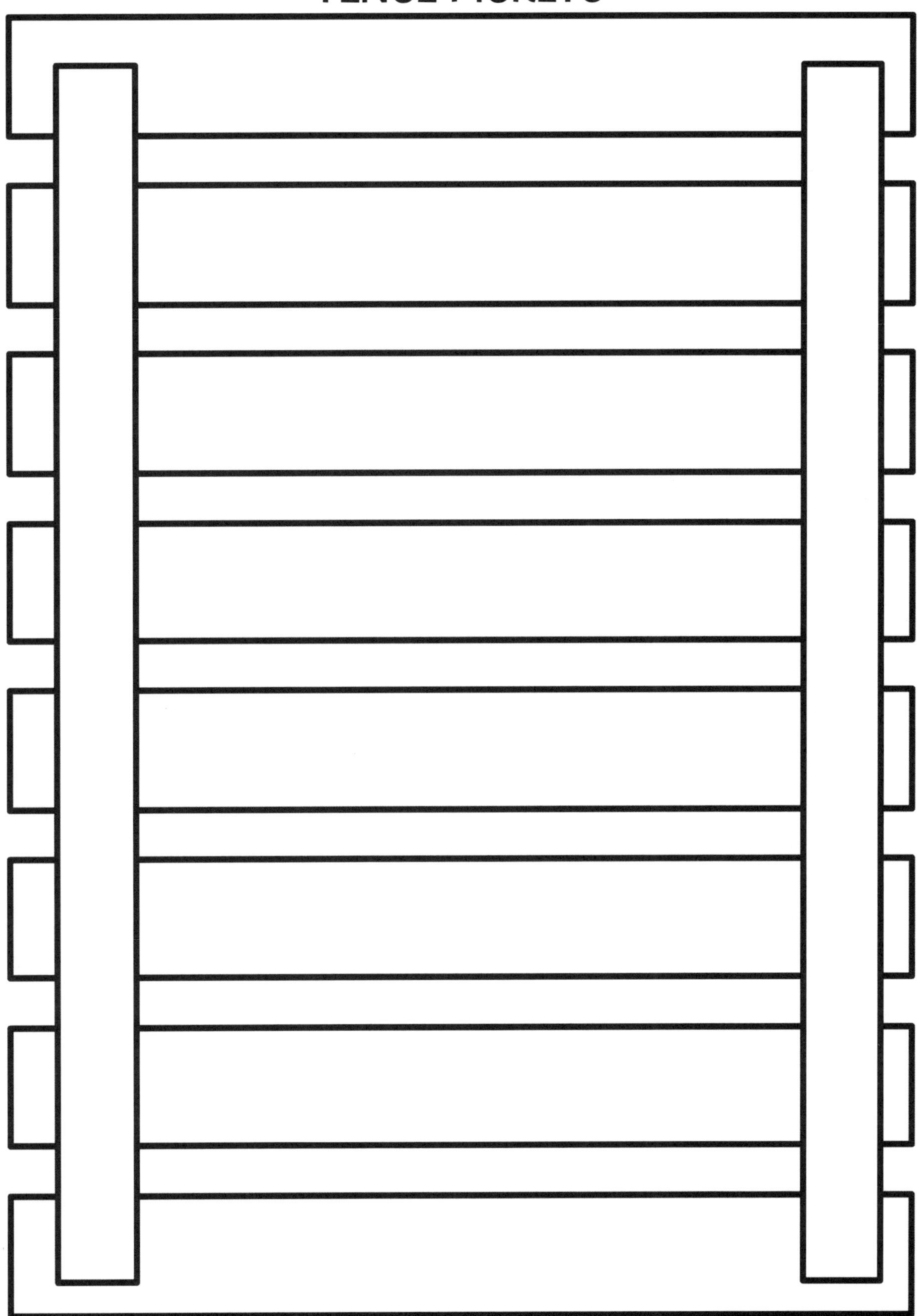

FENCE GATE

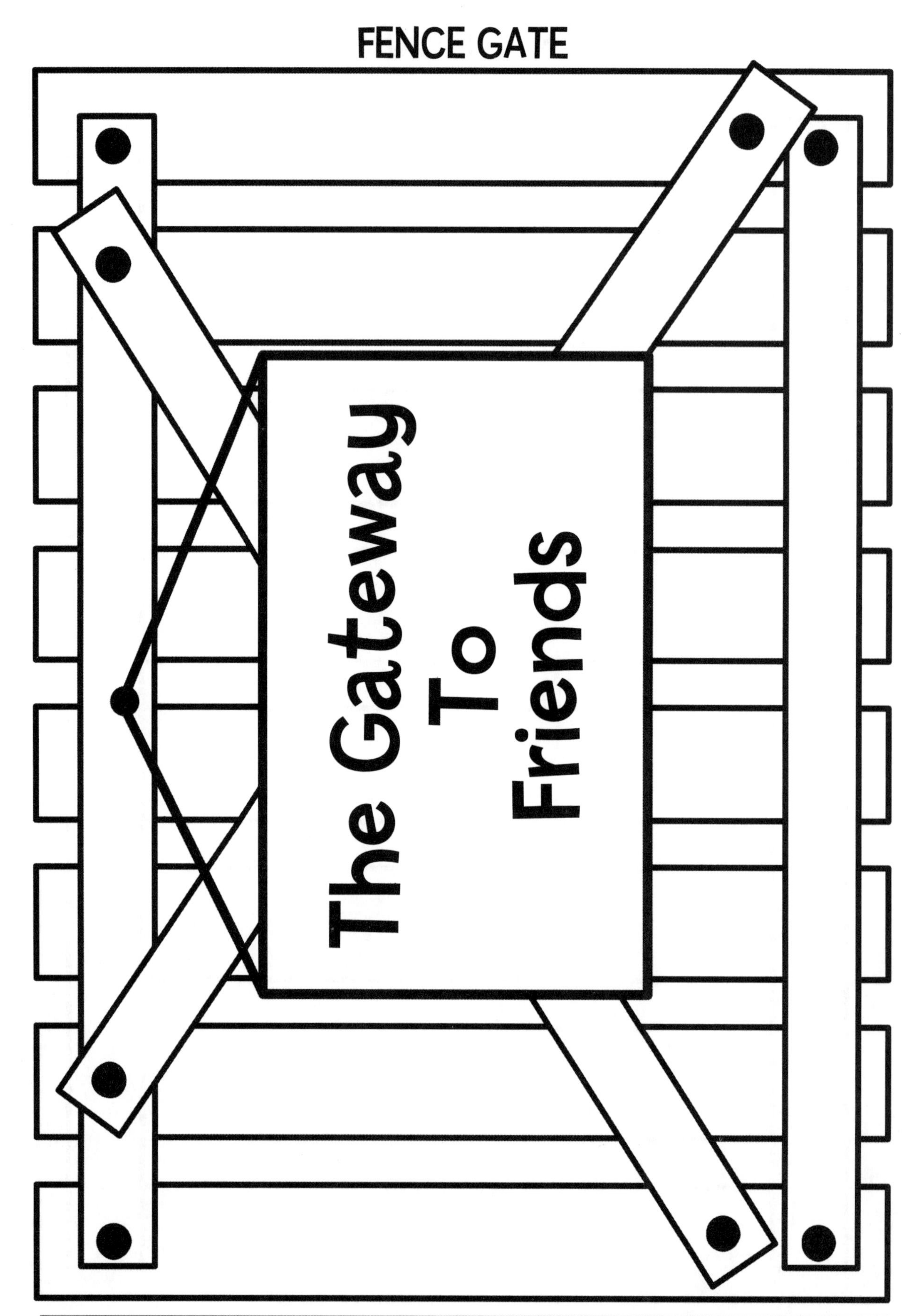

I TREASURE MY FRIENDS

TREASURE CHEST ITEMS

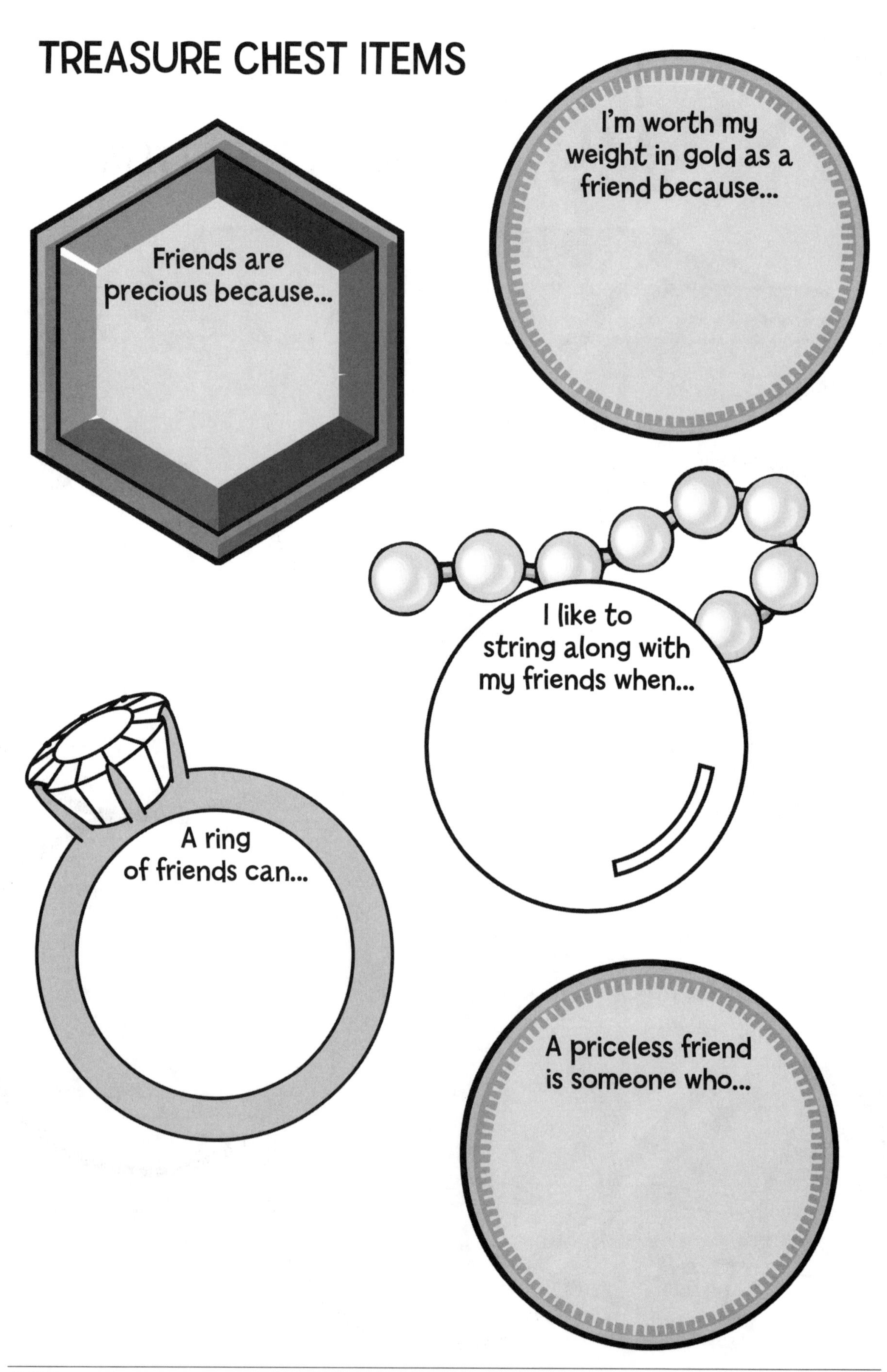

FLOWER PATTERN

JOINING-IN ROLE-PLAY CARDS

Joining In You see a group of students playing soccer and you want to play, too. The teams are already chosen and each side has the same number of players. ***What will you do?***	**Joining In** Two students are playing checkers. You love to play checkers and are very good at it. ***What will you do?***
Joining In A group of students you really want to be your friends are talking together. They don't notice you. You want to join in. ***What will you do?***	**Joining In** Two students who are really good friends are walking the track. You want to become their friend but know only one of them a little. You can't tell what they are discussing. ***What will you do?***
Joining In You're new to this school and it's time for recess. Outside, the students all run off to do their favorite things. ***What will you do?***	**Joining In** On Fridays, the teacher lets students sit anywhere they want at lunch. You want to join four students who always sit together. ***What will you do?***
Joining In It's time to select groups for social studies projects. You want to try being in a group with students you don't usually work with. ***What will you do?***	**Joining In** At the park on Saturday, you notice some kids from your school. You know them only a little, but they're always nice. You'd like to get to know them better. ***What will you do?***
Joining In The class has 30 minutes to play board games. You and your best friend want to play a board game that two other students have already chosen. ***What will you do?***	**Joining In** You really want the "popular" kids to be your friends, but they don't seem to feel the same way. Other kids in the class are nice, but you've never gotten to know them. ***What will you do?***

Cartoon Conflicts

Feeling Words:

____

____

____

____

____

____

____

____

____

____

____

____

Negative Exchange:

Positive Exchange:

Cartoon Conflicts

Feeling Words:

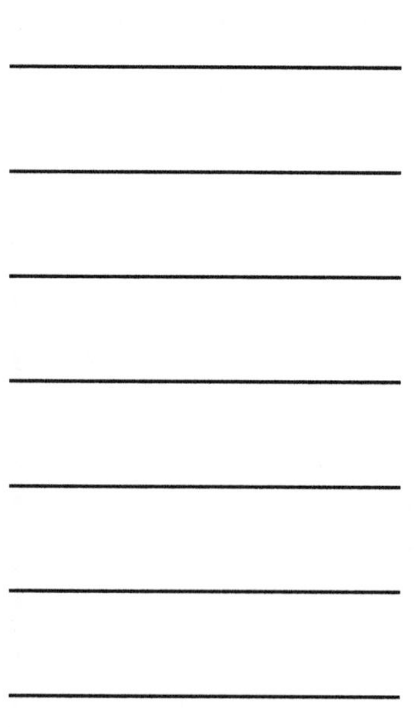

Negative Exchange:

Positive Exchange:

Cartoon Conflicts

Feeling Words:

____

____

____

____

____

____

____

____

____

____

____

____

Negative Exchange:

Positive Exchange:

Cartoon Conflicts

Negative Exchange:

Positive Exchange:

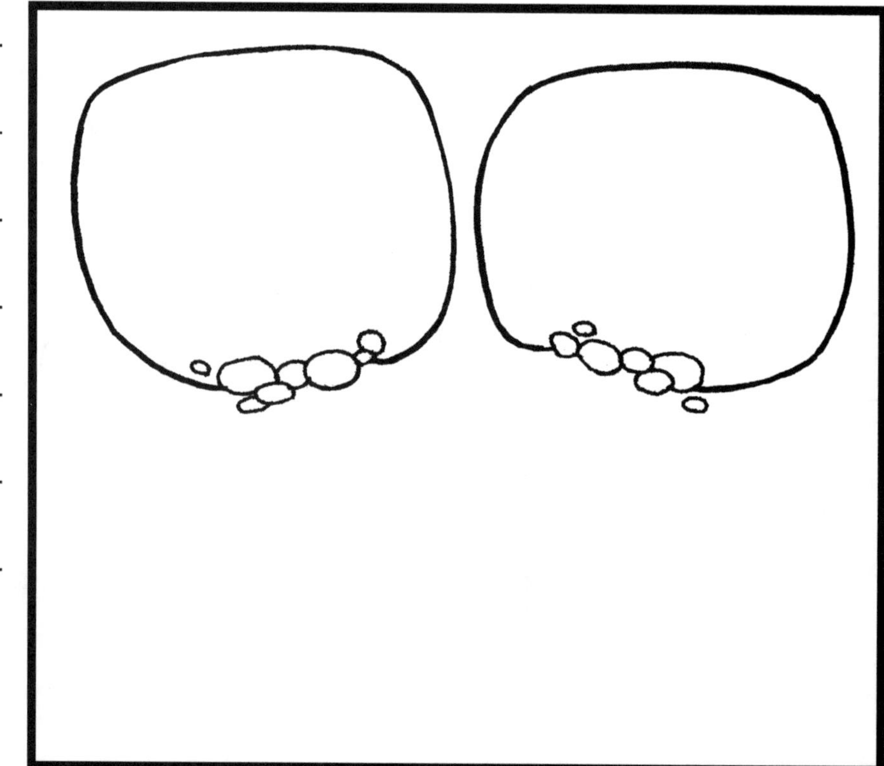

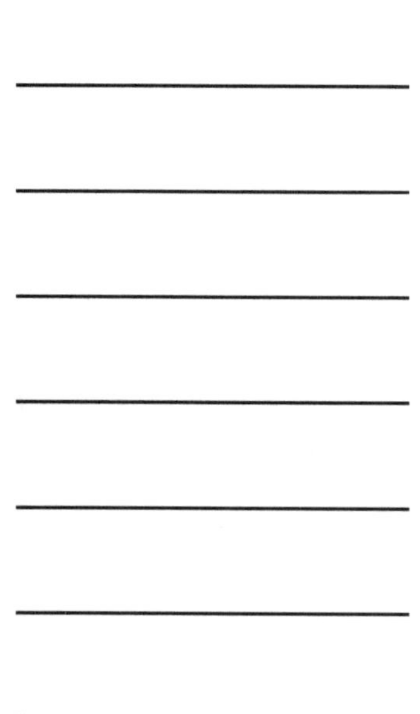

Cartoon Conflicts

Feeling Words:

____

____

____

____

____

____

____

____

____

____

____

____

Negative Exchange:

Positive Exchange:

Cartoon Conflicts

Feeling Words:

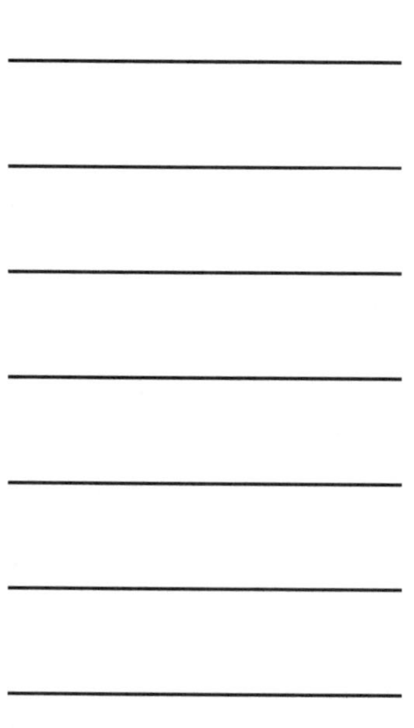

Negative Exchange:

Positive Exchange:

STICKY SITUATION CARDS

Sticky Situation
Each of your two best friends wants to be your only best friend.

Sticky Situation
Your mom will let you invite only one friend to a special event. You have two best friends.

Sticky Situation
Your best friend has started spending more time with a new boy/girl in class.

Sticky Situation
You've known your friend for a long time. Recently, though, you haven't enjoyed spending time with him/her. You have developed different interests.

Sticky Situation
Your best friend is very popular. How do you handle all the attention he/she gets?

Sticky Situation
You were invited to a party but your best friend was not. You really want to go.

Sticky Situation
One friend has told you some rumors that another friend is supposedly spreading about you.

Sticky Situation
You saw your friend do something wrong. The teacher is asking if you know anything about it.

Sticky Situation
A friend just told you a rumor about one of your other friends.

Sticky Situation
You are with a group of friends who just recently started letting you hang out with them. They all want to do something you know is wrong.

BROWNIE POINT CARDS

A bad friendship habit I need to break is...

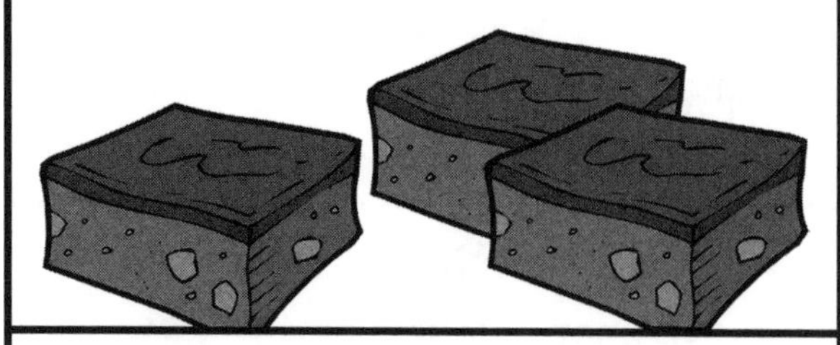

Things get messy with me and my friends when...

I stick with my friends when...

I'm best at being a friend when...

I would have to drop a friend who...

I need my friends to be patient with me when...

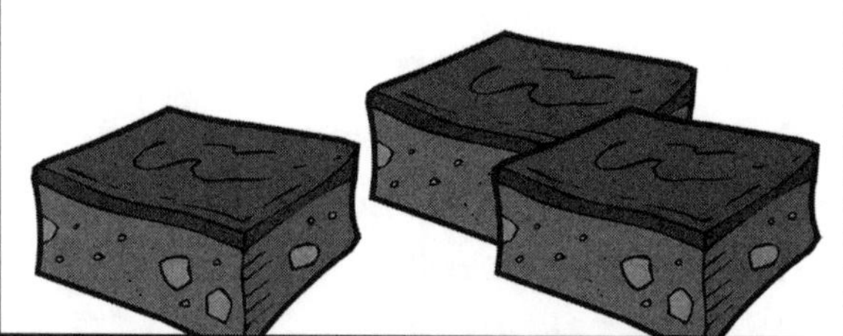

I would crumble if my friend...

Friends earn brownie points by...

FRIENDSHIP DISCUSSION CARDS

Something I would never do to make a new friend is...	Some kids are mean because ...
Something that could make me lose a friend is...	Some kids are popular because...
You know someone is a real friend when...	The hardest thing about being a friend is...
The hardest thing about making new friends is...	You can keep friends if you...
The best thing about having a friend is...	The main reason friends have arguments is...
Is it important to be friends with the popular kids? Explain.	What are the most important qualities in a friend?
It might be hard to be friends with someone who...	It's not a good idea to be friends with people who...

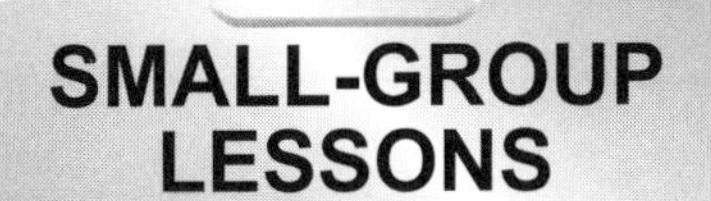

Grief/Loss

In presenting this topic, I use the same picture to introduce almost any discussion on grief. For me, the well represents the wishing we often do when someone dies. I explain the concept of *wishing wells*, then discuss the many wishes I have regarding my personal losses. Children will quickly add their own wishes. The stormy sky illustrates how dark and lonely grief feels. The rainbow represents hope in the sense that beauty can follow storms. Discussing this picture can fill an entire group session. A reproducible copy of this picture is on page 205.

Helping children cope with loss and grief is extremely important to me. Children are often confused and misinformed about these topics. In most cases, family members are also grieving, and children may not be able to talk with them about their questions or concerns. The counselor can provide a safe haven where questions are answered and fears are allayed. The issue of spiritual beliefs will come up, so the counselor needs to be prepared to respond.

These lessons attempt to address each of the specific tasks related to the grief process:

- Understanding death
- Remembering the deceased
- Commemorating the deceased
- Understanding feelings
- Identifying support systems

SMALL-GROUP LESSONS

Grief/Loss

GRADES K/1

GRADES 2/3

GRADES 4/5

ASCA STANDARDS, COMPETENCIES, AND INDICATORS FOR SMALL-GROUP LESSONS ON GRIEF/LOSS

Participation in these group activities will address the following ASCA standards, competencies, and indicators:

Domain	**A/ACADEMIC DEVELOPMENT**
A/A:2.3	Use communication skills to know when and how to ask for help when needed
A/A:3.1	Demonstrate the ability to work independently, as well as the ability to work cooperatively with other students

Domain	**C/CAREER DEVELOPMENT**
C/A:1.4	Learn how to interact and work cooperatively in teams

Domain	**PS/PERSONAL/SOCIAL DEVELOPMENT**
PS/A:1.1	Develop a positive attitude toward self as a unique and worthy person
PS/A:1.2	Identify values, attitudes and beliefs
PS/A:1.4	Understand change as a part of growth
PS/A:1.5	Identify and express feelings
PS/A:1.7	Recognize personal boundaries, rights and privacy needs
PS/A:1.9	Demonstrate cooperative behavior in groups
PS/A:1.10	Identify personal strengths and assets
PS/A:1.11	Identify and discuss changing personal and social roles
PS/A:1.12	Identify and recognize changing family roles
PS/A:2.1	Recognize that everyone has rights and responsibilities
PS/A:2.5	Recognize and respect differences in various family configurations
PS/A:2.6	Use effective communication skills
PS/A:2.7	Know that communication involves speaking, listening, and nonverbal behavior
PS/B:1.4	Develop effective coping skills for dealing with problems
PS/B:1.5	Demonstrate when, where, and how to seek help for solving problems and making decisions
PS/C:1.4	Demonstrate the ability to assert boundaries, rights, and personal privacy
PS/C:1.5	Differentiate between situations requiring peer support and situations requiring adult professional help
PS/C:1.6	Identify resource people in the school and community, and know how to seek their help
PS/C:1.10	Learn techniques for managing stress and conflict
PS/C:1.11	Learn coping skills for managing life events

Master Supply List For Small Group On Grief/Loss

Collect these supplies prior to presenting the group.
Place all special supplies in the same box as the lessons copied on cardstock.

GENERAL SUPPLIES:

- ☐ Chart paper and marker
- ☐ Scissors
- ☐ Pencils
- ☐ Pens
- ☐ Hole punches
- ☐ Stapler and staples
- ☐ Lined paper
- ☐ Yardsticks
- ☐ Rulers

ART SUPPLIES:

- ☐ Crayons or markers
- ☐ Drawing paper
- ☐ Cardboard or heavy paper
- ☐ Glue sticks/Glue
- ☐ Paint and brushes or contact paper
- ☐ Various art/craft supplies
- ☐ Black marker
- ☐ Construction paper (blue, other colors)
- ☐ Cardstock or heavyweight copy paper (white, red, green, tan, other colors)

MISCELLANEOUS SUPPLIES:

- ☐ Old magazines
- ☐ Small clear plastic soda bottles with lids
- ☐ Liquid soap
- ☐ Food coloring—different colors
- ☐ Small boxes (as large as a shoe box or as small as a jewelry gift box)
- ☐ Optional: Book on remembering someone who has died
- ☐ Several tubes of different-colored icing
- ☐ Optional: Lunch bags
- ☐ Optional: Fabric
- ☐ Optional: Fabric glue or needle and thread
- ☐ String, ribbon, or cording
- ☐ Small branches

- ☐ Small pots
- ☐ Plaster or clay
- ☐ Paper grocery bags
- ☐ Small nuts and bolts
- ☐ Small jar

COPY ON CARDSTOCK: *Note*: Heavyweight copy paper can be substituted for cardstock

- ☐ *Grief/Loss Small-Group Lessons* reproduced on white cardstock as a quick reference to each lesson's page number (page 180)
- ☐ *Bricks:* several copies reproduced on different shades of red cardstock and cut apart (page 207)
- ☐ *Tree Trunk:* one copy for each student, reproduced on tan or brown cardstock (page 208)
- ☐ *Leaves:* several copies reproduced on green cardstock and cut out (page 209)
- ☐ *Gift Tree Leaves:* one copy for each student, reproduced on green cardstock (page 213)
- ☐ *Journal Jar Topics:* one set reproduced on white cardstock and cut apart (pages 214-215)

ONE COPY FOR EACH STUDENT ON WHITE COPY PAPER:

- ☐ *Body Shape:* one for each student (page 206)
- ☐ *Gingerbread Man:* one for each student (page 210)
- ☐ *Face Shape:* one for each student (page 211)
- ☐ *Circles:* one for each student plus several extra copies (page 212)

Picture Diary
(Understanding)

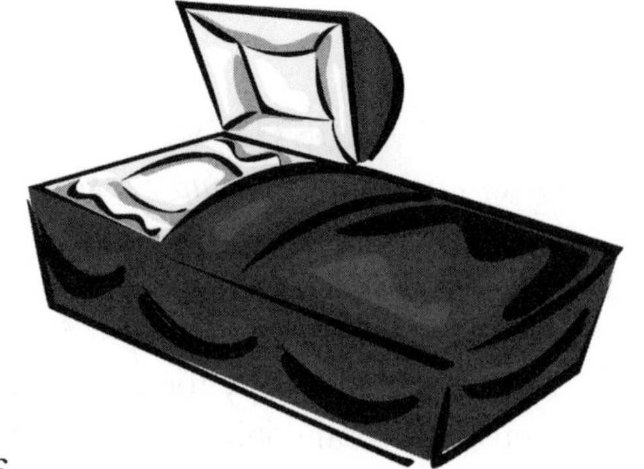

Materials:

For The Leader:
- ☐ Stapler and staples
- ☐ Scissors or paper cutter

For Each Student:
- ☐ Crayons or markers
- ☐ Several 9" x 12" sheets of drawing paper cut in half

Activity:

- ▶ Ask the students the name of the person who has died and their relationship to him/her. (Tom Smith—my grandfather)

- ▶ Give each student several sheets of drawing paper and crayons or markers.

- ▶ Ask the students to create several pictures to help you understand what has happened. Allow time for the students to complete a rough drawing of what is listed below, then to show/explain their drawings to the group. Before beginning, poll the students to see who attended the loved one's funeral. If no students attended a funeral, omit statements referring to the funeral. Allow those who did attend a funeral to draw the pictures. Have the students draw pictures that show:

    - death.
    - the person as they remember him/her.
    - what happened to the person who has died.
    - the funeral.
    - how they felt during the funeral.
    - how they feel when they think about the person who has died.
    - a place the two of them liked to go.

- ▶ Staple each student's drawings together to make a picture diary. Allow the students to take their diaries home.

Person Collage
(Remembering)

Materials:

For Each Student:
- ☐ Cardboard or heavy paper
- ☐ Glue stick
- ☐ Scissors

Have Available For The Group:
- ☐ Old magazines

Activity:

▶ Have the group members talk about the person who has died. Ask:

- What did that person love to do?
- What do you remember best about him/her?
- What did you and he/she like to do together?
- Where did you and he/she go together?

▶ Give each student a piece of cardboard or heavy paper, a glue stick, and scissors.

▶ Put the magazines in a place where they're accessible to the students.

▶ Using pictures cut from magazines, have each student create a collage that represents the person who has died. For example, a student may create a collage of a grandfather that includes pictures related to fishing, camping, hiking, and reading.

▶ Allow time for the students to complete their collages and share them with the group.

Churning Feelings
(Understanding Feelings)

Materials:

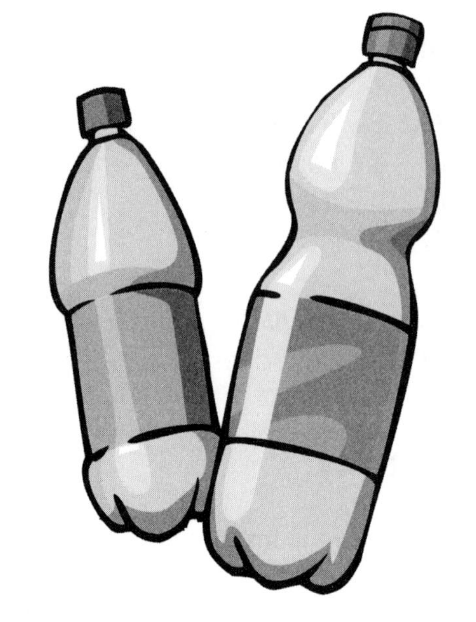

For The Leader:
- ☐ Small clear plastic soda bottle with lid

For Each Student:
- ☐ Small clear plastic soda bottle with lid

Have Available For The Group:
- ☐ Water
- ☐ Liquid soap
- ☐ Food coloring—different colors
- ☐ Glue

Preparation:

Make a Churning Feelings Bottle for demonstration purposes. Fill the soda bottle with water, liquid soap, and food coloring. Apply glue to the lip of the bottle. Screw on the lid.

Activity:

- Discuss the many feelings that occur when we lose someone we love—sadness, grief, anger, guilt, etc.
- Talk about the ways our bodies react to those feelings. Display the bottle you made earlier. Shake it vigorously to show how those feelings churn up inside us.
- Set the bottle aside and discuss how we can relieve those feelings—exercising, drawing pictures, talking with friends, talking with a trusted grown-up, going for a walk, reading a book, etc. After the discussion, call attention to the bottle, which should be much less bubbly and beginning to settle down.
- Allow the students to make their own Churning Feelings Bottles. Give each student a small clear plastic soda bottle with a lid. Tell the students to fill their bottle with water, liquid soap, and a few drops of food coloring, then to apply glue to the lip of the bottle and screw on the lid.
- The students may take their Churning Feelings Bottles with them as a reminder of the way feelings bubble up, then disperse over time.

My Memory Box
(Commemorating)

Materials:

For Each Student:
- ☐ Small box (as large as a shoe box or as small as a jewelry gift box)
- ☐ Glue or glue stick
- ☐ Scissors

Have Available For The Group:
- ☐ Old magazines
- ☐ Paint and brushes or contact paper
- ☐ Various art/craft supplies

Activity:

- ▶ Tell the students that many items may have special meaning to them or remind them of special times with the person who has died.
- ▶ Explain that they are going to create a special box in which to keep these mementos.
- ▶ Give each student a box supplied by you or brought from home, scissors, and glue.
- ▶ Allow time for the students to decorate the box. They may paint it or cover it with contact paper. Magazine pictures may be added. The box could be decorated to represent a theme. For example, a student who enjoyed fishing with his/her grandfather could decorate a box with fishing-related pictures. (Depending on the complexity or materials used, you may want to take two group sessions to complete this activity.)
- ▶ Discuss what could be kept in the box—ticket stubs, photographs, letters, dried flowers, etc.
- ▶ Send the boxes home with the students. Ask the students to bring the box to the next meeting, when they'll share with the group one item they decided to put in the box.

Wall of Support
(Identifying Support Systems)

Materials:

For The Leader:
- ☐ *Bricks:* several copies reproduced on different shades of red cardstock and cut apart (page 207)
- ☐ Scissors
- ☐ Black marker

For Each Student:
- ☐ *Body Shape* reproduced on white copy paper (page 206)
- ☐ Piece of blue construction paper
- ☐ Scissors
- ☐ Glue stick
- ☐ Crayons or markers
- ☐ Memory Boxes from Session 4

Have Available For The Group:
- ☐ Optional: Various art/craft supplies

Activity:

It is important for children to be aware of their support systems. This activity helps them identify friends, family, and other adults who may be helpful throughout the grief process.

- ▶ Begin the session by having the students describe one item they have chosen to put in their Memory Box.
- ▶ Give each student a copy of *Body Shape,* scissors, a piece of blue construction paper, a glue stick, and crayons or markers.
- ▶ Have each student color the body shape to represent him/herself. You may also have other art supplies available for the students to use to decorate the body shape.
- ▶ Have the students cut out the body shape and glue it from the center to the top of the construction paper.
- ▶ Discuss how the picture looks as though the student is floating in the sky. Explain that this is impossible. Without support, he/she would fall.

- Explain that everyone needs support, especially in times of grief.

- Ask the group members to identify people who can help them when they feel sad or mad or have a problem. On each brick, write the name of each person identified. Give the bricks to the student who suggested the names to glue under his/her body shape. This creates a "wall of support." (*Note:* Creating categories may help the students think of many different people—a friend, someone in school, a classmate, a relative, a neighbor, a teammate, etc.)

- Encourage the students to take their pictures with them and post them in a prominent place at home. The pictures can remind the students of the many people who can support them when they feel overwhelmed.

Picture Diary
(Understanding)

Materials:

For The Leader:
- ☐ Stapler and staples
- ☐ Scissors or paper cutter

For Each Student:
- ☐ Crayons or markers
- ☐ Several 9" x 12" sheets of drawing paper cut in half

Activity:

▶ Ask the students the name of the person who has died and their relationship to him/her.

▶ Give each student several sheets of drawing paper and crayons or markers.

▶ Ask the students to create several pictures to help you understand what has happened. Allow time for the students to complete a rough drawing of what is listed below, then to show/explain their drawings to the group. Before beginning, poll the students to see who attended the loved one's funeral. If no students attended a funeral, omit statements referring to the funeral. Allow those who did attend a funeral to draw the pictures. Have the students draw pictures that show:

- death.
- the person as they remember him/her.
- what happened to the person who has died.
- the funeral.
- how they felt during the funeral.
- how they feel when they think about the person who has died.
- a place the two of them liked to go.

▶ Staple each student's drawings together to make a picture diary. Allow the students to take their diaries home.

Memorial Tree
(Remembering)

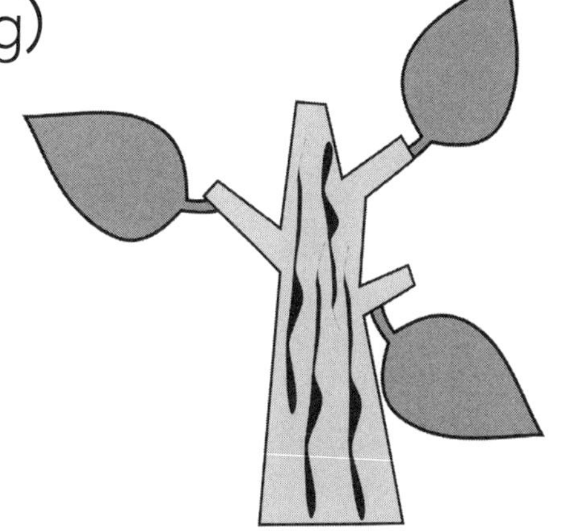

Materials:

For The Leader:

- ☐ *Leaves:* several copies reproduced on green cardstock and cut out (page 209)
- ☐ Scissors
- ☐ Optional: Book on remembering someone who has died

For Each Student:

- ☐ *Tree Trunk* reproduced on tan or brown cardstock (page 208)
- ☐ Glue stick
- ☐ Pencil

Activity:

- ▶ Begin by allowing each student to talk about what he/she misses most about the person who has died. It could be things they did together or something in the future that the deceased person won't be a part of. As students talk, ideas will emerge.
- ▶ Give each student a copy of *Tree Trunk*, a pencil, a glue stick, and two or three leaves.
- ▶ On each leaf, instruct the students to write a message to/about the loved one and ways he/ she is missed.
- ▶ Have the students glue the leaves onto the tree trunk.
- ▶ Allow time for each group member to share his/her Memory Tree with the group.
- ▶ Optional: Read a book about remembering someone who has died.

Feelings In My Body

(Understanding Feelings)

Materials:

For The Leader:
- ☐ Chart paper and marker
- ☐ Colored markers

For Each Student:
- ☐ Undecorated *Gingerbread Man* cookie (the larger, the easier)
- ☐ Several tubes of different-colored icing

  or
- ☐ *Gingerbread Man* reproduced on white copy paper (page 210)
- ☐ Crayons or markers

Preparation:

Draw a large outline of a gingerbread-type body shape on the chart paper.

Activity:

- ▶ Discuss the feelings we may have when someone we love dies.

- ▶ Discuss the parts of our bodies those feelings may affect. As each body part is mentioned, add graphic illustrations to the large body shape. Examples are:

  - Headaches—draw a lightning bolt in the head
  - Upset stomach—draw a red blob in the stomach area
  - Tears—draw blue teardrops near the eyes

- ▶ Option 1: Give each student one cookie. Set the tubes of colored icing where they are easily accessible to the students. Allow the students to decorate their gingerbread men, using colored icing to illustrate the body parts where their feelings are most evident.

- ▶ Option 2: Give each student a copy of *Gingerbread Man* and crayons or markers. Tell the students to color their gingerbread men, illustrating the body parts where their feelings are most evident.

▶ Discuss effective ways to release energy associated with the feelings mentioned by the students. Some suggestions are:

- running.
- walking.
- drawing.
- singing.
- listening to music.
- reading.
- talking with someone.

Memory Bag
(Commemorating)

Materials:

For The Leader: (If making fabric bags)
- ☐ Fabric
- ☐ Scissors
- ☐ Fabric glue or needle and thread
- ☐ String, ribbon, or cording

For Each Student:
- ☐ Small lunch bag or drawstring fabric bag

Have Available For The Group:
- ☐ Various art/craft supplies for decorating the bag

Preparation:

If you're making a drawstring fabric bag for each student:

- from the fabric, cut a circle approximately 12" in diameter.
- fold the outer edge over and stitch or glue it. Leave an opening through which to thread the string, ribbon, or cording.
- thread the string around the circumference of the circle.
- tie the ends of the string together, then pull the fabric to create the bag.

Activity:

- ▶ Tell the students that a Memory Bag holds special things they want to remember about the person who has died.

- ▶ Give each student a paper or fabric bag. Place the art supplies in a readily accessible area. Allow time for the students to decorate their bags.

- ▶ Discuss what the students might keep in their bags.

- ▶ The students may take the bags home, but should bring them to the next session, when they'll tell the group about one or more items in their bags.

Circles Of Friends
(Identifying Support System)

Materials:

For Each Student:
- ☐ *Face Shape* reproduced on white copy paper (page 211)
- ☐ *Circles* reproduced on white copy paper—make several extra copies (page 212)
- ☐ Large piece of construction paper
- ☐ Crayons or markers
- ☐ Scissors
- ☐ String or ribbon
- ☐ Glue stick

Activity:

- ▶ It's important for children to be aware of their support systems. This activity helps them identify friends, family, and other adults who may be helpful throughout the grief process.
- ▶ Begin the session by allowing students to share items from their Memory Bags.
- ▶ Give each student a copy of *Face Shape* and *Circles*, scissors, a large piece of construction paper, a glue stick, and crayons or markers.
- ▶ Instruct the students to color the face to represent themselves.
- ▶ Have the students cut out the face shape and glue it to the center of the construction paper.
- ▶ Discuss the need we all have for support, especially in times of grief.
- ▶ Ask the students to identify people who can help them when they're upset. As each student identifies a person, have him/her write the person's name on a circle. (*Note:* Have extra circles available.) Creating categories may help students think of:
    - a friend, someone in school.
    - a classmate.
    - a family member.
    - a neighbor.
    - a teammate, etc.

- Instruct the students to cut out their circles and glue them around the face. Give each student a long piece of string or ribbon.

- Have the students cut the ribbon/string into pieces long enough to reach from each circle to the face, then glue the pieces of the string/ribbon connecting each circle to the face (the student).

- Emphasize that many people can provide support. Students should take the completed paper with them and post it where they'll be reminded of the all the support they have.

Picture Diary
(Understanding)

Materials:

For The Leader:
- ☐ Stapler and staples
- ☐ Scissors or paper cutter

For Each Student:
- ☐ Crayons or markers
- ☐ Several 9" x 12" sheets of drawing paper cut in half

Activity:

- ▶ Ask the students the name of the person who has died and their relationship to him/her.
- ▶ Give each student several sheets of drawing paper and crayons or markers.
- ▶ Ask the students to create several pictures to help you understand what has happened. Allow time for the students to complete a rough drawing of what is listed below, then to show/explain their drawings to the group. Before beginning, poll the students to see who attended the loved one's funeral. If no students attended a funeral, omit statements referring to the funeral. Allow those who did attend a funeral to draw the pictures. Have the students draw pictures that show:
    - death.
    - the person as they remember him/her.
    - what happened to the person who has died.
    - the funeral.
    - how they felt during the funeral.
    - how they feel when they think about the person who has died.
    - a place the two of them liked to go.
- ▶ Staple each student's drawings together to make a picture diary. Allow the students to take their diaries home.

The Gift Tree
(Remembering)

Materials:

For The Leader:
- ☐ Small branches—one for each student
- ☐ Small pots— one for each student
- ☐ Plaster or clay

For Each Student:
- ☐ *Gift Tree Leaves* reproduced on green cardstock (page 213)
- ☐ Scissors
- ☐ Pencil

Have Available For The Group:
- ☐ Hole punches
- ☐ Ribbon

Preparation:

Fill each small pot with plaster/clay and insert a small branch. Make one pot for each student.

Activity:

- ▶ Discuss physical characteristics or traits the students may have inherited from the person who has died. These might include:
    - a sense of humor.
    - athletic ability.
    - a love of fishing.
    - height, eye color, etc.
- ▶ Give each student a copy of *Gift Tree Leaves*, scissors, and a pencil. Tell the students to cut out the leaves and punch a small hole in each one.
- ▶ Have students fill in the blank: "What ____ gave to me" on one side of a leaf and write the "gift" on the other side. Using ribbon, have the students tie each completed leaf to a branch.
- ▶ Have the students take the tree with them as a reminder of the gifts received from the person who has died. Encourage them to share the tree with family. You may want to provide additional leaves for them to add as other ideas occur to them.

Do's And Don'ts Of Grieving

(Understanding Feelings)

Materials:

For The Leader:

- ☐ Chart paper and marker or chalkboard and chalk

For Each Student:

- ☐ Lined paper
- ☐ Pencil or pen

Activity:

▶ Brainstorm ways grief can affect people. Write responses on the chart paper/chalkboard. Be sure to include physical, emotional, and mental effects. You could also include social and behavioral consequences. (Some students may suggest spiritual effects.)

▶ Allow the students to share relevant personal experiences.

▶ Discuss effective ways to cope with these responses. For example:

- Lack of energy may be due to grief. So it's a good idea to get more rest and eat healthful foods.
- Grief may affect concentration. It would be wise to ask the teacher to help you stay focused.
- Be willing to forgive a friend or family member who upset you when expressing his/her grief.

▶ Brainstorm things people do when grieving. Write these ideas on the chart paper/chalkboard. Guide the brainstorming so you end up with more positive reactions to grieving than negative ones.

▶ Give each student a piece of lined paper and a pencil or pen. Tell the students to write *The Do's And Don'ts Of Grieving* at the top of the paper. Then tell the students to divide the paper into two columns, labeling one column "Do's" and the other column "Don'ts."

▶ Using the list on the chart paper/chalkboard, decide which ideas belong in which column. As each item is assigned to a column, write *Do* or *Don't* next to it. Have the students copy these ideas in the correct columns on their papers.

▶ At the end of the discussion, each group member will have a list of *The Do's And Don'ts Of Grieving* to take home.

Memory Book
(Commemorating)

Materials:

For Each Student:
- ☐ 1-2 large paper grocery bags
- ☐ Several sheets of construction paper a bit smaller than the book covers
- ☐ 3 Sets of small nuts and fat, slightly shorter bolts

Have Available For The Group:
- ☐ Various art/craft supplies to decorate the book covers
- ☐ Yardsticks
- ☐ Hole punches

Preparation:

If possible, make a sample Memory Book to show the students.

Activity:

- ▶ Tell the students a Memory Book holds special items, pictures, and memories related to a person we have loved and lost. A Memory Book can be added to as time goes on.
- ▶ Discuss items a Memory Book might include—drawings, photographs, special mementos, descriptions of special times together, maps of places visited, ticket stubs from special events attended together, a letter to the deceased person expressing feelings, etc.
- ▶ Have each student make a Memory Book.
    - Give each student a large paper grocery bag, several sheets of construction paper, and three sets of small nuts and bolts.
    - Have the students separate the seams where the bag is glued.
    - Determine what size the book will be. The book should be slightly larger than the construction paper pages.
    - Tear two similar-sized rectangles from the paper bag. The best way to tear the bag is to place a yardstick over the material, hold it snugly, then tear along the edge. These pieces will be the front and back covers of the book.
    - Punch three holes on one side of the front cover, back cover, and construction paper pages.

- To bind the covers and pages together, thread the nuts through the punched holes. Secure each nut with a bolt.
- Have the students decorate their covers, using art supplies.

▶ Have the students write at least one memory or special thought in the book before leaving the session. Ask them to take their books home and add other items. Have the students bring their Memory Books to the remaining sessions to share them with the group. This is easier than having everyone share their books at the same session.

Pyramid Of Support

(Identifying Support Systems)

Materials:

For Each Student:

- ☐ 2 Large pieces of construction paper in contrasting colors
- ☐ Glue
- ☐ Scissors
- ☐ Pencil or pen
- ☐ Ruler

Activity:

It's important for students to be aware of their support systems. This activity will help students identify friends, family, and other adults who may be helpful throughout the grief process.

- ▶ Give each student scissors, a pen or pencil, glue, and a ruler. Have each group member select one piece of construction paper. Tell the students to cut out a triangle almost as large as the paper itself, then use the ruler to draw two or three horizontal lines and short, staggered vertical lines on it to create blocks. Have the students number each block, starting from the bottom and working up, then cut the blocks apart.

- ▶ Ask the students to identify people who can help them through their grief journey. Creating categories may help students can think of many different people: Suggested categories could be:

  - a friend.
  - someone in school.
  - a classmate.
  - a family member.
  - a neighbor.
  - a teammate, etc.

- ▶ Each student who identifies a person should write that person's name on one of the blocks.

- Group members may also decide to write a brief description of the way each person can help. Some suggestions are:

    - Counselor—will listen to me
    - Mom—will hug me
    - Friend—will play ball with me

- Have each student select a piece of construction paper of a contrasting color, then glue each block to the construction paper, building the pyramid from the bottom up.

- Reserve the top block of each pyramid for the student's self-portrait or name.

- Encourage the students to post their pyramids in a prominent place as a reminder of sources of support.

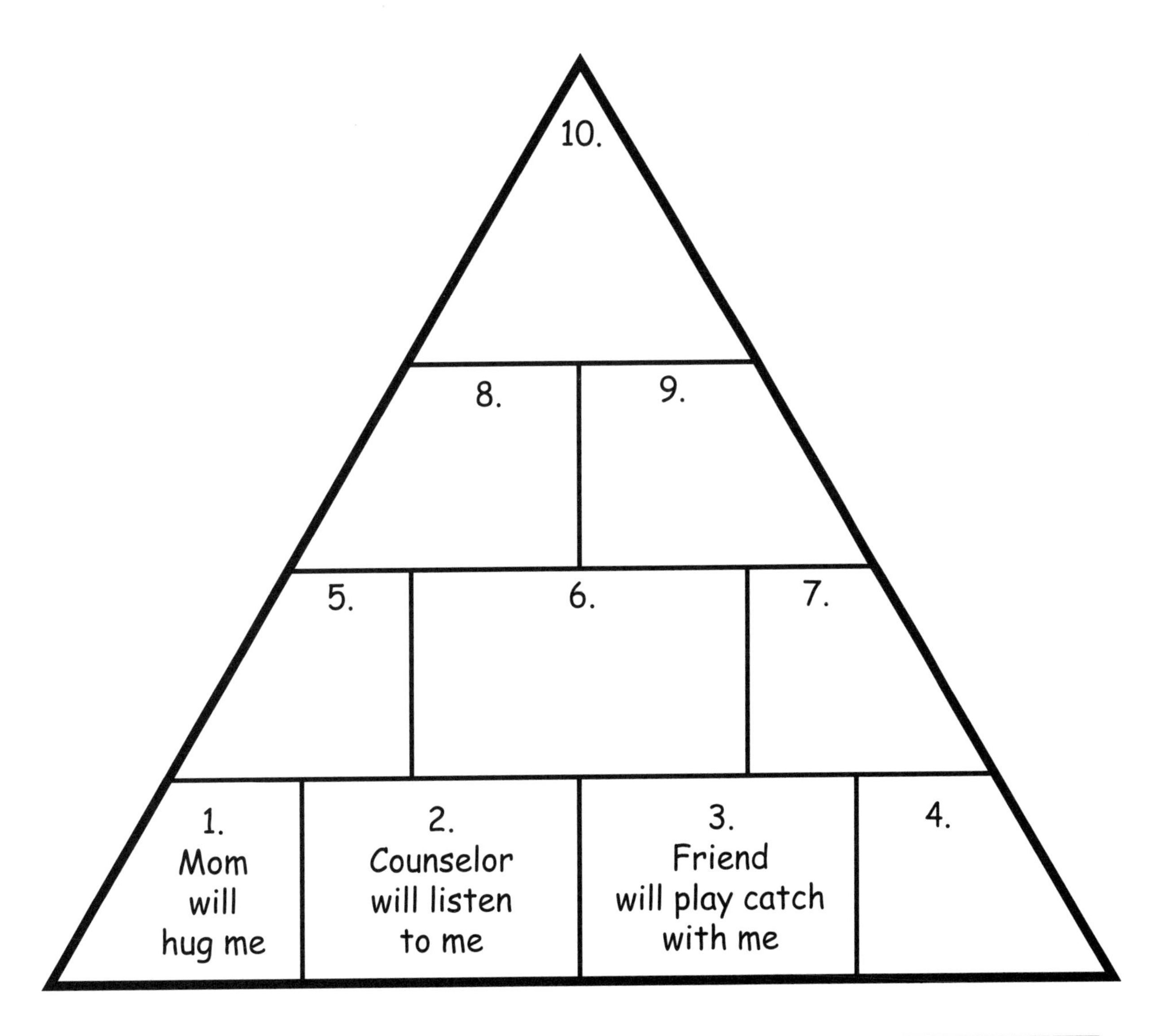

Journal Jar
(Final Lesson)

Materials:

For The Leader:

- ☐ *Journal Jar Topics* reproduced on white cardstock and cut apart (pages 214-215)
- ☐ Scissors
- ☐ Small jar

Preparation:

Place the *Journal Jar Topics* in a small jar. Place the jar in the center of the table.

Activity:

- ▶ Allow the students to select one card from the jar and answer the question on it.
- ▶ Continue until each student has had an opportunity to respond at least once.
- ▶ Toward the end of the session, stop the Journal Jar activity and have each student name one thing he/she has learned during the group sessions. Remind the students that you are available if they have concerns or questions in the future.

My
Rainbow

BODY SHAPE

BRICKS

TREE TRUNK

LEAVES

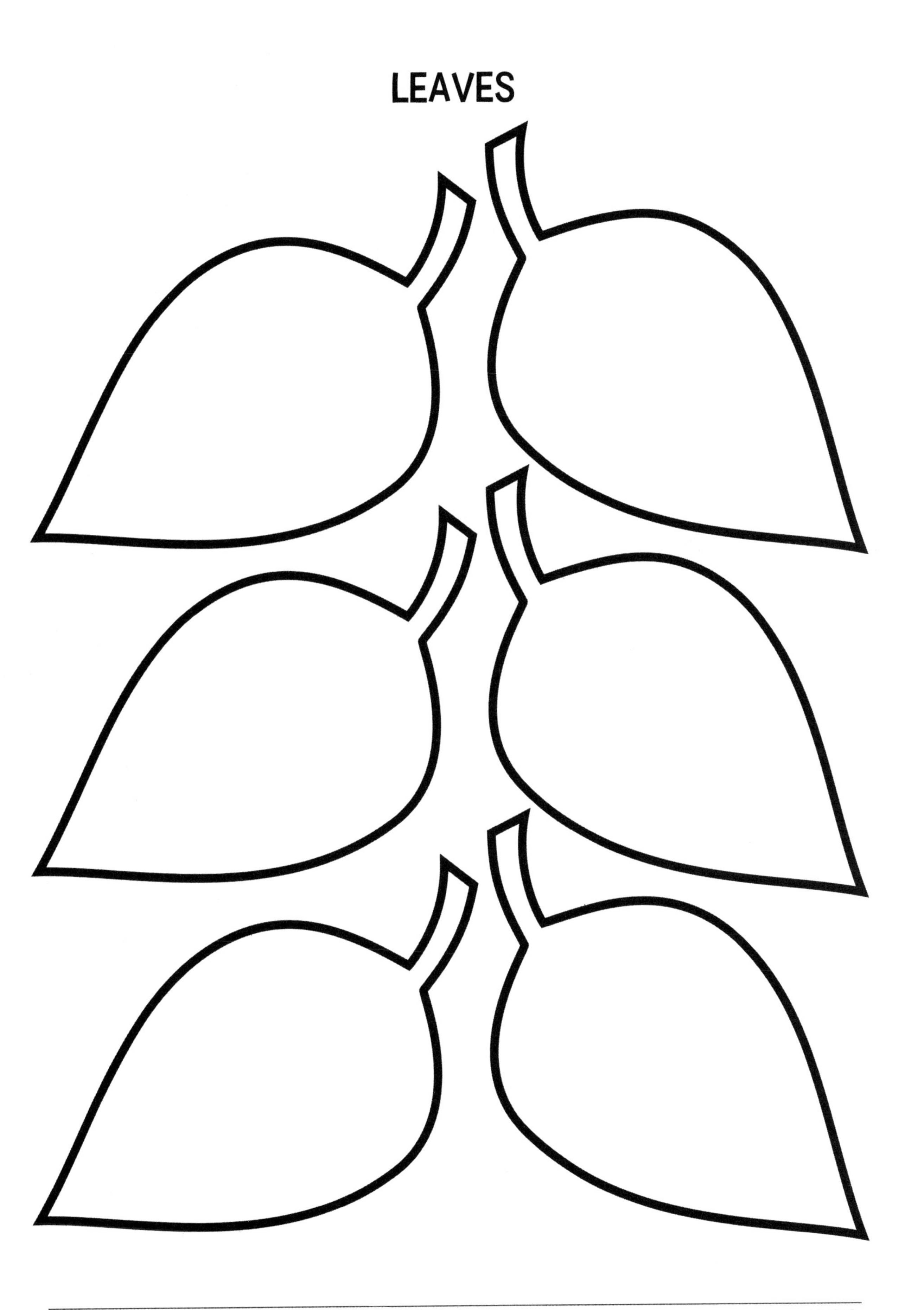

GINGERBREAD MAN

FACE SHAPE

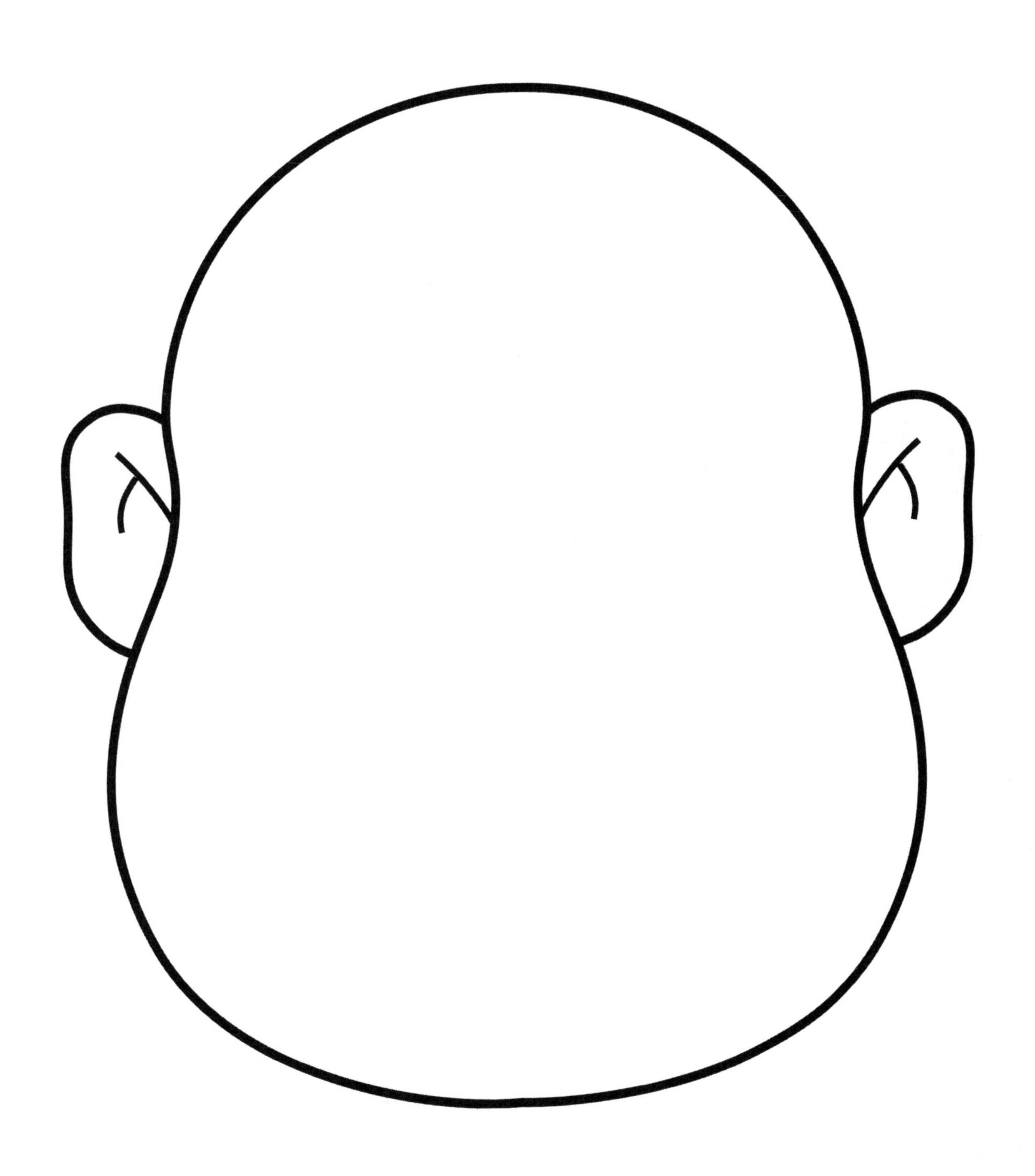

CIRCLES

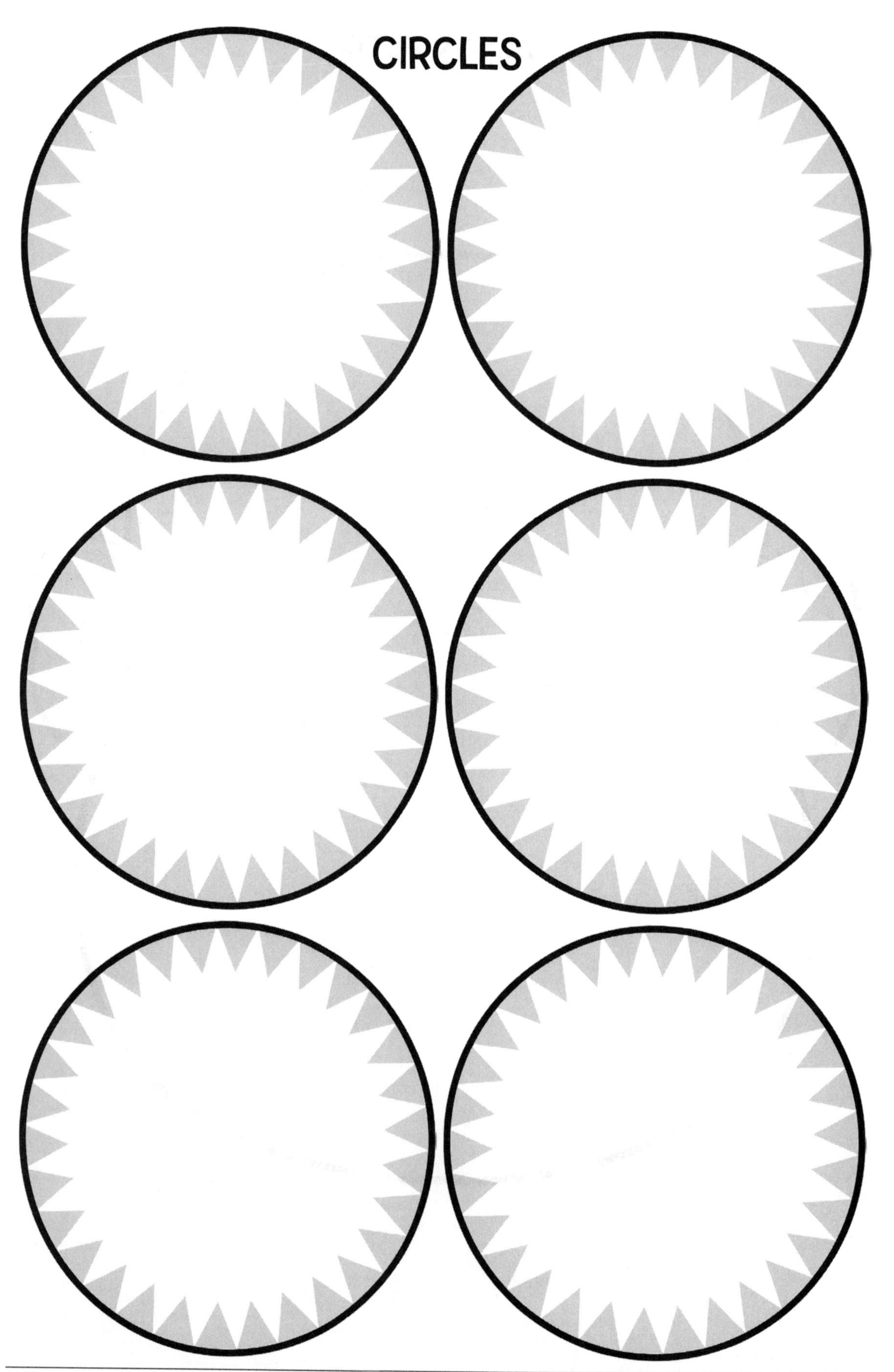

GIFT TREE LEAVES

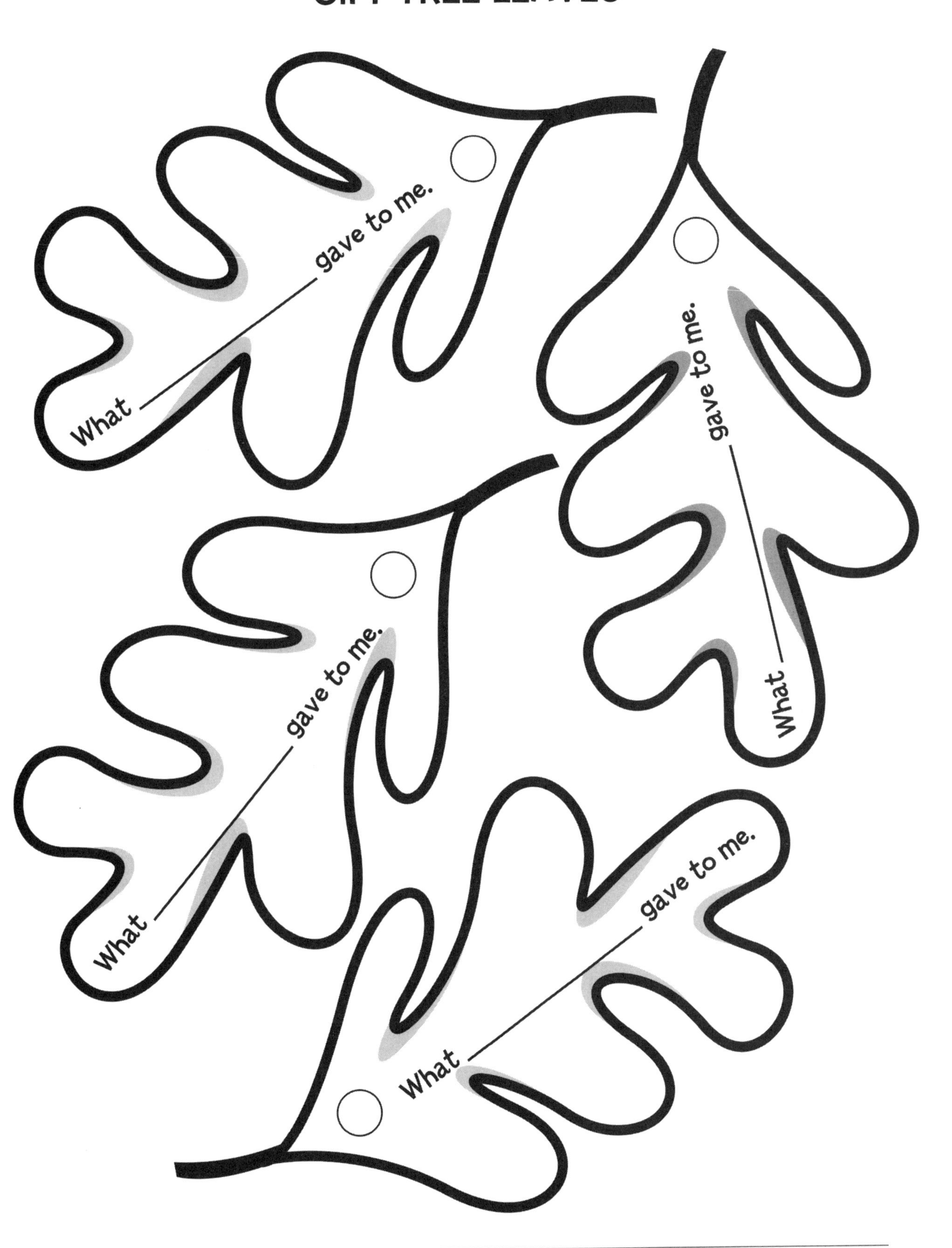

JOURNAL JAR TOPICS

Tell about something you received from the person who has died.	Name 3 people in school who will listen and talk with you.	Name 2 people in your family who listen to you when you are upset.
Name 3 friends who will listen and talk with you when you are sad.	Name 2 things you miss most about the person who has died.	Name some important future events that will be missed by the person who has died.
Say something you wish you could say to the person who has died.	Name 3 places in your body that are affected by feelings.	Name 3 ways to release energy caused by strong feelings.
What is death?	What do you remember best about the person who has died?	What happens at a funeral?
How do you feel when you think about the person who has died?	Talk about something you used to do with the person who has died.	Talk about a place you liked to go with the person who has died.
Talk about something the person who has died liked to do.	Name 5 (or more) different feelings you have had since the person died.	Name 2 healthful things you can do to help yourself feel better.
Name 3 traits you share with the person who has died.	Tell us what other family members say about the person who has died.	Name 2 ways that grief affects us emotionally.

Name 2 ways that grief affects us physically.	Name 2 ways that grief affects us mentally.	Name 2 ways that grief affects us spiritually.
Name 3 “don’ts” of grieving.	Name 3 “do’s” of grieving.	Tell how the next holiday might be different without the person who has died.
Name 1 special memory you have of the person who has died.	Name 2 ways someone in your support system can help you.	Name 3 people in your personal support system.
What does death look like?	Talk about what happened to the person who has died.	Talk about the funeral.
Name one thing in your Memory Box and tell why you chose to put it in your box.	Name a place you liked to go with the person who has died.	Name 3 things you received from the person who has died.

Self-Esteem

I believe that students who are referred for self-esteem issues really need encouragement to try new things. As they attempt these things and have some successes, their self-worth will increase. Achieving this in the small-group setting requires a unique approach. These lessons help students develop a better understanding of self. The activities require identifying personal strengths, traits, wishes, and interests. While identifying their own, students also hear from other students.

The lessons address these areas:

Grades K/1
Identifying personal strengths, traits, skills, and favorites
Appreciating names
Giving and receiving compliments
Identifying goals and wishes

Grades 2/3
Identifying personal strengths, skills, traits (positive and negative)
Identifying goals and wishes
Understanding personal outlook/perspective

Grades 4/5
Identifying personal strengths, skills, beliefs, feelings, ideas, and interests
Identifying goals and wishes
Understanding personal outlook/perspective
Understanding group membership/sense of belonging

SMALL-GROUP LESSONS

Self-Esteem

GRADES K/1

GRADES 2/3

GRADES 4/5

ASCA STANDARDS, COMPETENCIES, AND INDICATORS FOR SMALL-GROUP LESSONS ON SELF-ESTEEM

Participation in these group activities will address the following ASCA standards, competencies, and indicators:

Domain	A/ACADEMIC DEVELOPMENT
A/A:1.1	Articulate feelings of competence and confidence as a learner
A/A:1.3	Take pride in work and in achievement
A/A:1.5	Identify attitudes and behaviors which lead to successful learning
A/A:3.3	Develop a broad range of interests and abilities
A/A:3.5	Share knowledge
A/B:1.1	Demonstrate the motivation to achieve individual potential

Domain	C/CAREER DEVELOPMENT
C/A:1.3	Develop an awareness of personal abilities, skills, interests, and motivations
C/A:1.4	Learn how to interact and work cooperatively in teams
C/A:1.5	Learn to make decisions
C/A:1.6	Learn how to set goals
C/A:1.7	Understand the importance of planning
C/A:1.8	Pursue and develop competency in areas of interest
C/A:2.8	Understand the importance of responsibility, dependability, punctuality, integrity and effort in the work place
C/B:1.2	Identify personal skills, interests, and abilities and relate them to current career choices
C/C:1.2	Explain how work can help to achieve personal success and satisfaction
C/C:1.3	Identify personal preferences and interests which influence career choices and success
C/C:2.1	Demonstrate how interests, abilities, and achievement relate to achieving personal, social, educational and career goals.

Domain	PS/PERSONAL/SOCIAL DEVELOPMENT
PS/A:1.1	Develop a positive attitude toward self as a unique and worthy person
PS/A:1.2	Identify values, attitudes and beliefs
PS/A:1.3	Learn the goal setting process
PS/A:1.4	Understand change as a part of growth
PS/A:1.5	Identify and express feelings
PS/A:1.7	Recognize personal boundaries, rights and privacy needs
PS/A:1.9	Demonstrate cooperative behavior in groups
PS/A:1.10	Identify personal strengths and assets
PS/A:1.11	Identify and discuss changing personal and social roles
PS/A:2.1	Recognize that everyone has rights and responsibilities
PS/A:2.3	Recognize, accept, respect and appreciate individual differences
PS/A:2.4	Recognize, accept and appreciate ethnic and cultural diversity
PS/A:2.5	Recognize and respect differences in various family configurations
PS/A:2.6	Use effective communication skills
PS/A:2.7	Know that communication involves speaking, listening, and nonverbal behavior
PS/A:2.8	Learn how to make and keep friends
PS/B:1.1	Use a decision-making and problem-solving model
PS/B:1.4	Develop effective coping skills for dealing with problems
PS/C:1.4	Demonstrate the ability to assert boundaries, rights, and personal privacy
PS/C:1.6	Identify resource people in the school and community, and know how to seek their help

Master Supply List For Small Group On Self-Esteem

Collect these supplies prior to presenting the group.
Place all special supplies in the same box as the lessons copied on cardstock.

GENERAL SUPPLIES:

- ☐ Chart paper and marker
- ☐ Scissors
- ☐ Pencils
- ☐ Hole punches
- ☐ Stapler and staples
- ☐ Paper

ART SUPPLIES:

- ☐ Crayons or markers
- ☐ Cardstock or heavyweight copy paper (white, green, other colors)
- ☐ Construction paper (blue, other colors)
- ☐ Glue sticks/Glue
- ☐ Black fine-tip markers
- ☐ Glitter
- ☐ Black markers
- ☐ Manila paper
- ☐ Tape
- ☐ String
- ☐ Drawing paper
- ☐ Clay
- ☐ Various decorative art/craft supplies

MISCELLANEOUS SUPPLIES:

- ☐ Baby name book (optional)
- ☐ Felt
- ☐ Yarn or cord
- ☐ Wiggly eyes
- ☐ Pipe cleaners
- ☐ Dowel or paint stick
- ☐ Colorful candy-coated chocolates or similar small candies
- ☐ Serving spoon
- ☐ Small box
- ☐ Contact paper
- ☐ Paper lunch bags
- ☐ Coat hangers
- ☐ Old magazines
- ☐ Optional: Digital camera to take pictures of the students
- ☐ Inexpensive sunglasses
- ☐ Pink (rose-colored), green, blue, and orange cellophane
- ☐ Drinking straws
- ☐ Brown paint or woodgrain contact paper
- ☐ Cardboard tubes (toilet paper rolls)
- ☐ One simple magic trick that can be taught to group members

COPY ON WHITE CARDSTOCK: *Note*: Heavyweight copy paper may be substituted for cardstock

- ☐ *Self-Esteem Small-Group Lessons* as a quick reference to each lesson's page number (page 218)
- ☐ *Capability Cards:* one set reproduced and cut apart (pages 263-264)
- ☐ *Two People Looked Out From Prison.... Poster* (page 273)

ONE COPY FOR EACH STUDENT ON WHITE CARDSTOCK:

- ☐ *My Favorite Things* (page 248)
- ☐ *Clouds* (page 260)
- ☐ *Hot Air Balloons* (page 261)
- ☐ *Rainbow* (page 262)
- ☐ *Graduated Circles* (page 274)
- ☐ *Mask* (page 277)

COPY ON COLORED CARDSTOCK:

- ☐ *Star Shape:* one copy for each student on yellow cardstock, cut out (page 258)
- ☐ *Lemons:* one copy for each student on yellow cardstock (page 265)
- ☐ *Cherries:* one copy for each student on pink or red cardstock (page 266)
- ☐ *Leaf Templates:* one copy for each student on gold, orange, or green cardstock (page 269)

ONE COPY FOR EACH STUDENT ON WHITE COPY PAPER:

- ☐ *Flowers* (page 245)
- ☐ *Leaves* (page 246)
- ☐ *Flower Pot* (page 247)
- ☐ *Favorite Color* (page 249)
- ☐ *Favorite Food* (page 250)
- ☐ *Favorite Story* (page 251)
- ☐ *Favorite Instrument* (page 252)
- ☐ *Favorite Toy* (page 253)
- ☐ *Favorite Animal* (page 254)
- ☐ *Favorite Holiday* (page 255)
- ☐ *Favorite Place To Visit* (page 256)
- ☐ *Favorite Sport* (page 257)
- ☐ *Candy Game* (page 259)
- ☐ *Magician's Hat* (page 275)
- ☐ *Target* (page 278)

MULTIPLE COPIES ON WHITE COPY PAPER

- ☐ *Wish Clouds:* several clouds for each student, cut out (page 268)
- ☐ *Silhouette:* one copy for each student and the leader (pages 270-271)
- ☐ *Thought Bubbles:* one copy for each student and the leader (page 272)
- ☐ *Rabbits:* several rabbits for each student, cut out (page 276)

COPY ON COLORED COPY PAPER:

- ☐ *Magic Lamp:* one copy for each student and the leader on gold paper (page 267)

Bouquet of Me

Materials:

For Each Student:

- ☐ *Flowers* reproduced on white copy paper (page 245)
- ☐ *Leaves* reproduced on white copy paper (page 246)
- ☐ *Flower Pot* reproduced on white copy paper (page 247)
- ☐ Large piece of blue construction paper
- ☐ Glue stick
- ☐ Scissors
- ☐ Black fine-tip marker
- ☐ Crayons or markers

Activity:

- ▶ Explain that each group member will make a personal flower bouquet which identifies his/her individual strengths and characteristics.
- ▶ Give each student a copy of *Flowers, Leaves*, and *Flower Pot;* a large piece of blue construction paper; scissors; a glue stick; a black marker; and crayons or markers. Have the students write their names on the construction paper, cut out the flower pot, and glue it near the bottom of the blue construction paper. Tell the students to cut out the flowers and leaves, then color their flower pots, flowers, and leaves.
- ▶ Ask each group member to identify things he/she does well. You may need to encourage responses and provide basic ideas such as: helping others, riding a bike, helping Mom wash the dishes, etc.
- ▶ As each student identifies a strength or characteristic, have him/her write it on a cut-out flower, then glue the flower and a leaf on or above the flower pot.
- ▶ Continue this process until every student has several flowers in his/her pot.
- ▶ Review each student's bouquet, reading aloud his/her strengths and characteristics.
- ▶ Let the students take their completed papers with them.
- ▶ Ask the students to give you a note before the next session regarding how their parents selected their names. Research the meanings of some of the names.

Personal Headband

Materials:

For The Leader:

- ☐ Hole punch
- ☐ Glue
- ☐ Baby name book (optional)

For Each Student:

- ☐ 2" x 8" piece of colored construction paper or felt
- ☐ 2 pieces of yarn or cord

Have Available For The Group:

- ☐ Glitter
- ☐ Various art/craft supplies

Preparation:

Before beginning the session, collect the notes regarding how each student's parents selected his/her name. You may research the meanings of some names.

Activity:

- ▶ Discuss the importance of the students' names. Tell each student what the notes and your research taught you about his/her name.

- ▶ Use glue to write each student's name on the paper/felt rectangle. Let the students sprinkle glitter over their names. Group members may then add buttons, stars, or other decorations to their headbands.

- ▶ Punch a hole at each end of the rectangle. Thread yarn or cord through each hole. Tie a headband around each student's head and let the students wear their names proudly.

Caterpillar Of Compliments

Materials:

For The Leader:

- ☐ Different-colored construction paper circles—5 or more for each student, cut out
- ☐ Scissors
- ☐ Black marker

For Each Student:

- ☐ 1 Set of wiggly eyes
- ☐ Glue stick
- ☐ 1 Pipe cleaner, cut in half

Activity:

- ▶ Give each student one colored circle, a set of wiggly eyes, pipe cleaner sections, and a glue stick.
- ▶ Tell the students they will each be making a *Caterpillar Of Compliments*. Have the students glue the eyes and antennae (pipe cleaners) to their circle.
- ▶ Tell the students they will be adding to their caterpillar by complimenting one another.
- ▶ Go around the circle and let each group member say something positive about another student. Write each compliment on a colored circle and give it to the student receiving the compliment. Have the group member who has been complimented glue the compliment to the first circle of his/her caterpillar.
- ▶ Be sure everyone receives several compliments. At the end of the session, read each student's entire caterpillar aloud.
- ▶ Let the students take their *Caterpillars Of Compliments* with them. You may want to give the students extra paper circles so their teachers and family can add their own compliments.

Handprints

Materials:

For Each Student:

- ☐ Construction paper
- ☐ Manila paper
- ☐ Crayons or markers
- ☐ Glue stick
- ☐ Scissors

Activity:

- ▶ Encourage each student to name all the things he/she has learned to do—tie a shoe, walk, talk, count to *10*, say the alphabet, etc.

- ▶ Give each student a piece of construction paper, a piece of manila paper, scissors, a glue stick, and crayons or markers.

- ▶ Have each student trace his/her hand on manila paper, then cut it out.

- ▶ Continue the discussion on the skills students have acquired. As each skill is identified, help the student write it on a finger of the cut-out hand. (*Note:* If more than five skills are named, trace and cut out more hands.)

- ▶ Glue the hand(s) onto colored construction paper. Let the students take the paper home.

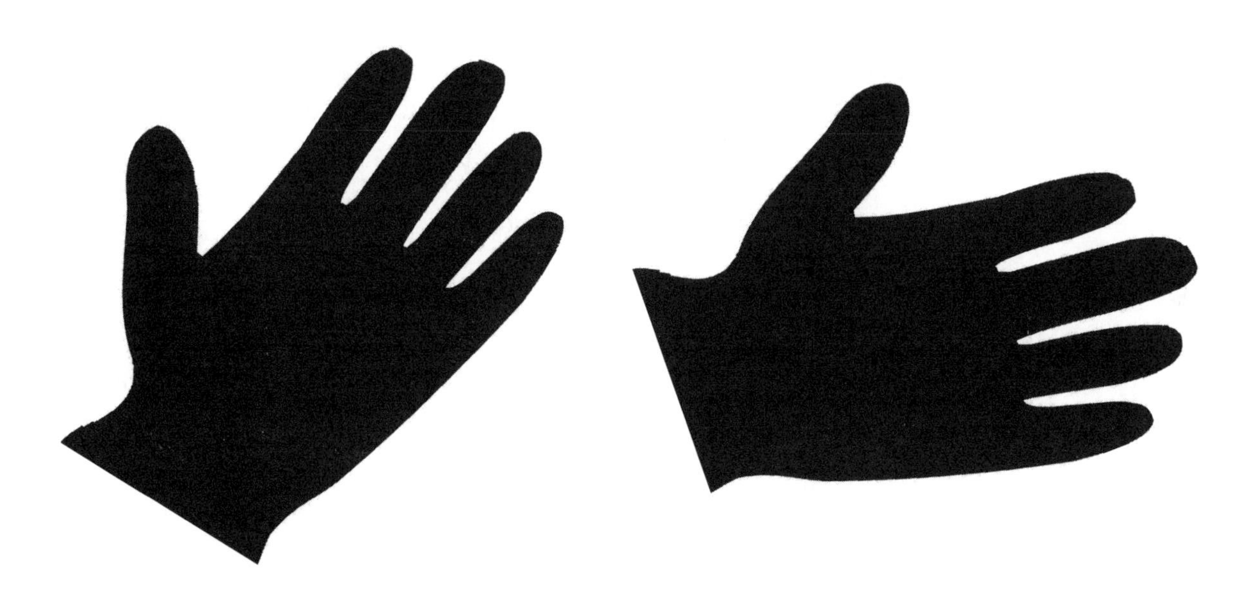

My Favorite Things

Materials:

For The Leader:

- ☐ Stapler and staples

For Each Student:

- ☐ *My Favorite Things* reproduced on white cardstock (page 248)
- ☐ *Favorite Color* reproduced on white copy paper (page 249)
- ☐ *Favorite Food* reproduced on white copy paper (page 250)
- ☐ *Favorite Story* reproduced on white copy paper (page 251)
- ☐ *Favorite Instrument* reproduced on white copy paper (page 252)
- ☐ *Favorite Toy* reproduced on white copy paper (page 253)
- ☐ *Favorite Animal* reproduced on white copy paper (page 254)
- ☐ *Favorite Holiday* reproduced on white copy paper (page 255)
- ☐ *Favorite Place To Visit* reproduced on white copy paper (page 256)
- ☐ *Favorite Sport* reproduced on white copy paper (page 257)
- ☐ Crayons or markers

Activity:

- ▶ Give each student a copy of *Favorite Color* and crayons or markers.
- ▶ Instruct the students to color their favorite color on the artist's palette. When everyone has finished, complete any or all of the other shapes.
- ▶ If there is enough time, allow the students to color each activity sheet.
- ▶ Give each student a copy of *My Favorite Things.* Using this page as a cover, staple the completed activity sheets together to make a booklet for each student. Allow time for the students to color the cover.
- ▶ Let each group member share his/her completed booklet with the group.
- ▶ Alternative Idea: Give each student a copy of *My Favorite Things* and crayons or markers. Instruct the students to write (or write for them) their favorite color on the artist's palette. When everyone has finished, complete any or all of the other shapes, then color the activity sheet.

Make A Wish

Materials:

For The Leader:
- ☐ Scissors

For Each Student
- ☐ Dowel or paint stick
- ☐ *Star Shape* reproduced on yellow cardstock and cut out (page 258)
- ☐ Tape
- ☐ Glue

Have Available For The Group:
- ☐ Various art materials

Activity:

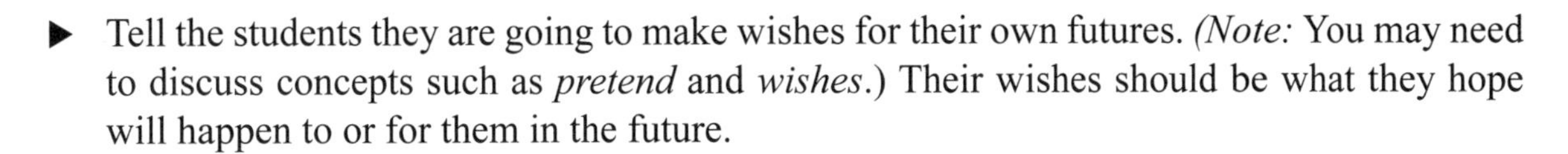

- ▶ Tell the students they are going to make wishes for their own futures. *(Note:* You may need to discuss concepts such as *pretend* and *wishes*.) Their wishes should be what they hope will happen to or for them in the future.

- ▶ Place the art supplies in a location where they are easily accessible to the students. Give each student a cut-out star, a dowel/paint stick, glue, and tape.

- ▶ Tell the students they're going to make Wishing Wands. Instruct the students to glue the star to one end of the dowel/paint stick, then tape the star in place until the glue dries.

- ▶ When the glue is dry, the students may add any decorative items they wish.

- ▶ Ask the students to hold their Wishing Wands. Go around the circle and ask each student:

    - What do you hope will be true when you are in fifth grade?
    - What do you hope will be true when you are in middle school/high school?
    - What do you hope will be true when you are a grown-up?
    - What will you have to do to make those wishes come true?

- ▶ Allow the students to take the wands with them as a reminder of the lesson.

Candy Beliefs

Materials:

For The Leader:

- ☐ Colorful candy-coated chocolates or similar small candies
- ☐ Serving spoon

For Each Student:

- ☐ *Candy Game* reproduced on white copy paper (page 259)
- ☐ Crayons of colors that match the candies to be used

(***Note:*** Be sure the use of candy is appropriate for use in your school district and for each group member. If you cannot use candy, you may substitute something suitable such as pieces of colored paper punched out with a hole punch. Or omit the *Candy Game* from your lessons.)

Activity:

- ▶ Give each student a copy of the *Candy Game* and crayons that match the colors of the candies to be used. Instruct the students to color each circle a different color. They may select which color to use for each circle and should not try and match anyone else's drawing.

- ▶ When the students have finished coloring the circles, give each student a spoonful of candy. Ask the students to line up the candy with the colored circles so all the red candies are with the circle they colored red and the green candies are with the green circle, etc. If there are any circles for which they have no matching candy, you may give them one. Have everyone count the candies they have. Give more to those who have fewer.

- ▶ Follow the worksheet instructions by giving each student a chance to respond to each statement. For example, the first statement asks students to tell one thing they are learning to do for each piece of candy they have. So a student with four pieces of candy matching the color of the first statement must identify four things he/she has learned.

- ▶ It's usually best if the students eat the candy as they respond to the statements so all the candy is gone by the end of the session.

Me Mobile

Materials:

For Each Student:
- ☐ Sheet of paper
- ☐ Pencil
- ☐ *Clouds* reproduced on white cardstock (page 260)
- ☐ *Hot Air Balloons* reproduced on white cardstock (page 261)
- ☐ *Rainbow* reproduced on white cardstock (page 262)
- ☐ Crayons or markers
- ☐ Scissors

Have Available For The Group:
- ☐ Hole punches
- ☐ String

Activity:

- ▶ Tell the students they will be identifying individual strengths and positive characteristics and will use these strengths and characteristics to create a *Me Mobile*.

- ▶ Give each student a copy of *Clouds, Hot Air Balloons,* and *Rainbow;* one sheet of paper; a pencil; scissors; and crayons or markers. On the piece of paper, have the students write their responses to these prompts:

  - Write one skill you possess—one thing you do well.
  - Write a word or phrase that someone who loves you would use to describe you.
  - Write a word or phrase a friend would use to describe you.
  - Write one thing you enjoy doing when you are not in school.
  - Write one thing you enjoy doing in school.
  - Write one word you would use to describe yourself.
  - Write one word your teacher would use to describe you.

- ▶ After everyone has finished writing, let the students read aloud what they wrote for the first prompt and, perhaps, make a brief statement regarding it. Be sure they use only positive responses. Then continue the process with the second prompt.

- ▶ Tell the students to write each of their listed responses on one of the hot air balloons or clouds. Then tell the students to write their names on the rainbows.

- ▶ Have the students cut out the balloons, rainbow, and clouds, then color the balloons and rainbow. Have the students punch a hole in each balloon and cloud, punch seven holes in the rainbow, then string the balloons and clouds from the rainbow.

- ▶ Tell the students they may take the mobile with them as a reminder of the lesson.

Capability Box

Materials:

For The Leader:

- Small box
- Contact paper
- Marker
- *Capability Cards:* one set reproduced on white cardstock and cut apart (pages 263-264)
- Scissors

Preparation:

Cover the small box with contact paper. Write *Capability Box* on each side of the box. Place the *Capability Cards* in the box.

Activity:

- Explain that every person has different capabilities. There are some things we can do and some things we can't do. Give personal examples and allow group members to share a few.

- Place the Capability Box in the center of the group.

- One at a time, have the students draw a *Capability Card* from the box, read the card, and discuss with the group whether it is something they can or cannot do. They may also discuss whether it is something they want to learn to do, are learning to do, or are not interested in doing.

- Review the various capabilities evident in the group members. Reinforce the idea that it's okay for us to have different capabilities.

Collage Bag

Materials:

For The Leader:
- ☐ Optional: Picture of each group member

For Each Student:
- ☐ Paper lunch bag
- ☐ Glue stick
- ☐ Scissors
- ☐ Drawing paper
- ☐ Crayons or markers

Have Available For The Group:
- ☐ Old magazines
- ☐ Various art/craft supplies

Lesson Preparation:

Following the activity instructions, make your own Collage Bag to serve as a personal example of the activity.

Activity:

- ▶ Give each student a paper lunch bag, glue stick, scissors, drawing paper, and crayons or markers. Have magazines and additional art supplies available for the students' use.
- ▶ Show the students your Collage Bag and talk about the pictures you chose and why you chose them.
- ▶ Instruct the students to cover their bags with pictures cut from magazines or drawings that symbolize what they wish for, dream of, believe in, or feel. The may put their own picture on the bag.
- ▶ Ask the students to present their completed bags to the group.
- ▶ Have the students take their bags home and fill them with things, or representations of things, that are particularly meaningful to them.
- ▶ Tell the students to bring their bags to the next meeting to share with the group.

Sweet-And-Sour Mobile

Materials:

For Each Student:

- ☐ *Lemons* reproduced on yellow cardstock (page 265)
- ☐ *Cherries* reproduced on pink/red cardstock (page 266)
- ☐ Glue stick
- ☐ Marker
- ☐ Scissors
- ☐ Coat hanger

Have Available For The Group:

- ☐ Hole punches
- ☐ Yarn
- ☐ Various colors of construction paper

Activity:

- ▶ Begin the lesson by having the students share their Collage Bags from the previous lesson.
- ▶ Tell the students that everyone has positive traits and things he/she needs to change. In fact, some personal traits can be both positive and negative (strong-mindedness or stubbornness). Explain that they will be identifying personal characteristics and determining if they are positive and/or negative.
- ▶ Give each student a copy of *Lemons* and *Cherries*, a marker, a glue stick, and scissors. Have the students cut out the cherries and the lemons.
- ▶ Have the students take turns identifying their personal traits. Determine if each trait identified is positive or negative and have the students write negative traits on the lemon and positive traits on the cherries. (*Note:* It may be easiest to elicit responses by asking the student to think of a word that someone else would use to describe him/her.)
- ▶ Tell the students to glue the shapes back to back (lemon to cherries) and punch a hole in the shapes. The simplest way to create a mobile is to use yarn to hang the items from a wire coat hanger. Two paper triangles can be drawn on construction paper, using the coat hanger as the pattern. Have the students write their names on the triangles, tie the shapes to the bottom of the hanger, then glue the paper triangles to cover the hanger.
- ▶ Alternate idea: Cherries could be things the student does well; lemons could be things the student is struggling to accomplish.

Make A Wish

Materials:

For The Leader:

- ☐ *Magic Lamp* reproduced on gold copy paper (page 267)
- ☐ Large piece of construction paper
- ☐ Scissors
- ☐ *Wish Clouds:* multiple copies reproduced on white copy paper and cut out (page 268)
- ☐ Marker
- ☐ Glue stick

For Each Student:

- ☐ *Magic Lamp* reproduced on gold copy paper (page 267)
- ☐ Large piece of construction paper
- ☐ Scissors
- ☐ Marker
- ☐ Glue stick

Preparation:

Using the activity instructions, make a sample Magic Lamp.

Activity:

- ▶ Show the sample Magic Lamp to the students. (If the students don't know the story of *Aladdin and the Magic Lamp,* tell a shortened version of it.) You may need to discuss the concepts of *pretend* and *fantasy*. Give each student a copy of the *Magic Lamp*, a piece of construction paper, scissors, a marker, and a glue stick.
- ▶ Instruct the students to make their own Magic Lamp by cutting the lamp out and gluing it near the bottom center of the construction paper, leaving room for the paper clouds to be glued around the lamp.
- ▶ Discuss the students' hopes and wishes for the future. For each wish/hope a student mentions, give him/her one paper cloud. Have the student write his/her wish/hope on the cloud, then glue the cloud around or above the lamp. Then discuss ways the students can make their wishes and dreams come true, emphasizing that no magic genie will suddenly appear and grant their wishes.
- ▶ The students may choose to write on each cloud one or two things they can do to help themselves realize their wishes.
- ▶ Students may take the completed paper with them.

Changing Your Outlook

Materials:

For The Leader:
- ☐ 4 pairs of inexpensive sunglasses
- ☐ Pink (rose-colored), green, blue, and orange cellophane
- ☐ Glue

For Each Student:
- ☐ One pair of inexpensive sunglasses
- ☐ Glue

Have Available For The Group:
- ☐ Various decorative art/craft supplies

Preparation:

Replace the lenses of four pairs of sunglasses with green, orange, blue, and pink cellophane.

Activity:

- ▶ Discuss how a person's outlook can influence what he/she thinks is happening and how he/she feels about what is happening. Emphasize that we can choose to be positive or to believe the positive, rather than the negative.

- ▶ Discuss the phrase, "seeing the world through rose-colored glasses." Provide an example by saying: "Oh, look! Those two girls are whispering. I bet they're talking about me."

- ▶ Then put on the sunglasses with rose-colored lenses and say: "Oh, look! Those two girls are whispering. I bet they're best friends talking about what they're going to do this weekend."

- ▶ Allow the students to try the exercise by putting on a pair of glasses and making a statement, then changing to the rose-colored glasses and making a positive statement. Examples:

    - green lens—being jealous of everyone
    - orange lens—being angry about everything
    - blue lens—being sad and depressed

- Give each student a pair of sunglasses and glue. Place various art supplies in a location readily accessible to the students.
- Let the students make their own sunglasses by gluing lots of decorative buttons, glitter, sequins, etc. to a pair of glasses.
- Discuss how the students are going to change their outlooks and be positive.
- As the students wear their glasses, have them name one thing they've learned from this group. Congratulate them on their hard work. Have them take their glasses with them as a reminder of what they learned in the group.

Me Tree

Materials Needed:

For Each Student:

- ☐ Pencil
- ☐ Piece of paper
- ☐ *Leaf Templates* reproduced on gold, orange, or green cardstock (page 269)
- ☐ Drinking straws
- ☐ Brown paint or woodgrain contact paper
- ☐ Cardboard tube (toilet paper roll)
- ☐ Scissors
- ☐ String
- ☐ Clay
- ☐ Glue
- ☐ Marker

Activity:

- ▶ Tell the students they will be identifying personal strengths and positive characteristics and writing them on cut-out leaves that will be affixed to the Me Tree each group member creates.

- ▶ Give each student a piece of paper and a pencil.

- ▶ Giving one prompt at a time, ask the students to identify a personal trait and write it on the paper. Possible prompts are:

  - identify a word your teacher (parent, friend, self, grandparent, coach) would use to describe you.
  - identify something you do well in school (at home, in the neighborhood, in Scouts).
  - identify something you enjoy doing alone (with friends, at school, at home, in a big group).

- ▶ Let the students tell what they wrote in response to the first prompt. Continue this process until you have given each prompt and the students have responded to it.

- ▶ Allow time for each student to make a Me Tree. Give each student a copy of *Leaf Templates*, straws, brown paint or woodgrain contact paper, a cardboard tube, scissors, string, clay, glue, and a marker.

▶ Have the students:

- wedge a piece of clay into the bottom of the tube.
- paint the cardboard tube with brown paint or cover it with woodgrain contact paper.
- tie a handful of straws together at the bottom. Spread the straws like a fan.
- push the straws into the top of the tube.
- cut several leaves from the *Leaf Templates*.
- write the items from your list on the *Leaf Templates*.
- glue the leaves to the straw branches.

▶ Students may take their trees with them as a reminder of the lesson.

All Of Me Inside My Head

Materials:

For The Leader and Each Student:
- ☐ *Silhouette* reproduced on on white copy paper (pages 270-271)
- ☐ *Thought Bubbles* reproduced on white copy paper (page 272)
- ☐ Large piece of colored construction paper
- ☐ Glue stick
- ☐ Marker
- ☐ Scissors

Preparation:

Following the activity instructions, make a sample silhouette. Cut out the *Boy* or *Girl Silhouette* and glue it onto the large piece of colored construction paper. Cut out the four *Thought Bubbles* and glue them above the silhouette.

Activity:

- ▶ Show the students the sample silhouette.
- ▶ Give each student a copy of the *Boy* or *Girl Silhouette*, a copy of *Thought Bubbles,* a large piece of colored construction paper, glue, scissors, and a marker. Have the students cut out their silhouette and glue it near the bottom of the construction paper.
- ▶ Then have the students cut out four bubbles.
- ▶ Discuss the fact that each person is a unique collection of thoughts, feelings, beliefs, and ideas. Taking each of the four areas separately, discuss possible thoughts, beliefs, feelings, and ideas. After a brief discussion, have each group member fill in his/her own thought bubble for that category. Then move to the next category.
- ▶ For example:
    - *Beliefs*: Family is important. School matters.
    - *Feelings*: I love my family. I have sympathy for animals. Pollution angers me.
    - *Thoughts*: I am worthwhile and good. I can't seem to do math.
    - *Ideas*: I want to make rivers cleaner. I want to discover something important.
- ▶ Allow time for the students to share their completed silhouettes.
- ▶ Students may take the finished silhouettes with them. You may need to provide a folder (folded construction paper works) to ensure privacy.

Mud Or Stars

Materials

For The Leader:

- ☐ *Two People Looked Out From Prison.... Poster* reproduced on white cardstock (page 273)
- ☐ Chart paper and marker or chalkboard and chalk

Activity:

- ▶ Display the poster where it can be seen by the entire group. Discuss the quote printed on the poster: *Two people looked out from prison bars; the one saw mud, the other stars.* Whether you see "mud" or "stars" as you encounter various experiences depends on your outlook on life. Your happiness and the way others see you can depend on your outlook.

- ▶ Brainstorm a list of "muds" or negative perspectives and "stars" or positive perspectives. Some examples could be:

  - Examples of *mud*: complaining, whining, being moody, rude behavior, helplessness
  - Examples of *stars*: being determined, prompt, courteous, careful

- ▶ Make two columns on the chart paper/chalkboard. Label one column "Muds" and the other column "Stars." As students give examples, write them in the appropriate column on the chart paper/chalkboard. Be sure to emphasize that outlooks change from day to day and person to person. In addition, people experience both kinds—no one is totally negative or positive all the time.

- ▶ Discuss how your outlook can influence whether others want to be around you.

Interest Inventories

Materials:

For The Leader:
- ☐ Chart paper and marker or chalkboard and chalk

For Each Student:
- ☐ Piece of paper
- ☐ Pencil

Activity:

- ▶ Brainstorm a list of things that could interest a person the age of the group members. As each thing is mentioned, write it on the chart paper/chalkboard.
- ▶ Give each student a piece of paper and a pencil. Ask the students to create four columns on the paper, then label the columns: "High Interest," "Some Interest," "Little Interest," and "No Interest."
- ▶ Have the students list each of the items from the brainstorming activity in one of the columns.
- ▶ Discuss the students' completed lists with the group. Emphasize that everyone has different interests and that particular interests are not good or bad.
- ▶ Discuss what the students might do about things of high interest.
- ▶ Discuss whether the students believe their interests will change and how.

Family Mobile

Materials:

For Each Student:

- ☐ *Graduated Circles* reproduced on white cardstock (page 274)
- ☐ Glue stick
- ☐ Scissors
- ☐ String
- ☐ Crayons or markers

Have Available For The Group:

- ☐ Old magazines
- ☐ Hole punches

Activity:

This activity helps group members recognize and acknowledge the many groups to which they belong.

- ▶ Give each student a copy of *Graduated Circles*, a glue stick, scissors, string, and crayons or markers. Place the magazines in a place easily accessible to the students.
- ▶ Have the students cut out the *Graduated Circles*. Explain that each circle represents a group to which the students belong.
    - The smallest circle represents home/family.
    - The next sizes could represent class, school, and neighborhood.
    - The largest circle represents the total human family.
- ▶ Have the students decorate or label their circles according to individual wishes. For example, the school circle could include pictures of classmates, teachers, supplies, or special events. The largest circle could be a collage of faces cut from magazines.
- ▶ Punch a hole in the top of each circle. String the completed circles together in a vertical line, with the smallest on top and the largest on the bottom.
- ▶ Discuss the completed mobiles, including how belonging to each group makes the students feel, and what obligations are put on them by the group.
- ▶ Close the lesson by discussing the impact or influence each group member has on his/her groups.
- ▶ Students may take their completed mobiles with them.

Make A Wish

Materials:

For The Leader:

- ☐ *Rabbits:* multiple copies reproduced on white copy paper and cut out (page 276)
- ☐ One simple magic trick that can be taught to the group members. (The easiest trick I've mastered is the coloring book with blank pages, black line drawings, and colored drawings. It's available at any trick shop. Most trick shops are willing to teach you other tricks, too.)

For Each Student:

- ☐ *Magician's Hat* reproduced on white copy paper (pages 275)
- ☐ Large piece of construction paper (not black)
- ☐ Glue stick
- ☐ Scissors
- ☐ Pencil

Activity:

- ▶ Give each student a copy of the *Magician's Hat,* a large piece of construction paper, a glue stick, scissors, and a pencil.
- ▶ Have the students cut out the *Magician's Hat* and glue it in the center of the large piece of construction paper, top side down.
- ▶ Discuss magic tricks and "pulling rabbits out of a hat."
- ▶ Ask the group members to identify their wishes for the future. As each student identifies a wish, give him/her a rabbit shape. Have the students write their wishes on the rabbits, then glue each rabbit around their magician's hat.
- ▶ Perform the coloring book (or any other trick you've learned) for the group. Explain that group members can make the same magic as magicians—*if* they know the "tricks of the trade." Show them how your trick is performed.
- ▶ Discuss what would be necessary to make each of their dreams come true. Suggestions or ideas generated by the group can be written on the rabbits.
- ▶ Have the students take their completed project with them.

Inside/Out

Materials:

For Each Student:

- ☐ *Mask* reproduced on white cardstock (page 277)
- ☐ Pencil
- ☐ Scissors

Activity:

This activity gives students the opportunity to clarify what they believe about their personal images.

- ▶ Tell the group members that each of us has two (or more) self-images—the one the outside world sees and what we see from the inside.
- ▶ Give each student a copy of *Mask*, scissors, and a pencil. Have the students cut out their masks.
- ▶ On the outside of the mask, instruct the students to write words that describe what the world believes to be true of them. Encourage other group members to contribute *positive* ideas about how they view their classmates. For example, some students may not realize classmates see them as popular or smart.
- ▶ On the inside of the mask, which only they can see, have the students write words that they know are true about them. This might be something the individual is sure no one realizes about him/her. For example, someone thought to be friendly by others may actually consider him/herself shy.
- ▶ Give the students an opportunity to first discuss how the outside world sees them, then discuss how they see themselves.

Setting A Goal

Materials:

For Each Student:
- ☐ *Target* reproduced on white copy paper (page 278)
- ☐ Pencil

Activity:

- ▶ Ask the group members to identify one personal or academic goal they hope to achieve this year.
- ▶ Give each student a copy of *Target* and a pencil.
- ▶ Instruct the students to write that goal in the center circle of the *Target* sheet.
- ▶ Have the students share their individual goals with the group. You may need to help them make their goals realistic and measurable.
- ▶ Brainstorm things students can do to achieve their goals. Encourage the students to identify realistic and meaningful steps toward each goal.
- ▶ Have the students write these steps on the concentric circles surrounding the center goal.
- ▶ Allow each student to talk about his/her goal and the steps he/she can take to achieve it.
- ▶ Encourage the students to keep their *Target* sheet in a location where they will see it often and be reminded to work toward the goal.
- ▶ Remind the students that this is the final session. Ask each of them to identify one thing he/she has learned. Congratulate the students on their hard work.

FLOWERS

LEAVES

FLOWER POT

MY
FAVORITE
THINGS
JULY
1
2
3
4
5
6
35
ADIg

FAVORITE COLOR

FAVORITE FOOD

FAVORITE STORY

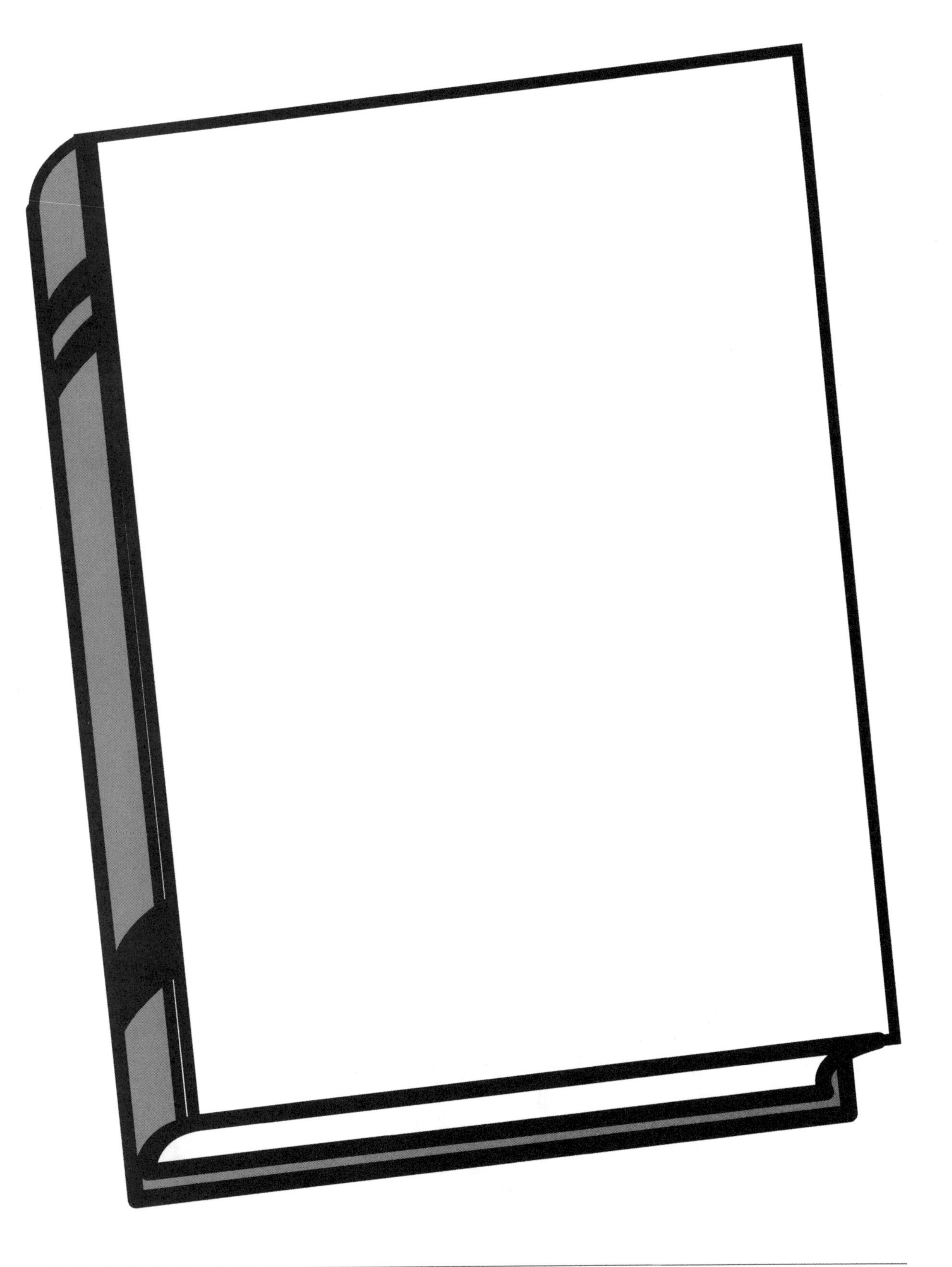

FAVORITE
INSTRUMENT

FAVORITE TOY

FAVORITE ANIMAL

FAVORITE HOLIDAY

FAVORITE PLACE TO VISIT

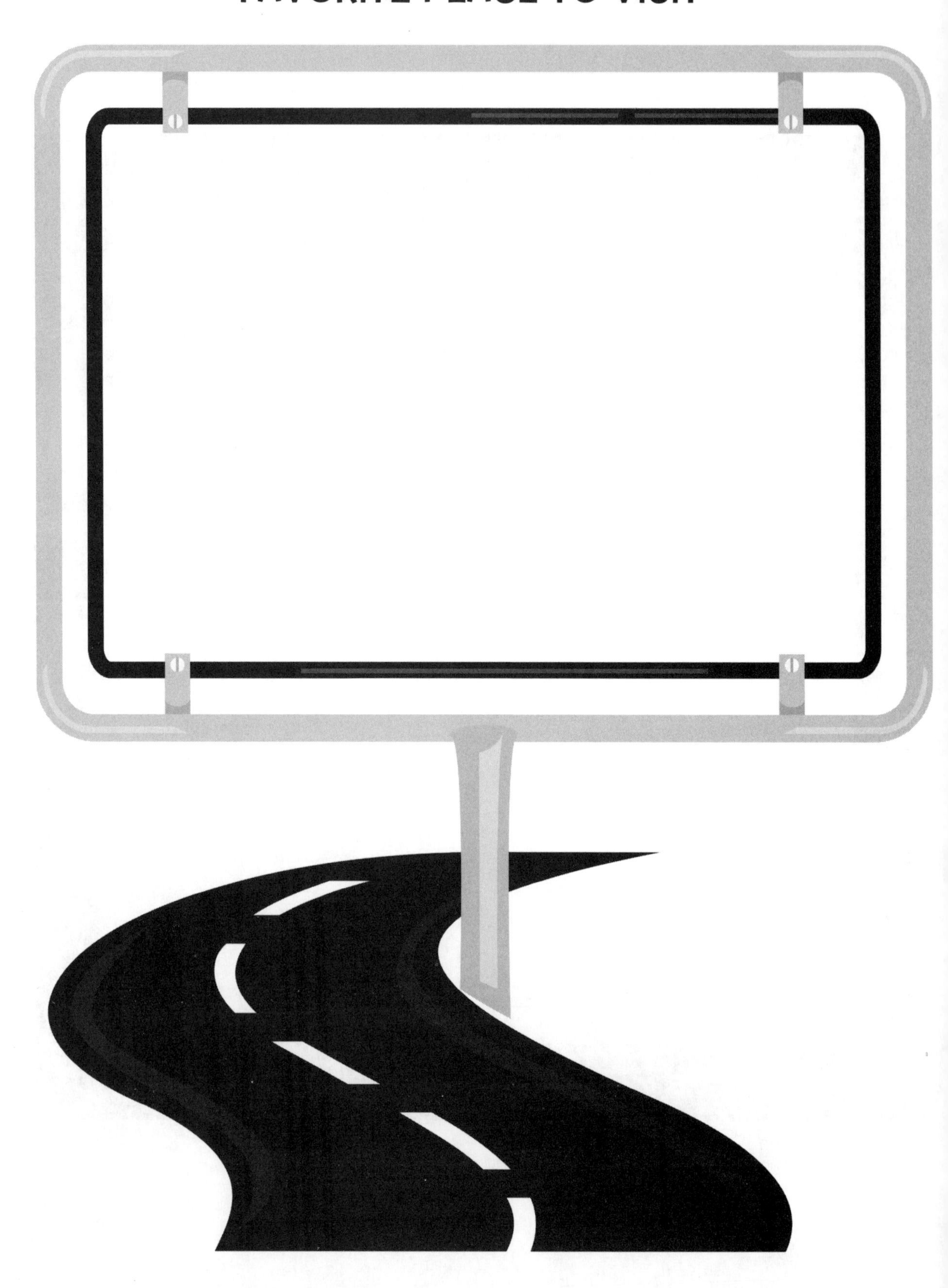

FAVORITE SPORT

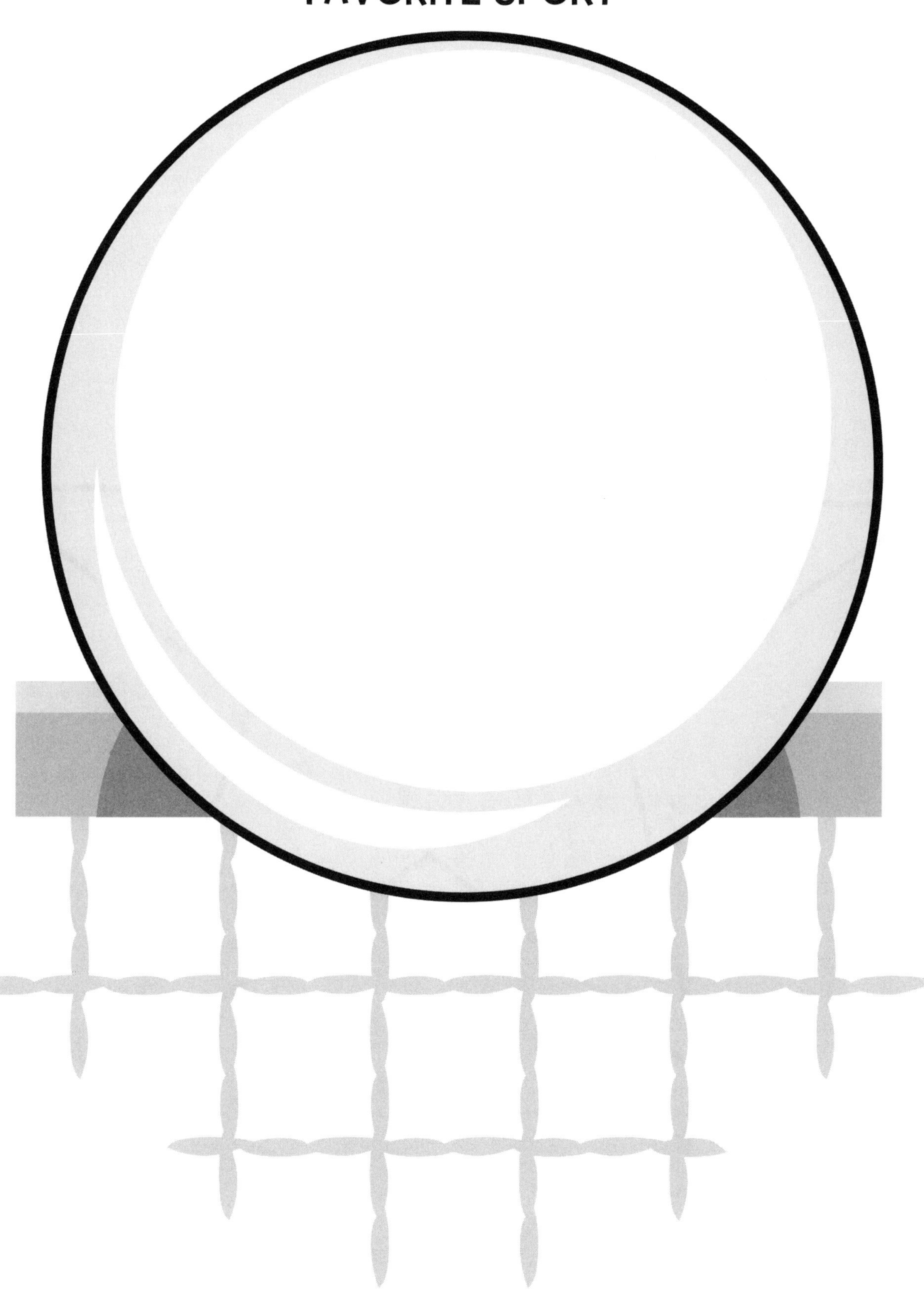

STAR SHAPE

Candy Game

For every ◯, name something you are learning to do.

For every ◯, name something you can already do well.

For every ◯, name something that makes you a good member of your class.

For every ◯, name something that makes you feel proud of yourself.

For every ◯, name something you wish you could change about yourself.

For every ◯, name a goal you have and what you are doing to achieve it.

CLOUDS

HOT AIR BALLOONS

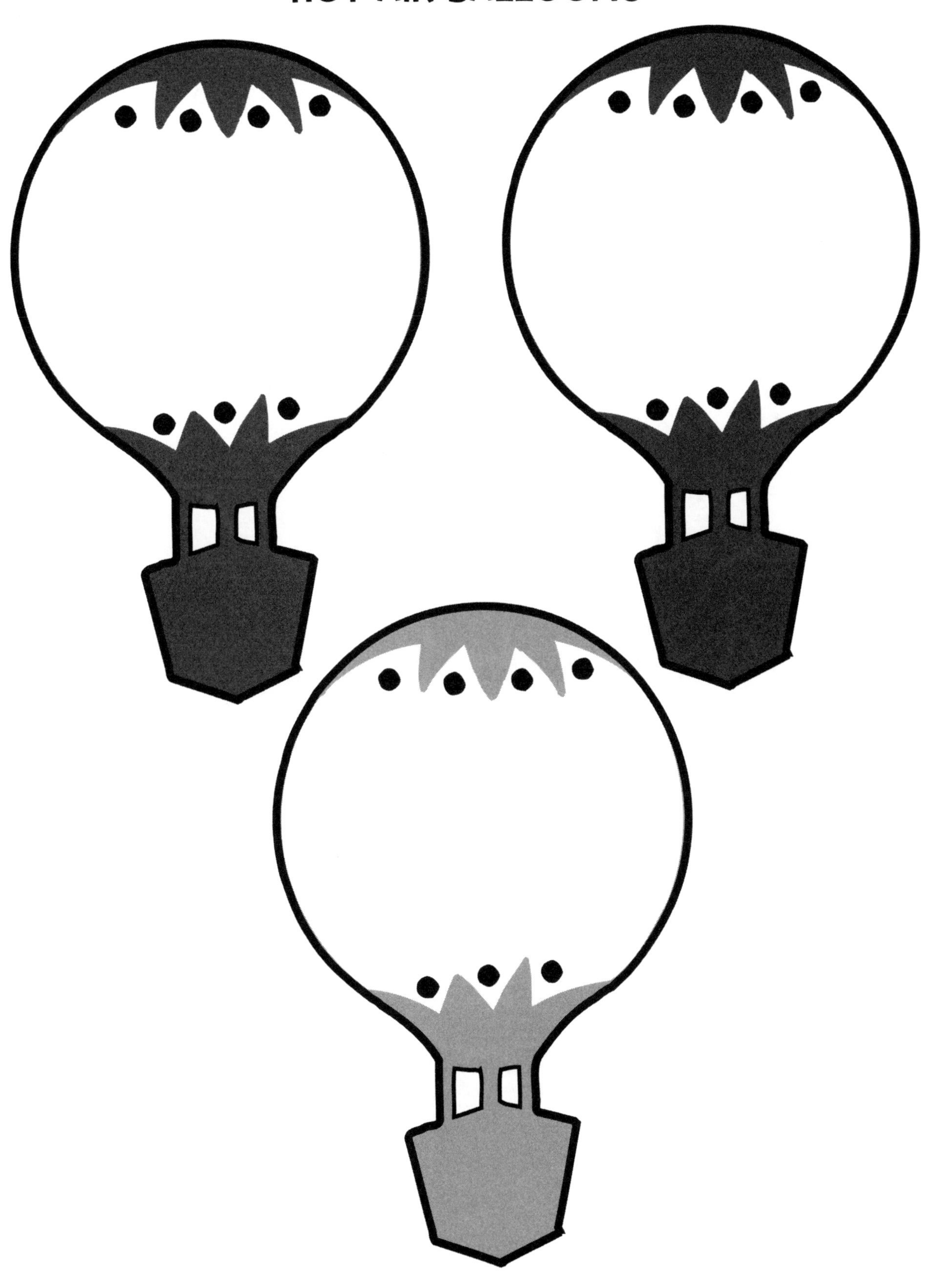

RAINBOW

CAPABILITY CARDS

Capability Card **Ride A Bike**	Capability Card **Read**
Capability Card **Speak Spanish**	Capability Card **Skate**
Capability Card **Draw**	Capability Card **Run Fast**
Capability Card **Sing**	Capability Card **Please My Teacher**
Capability Card **Tie My Shoe**	Capability Card **Solve Math Problems**
Capability Card **Type**	Capability Card **Play A Sport**

CAPABILITY CARDS

Capability Card **Dance**	Capability Card **Write A Poem**
Capability Card **Hop On One Foot**	Capability Card **Grow Flowers**
Capability Card **Swim**	Capability Card **Write Creative Stories**
Capability Card **Make People Laugh**	Capability Card **Make Friends**
Capability Card **Play An Instrument**	Capability Card **Make The Honor Roll**
Capability Card **Help My Parents**	Capability Card **Write Neatly**

LEMONS

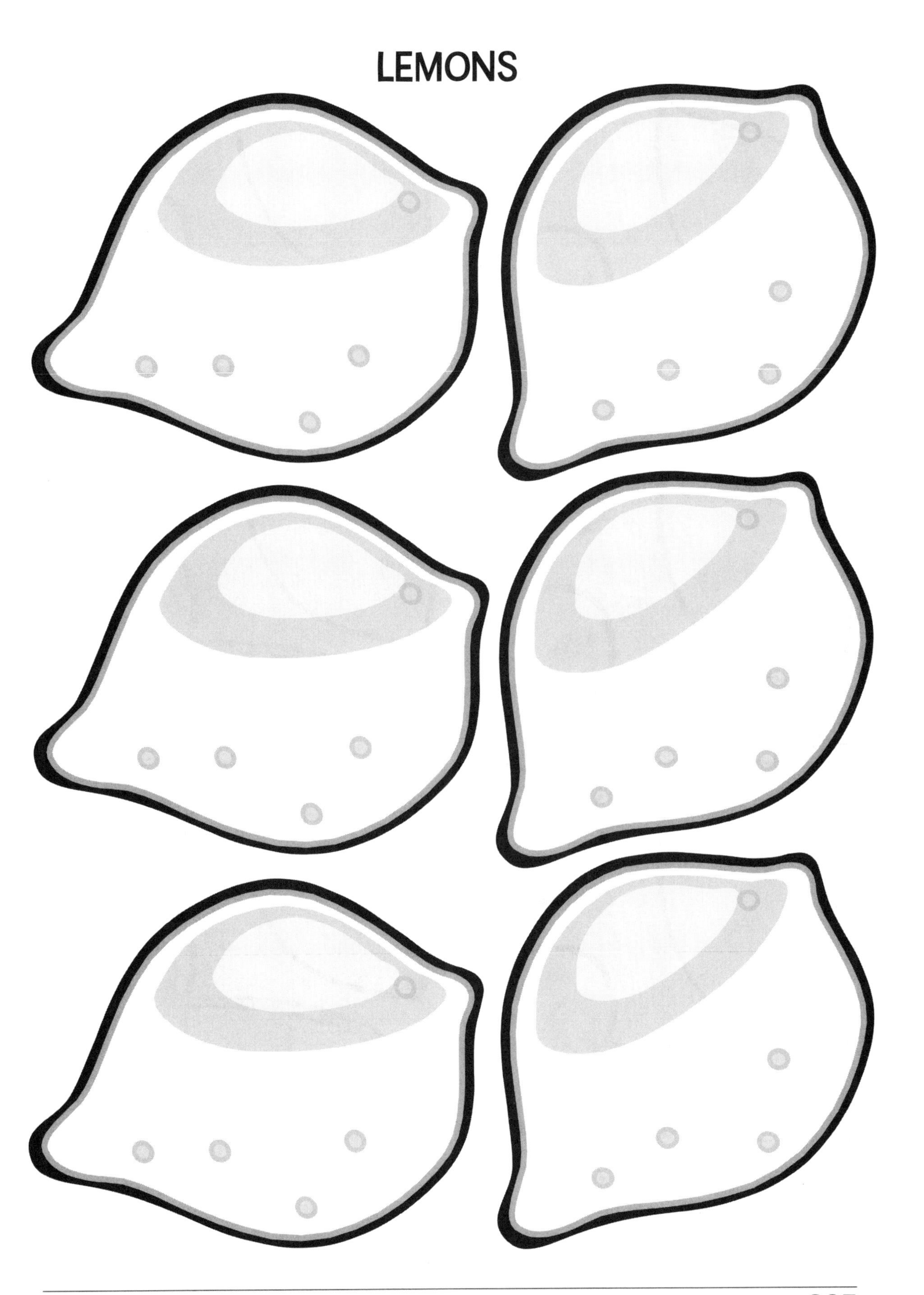

CHERRIES

MAGIC LAMP

WISH CLOUDS

LEAVE TEMPLATES

BOY SILHOUETTE

GIRL SILHOUETTE

THOUGHT BUBBLES

Two people looked out from prison bars; the one saw mud, the other stars.

GRADUATED CIRCLES

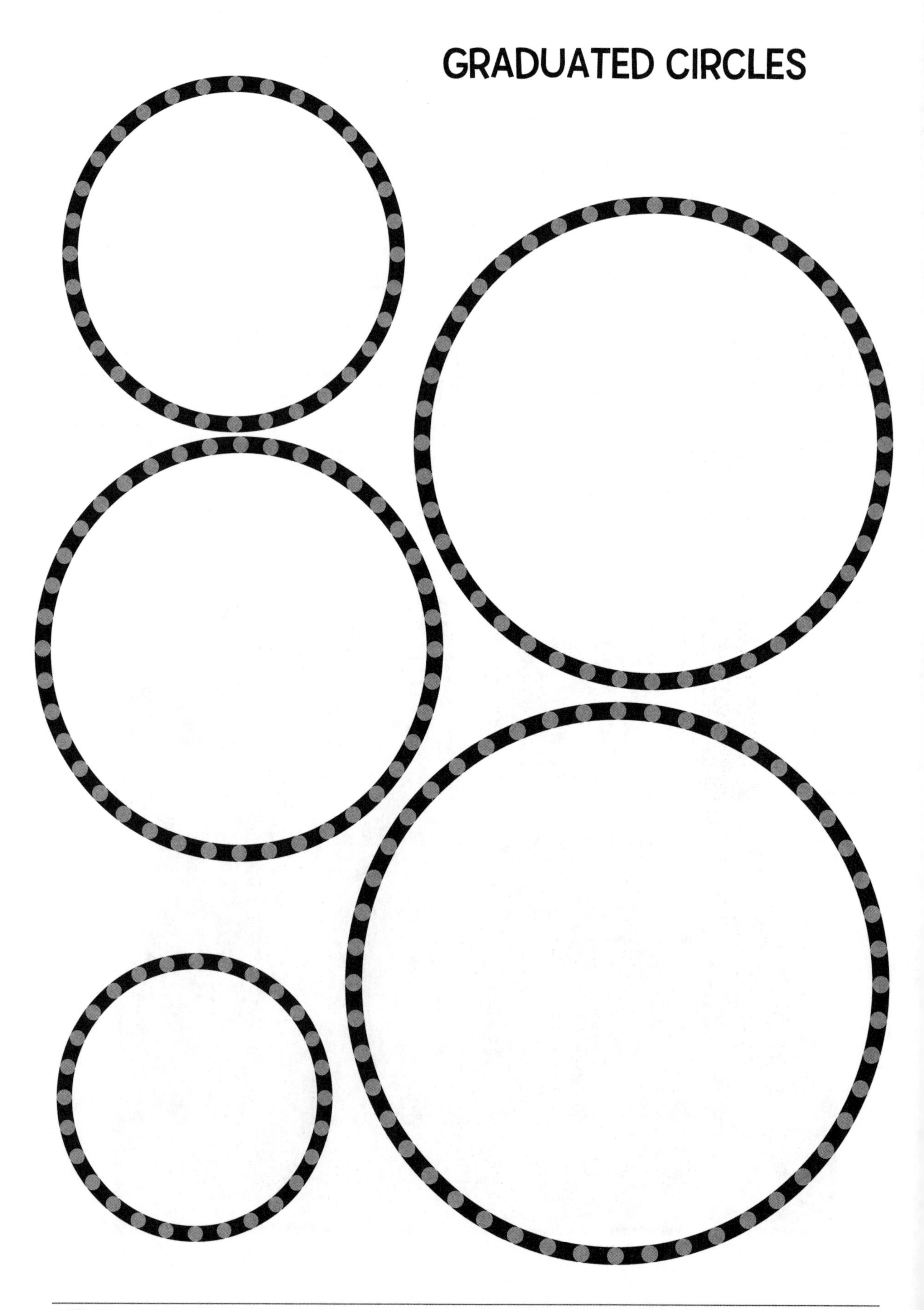

MAGICIAN'S HAT

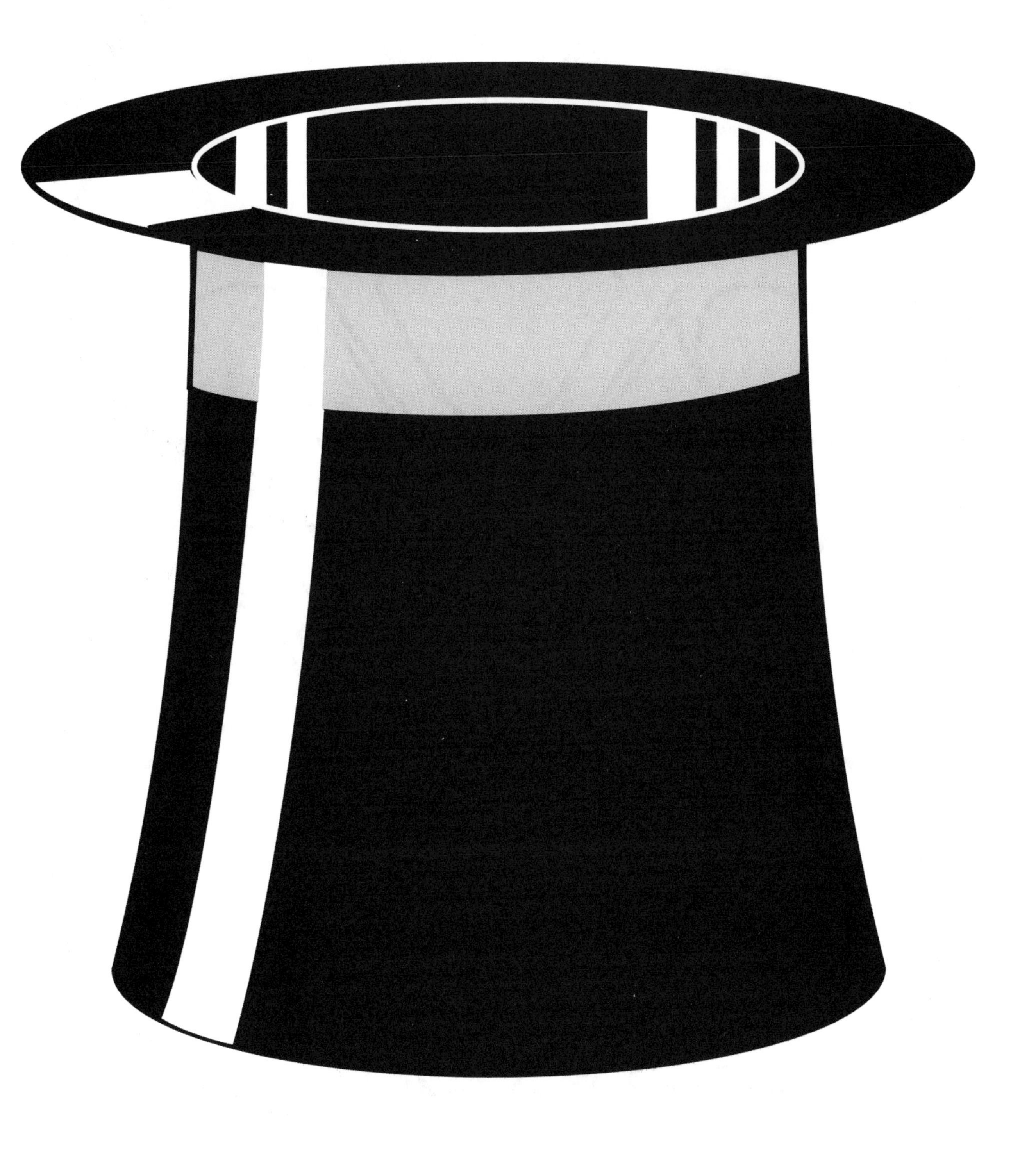

RABBITS

MASK

TARGET

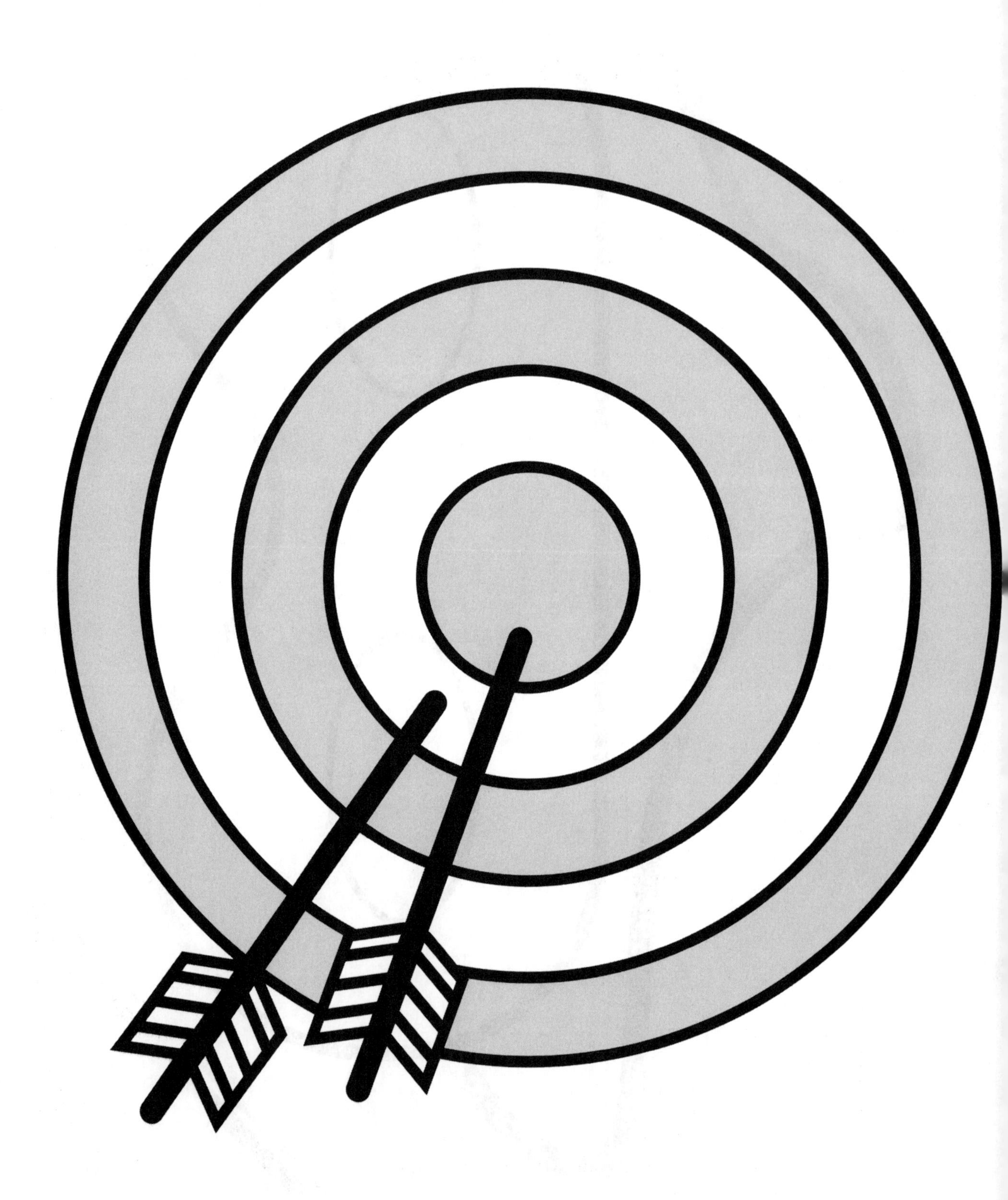

SMALL-GROUP LESSONS

Study Skills

Study skills are best taught by the classroom teacher. But it often becomes necessary for counselors to teach those students who do not absorb these tricks of effective studying. I always begin these groups by explaining that there is no magic formula for getting good grades. That requires work. But I can teach students how to work more effectively. I emphasize that I know these ideas work, but it is up to each individual to implement them.

You will notice that these group sessions begin at Grade 2. I do not believe study skills can be taught in the small-group setting for children in Kindergarten and Grade 1. A student in Kindergarten or Grade 1 who listens and participates will be a successful student. It would be more helpful to identify why an unsuccessful K or Grade 1 student is not listening or participating and to provide an intervention for that specific concern.

I suggest you identify students based on the grades attained the first quarter of the school year. Select students who have no identifiable factors contributing to their lack of success in school. For example, students who do not have a known disability, appear to have the requisite cognitive abilities, and may not be receiving any other kind of academic support in the school are good candidates for participation. The main skill areas for each group are:

Grades 2/3
Listening and learning
Being prepared
Using study time effectively
Following directions
The importance of reading
Goal-setting with public accountability
How behavior affects learning
Developing personal motivation and satisfaction

Grades 4/5
Being prepared
Study tools—creating personal study helpers
Using study time effectively
Good listening habits
Reading rates
How to use and read a textbook
How to study for a test
Concentration—understanding and practicing it
Accomplishments—developing personal motivation
Study reminders—general wrap-up

SMALL-GROUP LESSONS

Study Skills

GRADES 2-5

GRADES 2/3

GRADES 4/5

ASCA STANDARDS, COMPETENCIES, AND INDICATORS FOR SMALL-GROUP LESSONS ON STUDY SKILLS

Participation in these group activities will address the following ASCA standards, competencies, and indicators:

Domain	**A/ACADEMIC DEVELOPMENT**
A/A:1.1	Articulate feelings of competence and confidence as a learner
A/A:1.2	Display a positive interest in learning
A/A:1.3	Take pride in work and in achievement
A/A:1.5	Identify attitudes and behaviors which lead to successful learning
A/A:2.1	Apply time management and task management skills
A/A:2.2	Demonstrate how effort and persistence positively affect learning
A/A:2.3	Use communication skills to know when and how to ask for help when needed
A/A:3.1	Take responsibility for their actions
A/A:3.1	Demonstrate the ability to work independently, as well as the ability to work cooperatively with other students
A/A:3.3	Develop a broad range of interests and abilities
A/A:3.4	Demonstrate dependability, productivity and initiative
A/A:3.5	Share knowledge
A/B:1.1	Demonstrate the motivation to achieve individual potential
A/B:1.2	Learn and apply critical thinking skills
A/B:1.3	Apply the study skills necessary for academic success at each level
A/B:1.4	Seek information and support from faculty, staff, family, and peers
A/B:1.7	Become self-directed and independent learners
A/B:2.5	Use problem-solving and decision-making skills to assess progress toward educational goals
A/B:2.6	Understand the relationship between classroom performance and success in school
A/C:1.6	Understand how school success and academic achievement enhance future career and avocational opportunities

Domain	**C/CAREER DEVELOPMENT**
C/A:1.4	Learn how to interact and work cooperatively in teams
C/A:1.5	Learn to make decisions
C/A:1.6	Learn how to set goals
C/A:1.7	Understand the importance of planning
C/A:2.1	Acquire employability skills such as working on a team, problem-solving and organizational skills
C/A:2.9	Utilize time- and task-management skills
C/C:2.3	Learn to work cooperatively with others as a team member

Domain	**PS/PERSONAL/SOCIAL DEVELOPMENT**
PS/A:1.3	Learn the goal setting process
PS/A:1.6	Distinguish between appropriate and inappropriate behaviors
PS/A:1.8	Understand the need for self-control and how to practice it
PS/A:1.9	Demonstrate cooperative behavior in groups
PS/A:2.1	Recognize that everyone has rights and responsibilities
PS/A:2.6	Use effective communication skills
PS/A:2.7	Know that communication involves speaking, listening, and nonverbal behavior
PS/B:1.1	Use a decision-making and problem-solving model
PS/B:1.2	Understand consequences of decisions and choices
PS/B:1.3	Identify alternative solutions to a problem
PS/B:1.4	Develop effective coping skills for dealing with problems
PS/B:1.5	Demonstrate when, where, and how to seek help for solving problems and making decisions
PS/B:1.9	Identify long- and short-term goals
PS/B:1.10	Identify alternative ways of achieving goals
PS/C:1.6	Identify resource people in the school and community, and know how to seek their help

Master Supply List For Small Group On Study Skills

Collect these supplies prior to presenting the group.
Place all special supplies in the same box as the lessons copied on cardstock.

GENERAL SUPPLIES:

- ☐ Chart paper and marker
- ☐ Scissors
- ☐ Pencils
- ☐ Pens
- ☐ Paper
- ☐ Index cards

ART SUPPLIES:

- ☐ Crayons or markers
- ☐ Tape
- ☐ Glue/Glue sticks
- ☐ $^{3}/_{4}$" pompoms—16 of the same color for each student
- ☐ Soft foam strips $^{1}/_{2}$" wide by 10" long, the same color as the pompoms
- ☐ Wiggly eyes
- ☐ Pipe cleaners
- ☐ Foam sheets in different colors
- ☐ Paint or markers
- ☐ Black markers
- ☐ Drawing paper
- ☐ Cardstock or heavyweight copy paper (white)
- ☐ Decorative cord
- ☐ Decorative hole punchers
- ☐ Pinking shears
- ☐ Beads
- ☐ Various art/craft supplies

MISCELLANEOUS SUPPLIES:

- ☐ Colorful candy-coated chocolates or similar small candies
- ☐ Serving spoon
- ☐ Selected passage to be read aloud with several comprehension questions
- ☐ Boxes with lids (Other containers may also be used: tote bag, gift bag, etc.)
- ☐ List of supplies (use a beginning–of-year grade-level supply list)
- ☐ A few "starter" supplies from the beginning–of-year grade-level supply list (paper, pencils, crayons, glue, tape, etc.)
- ☐ Timer
- ☐ CD and CD player or radio
- ☐ Video (Interesting video that students will enjoy)

- ☐ Sample assignments: math worksheet, spelling list, and reading passage with comprehension questions
- ☐ Optional: Empty containers with pictures that do not relate to the products, such as a shortening can with a picture of fried chicken or cereal box with a picture of sports equipment
- ☐ Button or badge maker (if not available, name tag holders will work)
- ☐ Magnetic sheeting (Alternative—a wooden clothespin)
- ☐ Reading selections of different levels and content (one easy short story, a paragraph from a science or social studies book, a math word problem, directions for completing an origami fold)
- ☐ Sample graphic organizers
- ☐ Video/DVD of a cartoon

COPY ON WHITE CARDSTOCK: *Note*: Heavyweight copy paper may be substituted for cardstock

- ☐ *Study Skills Small-Group Lessons* as a quick reference to each lesson's page number (page 280)
- ☐ *Listening Poster* (page 306)
- ☐ *Grid Pattern Pictures:* one copy for the leader (pages 308-313)
- ☐ *School-Related Shapes Template:* several copies cut out (pages 314-315)
- ☐ *Bookmark #3:* multiple copies cut apart (page 324)

COPY ON COLORED CARDSTOCK:

- ☐ *Bookmark #1:* multiple copies on different colors of cardstock and cut apart (page 322)
- ☐ *Bookmark #2:* multiple copies on different colors of cardstock cut apart (page 323)

ONE COPY FOR EACH STUDENT ON WHITE COPY PAPER:

- ☐ *Candy Game* (page 305)
- ☐ List of supplies (use a beginning-of-year grade-level supply list obtained from the classroom teacher)
- ☐ *Grid Pattern* (page 307)
- ☐ *Schedule Sheet* (page 316)
- ☐ *Are You Listening?* (page 317)
- ☐ *SQ3R* (page 319)
- ☐ *Test Study Time Tips* (page 320)
- ☐ Spelling words taken from a class list
- ☐ *Concentration Tips* (page 321)

Candy Game

Materials:

For The Leader:

- ☐ Colorful candy-coated chocolates or similar small candies
- ☐ Serving spoon

For Each Student:

- ☐ *Candy Game* reproduced on white copy paper (page 305)
- ☐ Crayons of colors that match the candies to be used

(***Note:*** Be sure the use of candy is appropriate for use in your school district and for each group member. If you cannot use candy, you may substitute something suitable such as pieces of colored paper punched out with a hole punch. Or omit the *Candy Game* from your lessons.)

Activity:

- ▶ Give each student a copy of the *Candy Game* and crayons that match the colors of the candies to be used. Instruct the students to color each circle a different color. They may select which color is used for each circle and should not try and match anyone else's choices.

- ▶ When the students have finished coloring the circles, give each one a spoonful of candy. Ask the students to line up the candy with the colored circles so all the red candies are with the circle colored red and the green candies are with the green circle, etc. If there are any circles for which they have no matching candy, you may give them one. Have everyone count the candies they have. Give more to those who have fewer.

- ▶ Follow the worksheet instructions by giving each student a chance to respond to each statement. For example, the first statement asks students to name a way to study spelling words. A student who has four pieces of matching-colored candy for this first statement must identify four ways to study spelling words.

- ▶ It is usually best if the students eat the candy as they respond to the statements so all the candy is gone by the end of the session.

Listening And Learning

Materials:

For The Leader:

- ☐ *Listening Poster* reproduced on white cardstock (page 306)
- ☐ Tape
- ☐ A selected passage to be read aloud with several comprehension questions

For Each Student:

- ☐ Paper
- ☐ Pencil

Activity:

- ▶ Tape the *Listening Poster* in a place where the students can see it.
- ▶ Introduce the lesson by asking, "Can we do two things at once?" Allow a reasonable amount of time for discussion.
- ▶ Tell the students that the group will conduct an experiment to prove or disprove the possibility of doing two things at once.
- ▶ Give each student a piece of paper and a pencil. Then say, "As I read, write the directions from your classroom to my room. Try to write quickly and give only important information." (You may want to give an example: To get to the gym, leave the classroom and turn right. Go to the end of the hallway and turn right. The first door on your left is the gym.) Be sure a newcomer would be able to follow your directions easily.
- ▶ As the students write the directions, read several paragraphs of a story aloud. Remind the students to continue writing. After reading the paragraphs, collect the students' writings and ask several story-related comprehension questions. Review the written directions and the level of comprehension achieved.
- ▶ Discuss how well the students did and why.
- ▶ Reflect on the poster statement: *Listening is a learned skill that requires concentration without distraction.*
- ▶ Identify listening skills the students need to develop in order to improve their study habits.

Homework Survival Kit

Materials:

For Each Student:

- ☐ Box with lid (or other container)
- ☐ Crayons or markers
- ☐ List of supplies (use a beginning–of-year grade-level supply list)
- ☐ Tape or glue
- ☐ Pencil or pen
- ☐ A few "starter" supplies from the supply list

Activity:

- ▶ Discuss time wasters that can prevent students from completing homework (television, not having supplies handy, not knowing what to do or how to do it, daydreaming, radio, etc.).
- ▶ Explain that the Homework Survival Kit is a box or drawer at home in which all homework supplies are kept.
- ▶ Discuss how organizing supplies can help students complete homework more quickly.
- ▶ Tell the students they will each be making a Homework Survival Kit.
- ▶ Give each student a box or other container, crayons or markers, tape or glue, a pen or pencil, and the list of supplies. Discuss why the listed supplies are important to include in the kit. Allow the students to list their own suggestions for items to keep in the kit. Tell the students to tape/glue the supply list to the inside of the box's lid.
- ▶ Allow the students to decorate their kits.
- ▶ Give each student a few "starter" supplies to include in his/her kit. Encourage the students to complete their kits at home.

Working Well

Materials:

For The Leader:
- ☐ Timer
- ☐ Video and video player
- ☐ CD and CD player or radio

For Each Student:
- ☐ A few sample assignments: math worksheet, spelling list, and reading passage with comprehension questions
- ☐ Pencil

Activity:

- ▶ Discuss common distractions that occur while working and their possible impact:

    - Watching TV while doing homework—may take you longer to complete it
    - Talking with a friend while you're working on math—may make careless errors
    - Listening to a favorite radio station while writing a story—may not get much completed
    - Other examples from the students

- ▶ Give each student a math worksheet and a pencil. Ask the students to complete the worksheet in three minutes. Before the students begin, tell them that it's OK (even required) for them to talk with each other while they work. After three minutes, check their progress.

- ▶ Give each student a spelling list. Ask the students to write a sentence for each word on the sheet. When they start to work, begin the video. (Make sure it's an interesting video that they will enjoy.) After five minutes, see how much work the students have accomplished.

- ▶ Give each student a reading passage. Ask the students to read the passage and answer the questions (worksheet format) at the end. Before they begin work, select a music station (or CD) which features current popular music. Play it while they work. After three minutes, check the students' progress.

- ▶ Discuss each distraction's impact.

- ▶ Work together and make a plan for working more efficiently.

(*Note:* You may wish to repeat one of the activities without the distraction and compare the amount of work accomplished in the same time period.)

Following Directions

Materials:

For The Leader:

- ☐ *Grid Pattern Pictures* reproduced on white cardstock and cut apart (pages 308-313)
- ☐ Scissors
- ☐ Chart paper and marker
- ☐ Tape

For Each Student:

- ☐ *Grid Pattern* reproduced on white copy paper (page 307)
- ☐ Pencil

Preparation:

Reproduce and cut apart the *Grid Pattern Pictures*. On the chart paper, draw a grid pattern the exact size as the grid pattern pictures. Put the chart paper in a place it where the students cannot see it.

Activity:

- ▶ Discuss the following questions:
    - Why should we follow directions and when is following directions important?
    - What makes following directions challenging?
    - What happens if directions aren't followed?
- ▶ Give each student a copy of the *Grid Pattern* and a pencil.
- ▶ Tell the students you're going to show them one section of the grid at a time. Their job is to reproduce that section as closely as they can. Show the picture sections one at a time in random fashion, identifying in which section on their sheet they should reproduce the lines. Then tape that picture to its corresponding square on the chart paper. Remember to keep the chart paper hidden from the students.
- ▶ After the students have drawn all 12 grid pictures, show them the completed picture on the chart paper. If the students have followed the directions, they should have a mouse (or close to it) when they have completed the activity.
- ▶ Discuss the importance of following directions exactly.

Bookworm

Materials:

For The Leader:

- ☐ Optional: Empty containers of various products labeled with pictures that do not relate to the products

For Each Student:

- ☐ $^{3}/_{4}$" pompoms—16 of the same color
- ☐ 2 pieces of foam cut into strips $^{1}/_{2}$" wide by 10" long, the same color as the pompoms
- ☐ 2 Wiggly eyes
- ☐ 1 Pipe cleaner
- ☐ Glue

Preparation:

Following the activity instructions, make a sample Bookworm to use as a visual.

Activity:

- ▶ Discuss the importance of reading and how it relates to all subject areas in school as well as in real life. (*Note:* It can be enlightening to bring empty food containers labeled with pictures that do not relate to the products that were in the containers. Ask the students what they might think each one contained if their only clue to the product inside was the picture on the outside.)

- ▶ Show the students the Bookworm sample and tell them they'll each make a Bookworm that will serve as their reminder of the importance of reading.

- ▶ Give each student two same-color foam strips, a pipe cleaner, 16 pompoms that match the color of the foam strips, two wiggly eyes, and glue. Have the students make their Bookworms as follows:

    - Glue the pipe cleaner to one foam strip.
    - Glue the second foam strip over the pipe cleaner.
    - Glue the pompoms to one side of the strips, placing them as close to each other as possible so there will be fewer gaps when the Bookworm is bent into shapes.
    - Glue the wiggly eyes to the first pompom.

- ▶ Encourage the students to set a goal of reading for a specific number of minutes every night. You may also have them maintain a reading log showing how much time they spend reading each day.

Commitment Button

Materials:

For The Leader:

- ☐ Chalkboard and chalk or chart paper and marker

Have Available For The Group:

- ☐ Button or badge maker
- ☐ Various art/craft supplies

Activity:

- ▶ Discuss some things the students could do to become better students. List their ideas on the chart paper/chalkboard.

- ▶ Ask each group member to select one thing on the list he/she can do during the next week.

- ▶ Place the materials for making buttons or badges in a place easily accessible to the students. Have each student design, make, and wear a button or badge proclaiming something to which he/she is committed. For example, a button could have a simple statement: "I will do my homework every night." Or "I will keep my desk area clean and organized." Perhaps one button could have an ear on it with the word *listen* under it.

- ▶ Alert the teachers to the task being undertaken by the students so they can provide encouragement and reminders.

- ▶ Ask the students to wear their buttons for the week and be prepared to answer these questions at the next group meeting:

  - Did you always wear your button?
  - Did you mind wearing your button?
  - How did others react to your button?
  - Did wearing your button help you meet your goal?

Teacher Pleasing

Materials:

For The Leader:

- ☐ Chart paper and marker or chalkboard and chalk

For Each Student:

- ☐ Index cards—one card for each behavior symbol/picture drawn on the chart paper/chalkboard
- ☐ Index cards—one card for each good habit listed on the chart paper/chalkboard
- ☐ Crayons or markers

Activity:

- ▶ Ask the students the following questions relating to the buttons they wore during the week:
  - Did you always wear your button?
  - Did you mind wearing your button?
  - How did others react to your button?
  - Did wearing your button help you meet your goal?
- ▶ Brainstorm behaviors that annoy teachers. List them on the chart paper/chalkboard as they are mentioned. Some answers could be:
  - talking in class.
  - not being prepared.
  - not having the right materials.
  - wasting time.
  - not listening.
  - yelling out answers.
  - bothering other students.
- ▶ Discuss why these behaviors might bother teachers (interrupts learning, teacher has to repeat things, students don't learn as well, shows disinterest or disrespect, etc.).
- ▶ Discuss how these behaviors might interfere with a student's own learning.
- ▶ Decide on certain symbols or pictures which might remind students to avoid these behaviors. For example, a picture of an open mouth for yelling out, a picture of an ear with a hand over it for not listening, etc. Draw each symbol or picture on the chart paper/chalkboard.

- Give each student crayons or markers and one index card for each symbol or picture the students have decided upon. Allow time for each group member to make a set of cards with these pictures/symbols on them. Then add the ⃠ symbol over each.

- Brainstorm the habits of a good student (well behaved, prepared, completes tasks on time, is organized, etc.). List each good habit mentioned on the chart paper/chalkboard.

- Give each student one index card for each good habit listed. Have each group member make a set of positive cards to remind him/her to do these things.

- Group members may take their cards with them as reminders.

Accomplishments

Materials:

For Each Student:

- Black marker
- Scissors
- Glue

Have Available For The Group:

- *School-Related Shapes Templates*—several copies reproduced on white cardstock and cut out (pages 314-315)
- Foam sheets in different colors
- Paint or markers
- Magnetic sheeting (Alternative—a wooden clothespin)

Activity:

- Discuss the importance of the students recognizing and celebrating their personal accomplishments. Say:
    - We need not depend on others to recognize our personal accomplishments, although it's nice when others recognize that we've worked hard and met a personal goal.
    - We can find a way to celebrate ourselves.
- Tell the students that one way to celebrate personal accomplishments is to display their own work in their rooms or study areas. This can serve as a reminder of what they can accomplish when they are diligent with their studies.
- Place the cut-out *School-Related Shapes Templates*, different-colored foam sheets, paint or markers, and magnetic sheeting or wooden clothespins on a table. Give each student glue, a black marker, and scissors. Tell the students they are going to make magnets to use to display their personal accomplishments. Then give the following directions:
    - Using the *School-Related Shapes Templates*, choose one shape, trace it onto the appropriate color foam, and cut it out. (Apples, pencil, ruler, school house, etc.)
    - Use paint or markers to complete the shape details. For example, use a marker to add windows and a door to the school house or numbers and measurement marks to the ruler. Or use a pink marker to add an eraser to the yellow pencil and use a black marker to write *#2* on the side.
    - Glue magnetic sheeting to the back of the shape. (*Note*: If the students do not have a board on which to affix the magnet, you may need to use a wooden clothespin to hold the paper or project being displayed.)

Your Study Place

Materials:

For Each Student:

- ☐ Crayons or markers
- ☐ Drawing paper

Activity:

- ▶ Discuss where group members do homework. Tell them it is important to have a special place to study.

- ▶ Talk about places that are *not* appropriate places to do homework. For example, the kitchen table is not usually a good place to study. It is the center of activity and may encourage too much dependence on a parent for help.

- ▶ Go over the tools needed for proper study.

    - Good light
    - Writing surface (desk or table)
    - Homework materials (texts, assignments, paper, pencils, pens, etc.)
    - Extras—dictionary, atlas, bulletin board, radio, etc. (*Note:* Including a radio may be controversial. However, I believe playing soft music can help create an atmosphere of learning while masking background distractions.)
    - Some method of storage or way of easily moving items when necessary (box, crate)

- ▶ Give each student a piece of drawing paper and crayons or markers. Have the students draw a picture representing the perfect place to study at home. The preferred elements should be clearly labeled. Let the students take their drawings home. Encourage them to work toward establishing an area as much like their drawing as possible.

Effective Use Of Time

Materials:

For Each Student:

- ☐ 2 pieces of 8½" x 11" white cardstock
- ☐ Crayons or markers
- ☐ *Schedule Sheet* reproduced on white copy paper (page 316)
- ☐ Pencil

Activity:

- ▶ Discuss the "great time robbers"—laziness, distractions, procrastination, and daydreaming.

- ▶ Discuss when and where homework should be completed.

    - Best if done at a desk
    - Need good lighting
    - Should be done at same time every day
    - Sufficient time should be budgeted
    - Best if done in daylight hours

- ▶ Give each student two 8½" x 11" pieces of white cardstock and crayons or markers. Have the students create "reminder" signs they can post in their homework area. Signs should give positive suggestions or remind them to stay on task. Use the previous discussions as a guide for making the posters.

- ▶ Give each student a copy of the *Schedule Sheet* and a pencil. Have the students fill in the side that tells how they plan to spend their time (school, homework, soccer practice, etc.). The other side should be left blank and completed each day with how they actually spent their time (watching TV, soccer, homework, shopping, etc.)

- ▶ Tell the students to bring their completed *Schedule Sheets* to the next session.

Good Listening Habits

Materials:

For The Leader:
- ☐ *Are You Listening? Leader's Directions* (page 318)

For Each Student:
- ☐ *Are You Listening?* reproduced on white copy paper (page 317)
- ☐ Crayons or markers

Activity:

- ▶ Discuss the *Schedule Sheets* completed by the students in Session #2. Discuss why the students' schedules worked or didn't work.

- ▶ Introduce the following good-listening habits:

  - Eyes on speaker
  - Ears listening
  - Hands/feet/body still
  - Distractions intentionally ignored
  - Mouth closed and quiet
  - Mind focused and thinking
  - Pencil in hand

- ▶ Discuss the possible consequences of not listening in class:

  - Not knowing what to do, how to do it, or when to do it

- ▶ Then discuss possible distractions in class or at home:

  - Someone talking
  - Someone trying to get the student's attention
  - A TV or music playing in the background
  - Someone tapping a pencil

- ▶ Give each student a copy of *Are You Listening?* and crayons or markers. Tell the students you'll give them directions but will only say each instruction once. Emphasize that nothing will be repeated.

- ▶ Designate one group member to distract others and interfere with their listening. Begin reading the *Are You Listening? Leader's Directions* while the distracter goes to work.

- ▶ Discuss how well the students completed their task.

- ▶ Ask the students to bring their social studies book (or science book) to the next session.

Make Your Own Study Tools

Materials:

For Each Student:
- ☐ Textbook (social studies or science) currently being used in his/her classroom
- ☐ Index cards
- ☐ Pencil or pen

Activity:

- ▶ Discuss how making study tools can help students remember facts for a test.
- ▶ Make sure each student has brought a textbook.
- ▶ Tell the students that one study tool is flash cards made up of information found in their textbook. Have them open their books to a chapter they're currently studying.
- ▶ As a group, go through the chapter and determine what things should be included on each index card.
- ▶ Give each student index cards and a pencil or pen. Allow time for the students to make the flash cards. Only one fact should be written on each card.
- ▶ Discuss how the flash cards can be used—partners asking each other questions, writing on the back a question whose answer is the fact on the front, etc.
- ▶ Conclude the session by asking questions based on the flash cards. The students will be surprised at how much they remember, just from writing the facts.
- ▶ Before dismissing the students, tell them to bring their social studies book to the next meeting.

SQ3R—Reading A Textbook

Materials:

For Each Student:

- ☐ Social studies book currently being used in the student's classroom
- ☐ *SQ3R* reproduced on white copy paper (page 319)

Activity:

- ▶ Explain that the students will be learning a method of reading their textbooks—SQ3R.
- ▶ Give each student a copy of *SQ3R* (Survey, Question, Read, Recite, Review) and explain each component. Choose a chapter the from the students' social studies book that they have not already studied in class.
  - **S**urvey—Read only the chapter title, subtitles, italicized terms, boldface type. Think about what they imply the chapter will discuss.
  - **Q**uestion—Go to the first major heading. Anticipate what will be in that section. Using the interrogatives *who, what, where, when*, and *why,* turn heading #1 into questions. Write those questions. (Relate this technique to the previous lesson on creating study tools on index cards. The **Q**uestion step written on an index card becomes a study tool.)
  - **R**ead—Read the chapter section by section for the purpose of answering the questions written in the previous step.
  - **R**ecite—After you read a section, cover the page(s) and recite what you can remember.
  - **R**eview—Look at the section and see if you missed any important information.
- ▶ Repeat S, Q, R, R, R for each section in the chapter.
- ▶ Explain that this process involves active reading, which sharpens comprehension. Ask the students to try using it for future study sessions.

Reading Rates

Materials:

For The Leader:

- ☐ Reading selections of different levels and content (one easy short story, a paragraph from a science or social studies book, a math word problem, directions for completing an origami fold)
- ☐ Overhead projector and transparency or chart paper and marker

Preparation:

Copy the reading selections onto the chart paper or transparency.

Activity:

▶ Tell the students that a good reader:

- reads for understanding.
- reads for pleasure.
- scans or looks for specific information.

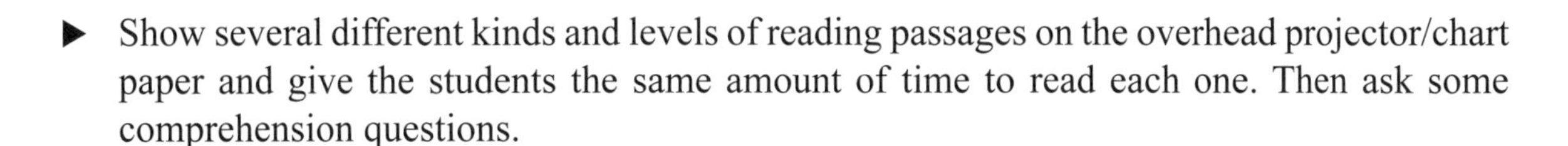

▶ Show several different kinds and levels of reading passages on the overhead projector/chart paper and give the students the same amount of time to read each one. Then ask some comprehension questions.

▶ Discuss why the students could answer some questions and not others. For example, few students will be able to answer the science or social studies questions because of the difficult words, complex information, etc.

▶ Discuss the importance of allowing various amounts of time to read and understand, depending on what is being read and the complexity of the material.

▶ Have the students reread the passages, this time allowing appropriate lengths of time. (*Note:* You may want to model the different rates of reading.)

How To Study For A Test

Materials:

For The Leader:

- ☐ Sample graphic organizers
- ☐ Chart paper and marker or chalkboard and chalk

For Each Student:

- ☐ *Test Study Time Tips* reproduced on white copy paper (page 320)
- ☐ Spelling words taken from a class list, reproduced on white copy paper

Activity:

- ▶ Give each student a copy of the *Test Study Time Tips.*

- ▶ Review each of the following tips:

  - Write the information you need to know on index cards, creating flash cards. Write a question on one side of the card and the answer on the back.
  - Go through the flash cards you created and try to answer the questions. If you are successful, place that card in the discard pile. If you cannot answer the question, look at the answer and place the card in the review pile.
  - Go through the review pile.

- ▶ Demonstrate the use of a graphic organizer for studying. On the chart paper/chalkboard, provide a few sample graphic organizers.

  - Working as a group, create an example by discussing something currently being studied in class. Write the graphic organizer on the chart paper/chalkboard.

- ▶ Give each student the list of spelling words. Using these tips, practice studying for a spelling test:

  - Read the word aloud and spell it.
  - Trace the word in the air with your finger as you spell it aloud again.
  - Use the word in a sentence.
  - Say the word and spell it aloud three times.
  - Close your eyes, say the word, and spell it.
  - Write the word.
  - Check to see if you spelled it correctly.
  - Have someone give you a practice test.
  - Repeat the process for any words you miss.

Concentration

Materials:

For The Leader:

- ☐ Video/DVD of a cartoon and Video/DVD player or radio turned to a popular station

For Each Student:

- ☐ *Concentration Tips* reproduced on white copy paper (page 321)
- ☐ Activity or chapter review from a textbook being used by the students, reproduced on white copy paper

Activity:

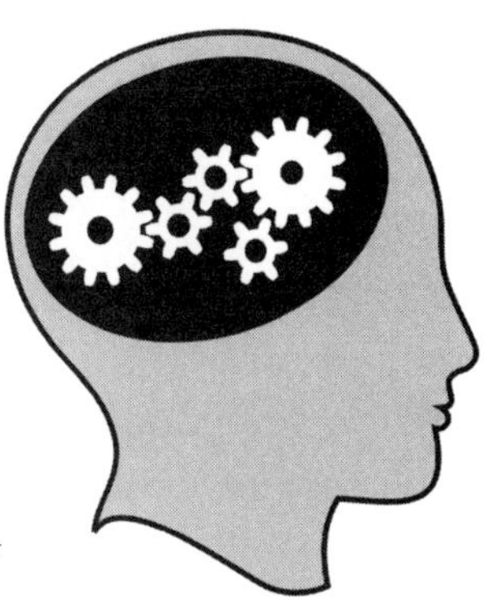

- ▶ Give each student a copy of the *Concentration Tips.*
- ▶ Go over the tips for improving concentration.
  - Breakfast is essential.
  - Be well rested.
  - Exercise makes you feel better and keeps your body chemistry in good condition.
  - Study with a pencil in your hand.
  - Keep a water bottle nearby.
  - A quiet place for study is best.
  - Control TV viewing—more than 10 hours/week may reduce the ability to study and concentrate.
  - Consider .listening to quiet music on a headset—or "white noise" (oceans sound, surf, etc.).
  - Plan a small break between 20-minute study segments.
- ▶ Give each student a copy of the lesson to be studied (an activity or chapter review from a textbook).
- ▶ Advise the students that they will have 10 minutes to study and learn as much as they can.
- ▶ While studying, play an entertaining video or popular music. Provide no pencils or papers or other supplies.
- ▶ After 10 minutes, ask some basic questions from the lesson.
- ▶ Discuss how the video/music and lack of other materials affected the students' ability to concentrate and learn.

Accomplishments

Materials:

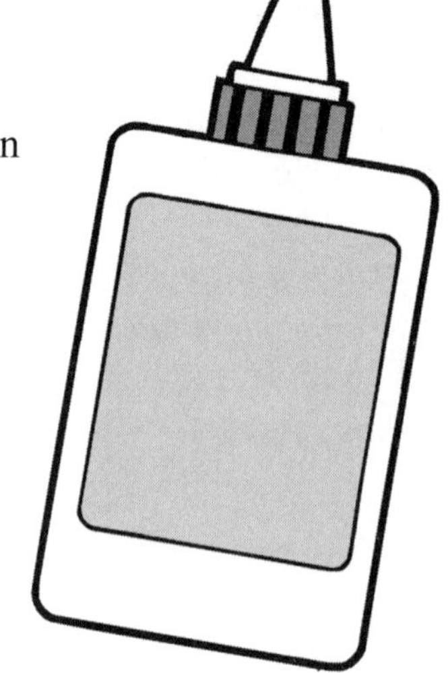

Have Available For The Group:
- ☐ *School-Related Shapes Templates*—several copies reproduced on white cardstock and cut out (pages 314-315)
- ☐ Foam sheets in different colors
- ☐ Paint or markers
- ☐ Magnetic sheeting (Alternative—a wooden clothespin)

For Each Student:
- ☐ Black marker
- ☐ Scissors
- ☐ Glue

Activity:

▶ Discuss the importance of the students recognizing and celebrating their personal accomplishments. Say:

- We need not depend on others to recognize our personal accomplishments, although it's nice when others recognize that we've worked hard and met a personal goal.
- We can find a way to celebrate ourselves.

▶ Tell the students that one way to celebrate personal accomplishments is to display their own work in their rooms or study areas. This can serve as a reminder of what they can accomplish when they are diligent with their studies.

▶ Place the cut-out *School-Related Shapes Templates*, different-colored foam sheets, paint or markers, and magnetic sheeting or wooden clothespins on a table. Give each student glue, a black marker, and scissors. Tell the students they are going to make magnets to use to display their personal accomplishments. Then give the following directions:

- Using the *School-Related Shapes Templates*, choose one shape, trace it onto the appropriate color foam, and cut it out. (Apples, pencil, ruler, school house, etc.)
- Use paint or markers to complete the shape details. For example, use a marker to add windows and a door to the school house or numbers and measurement marks to the ruler. Or use a pink marker to add an eraser to the yellow pencil and use a black marker to write *#2* on the side.
- Glue magnetic sheeting to the back of the shape. (*Note*: If the students do not have a board on which to affix the magnet, you may need to use a wooden clothespin to hold the paper or project being displayed.)

Bookmark And Reading Tip Reminders

Materials:

For The Leader:

- ☐ Chart paper and marker or chalkboard and chalk

For Each Student:

- ☐ Scissors
- ☐ One 12" piece of decorative cord
- ☐ Glue stick

Have Available For The Group:

- ☐ *Bookmarks #1* reproduced on different colors of cardstock and cut apart (page 322)
- ☐ *Bookmark #2* reproduced on different colors of cardstock and cut apart (page 323)
- ☐ *Bookmark #3* reproduced on white cardstock and cut apart (page 324)
- ☐ Decorative hole punchers
- ☐ Pinking shears
- ☐ Beads

Preparation:

Cut the decorative cord into 12" lengths. Reproduce enough copies of *Bookmark #1* for each student to have one rectangle. Reproduce enough copies of *Bookmarks #2* and *#3* for each student to have two rectangles of each one.

Activity:

- ▶ Discuss the study skills and test tips the group has learned.
- ▶ Create a list of important or favorite tips learned during the group. Write them on the chart paper/chalkboard as they are mentioned.
- ▶ Tell the students they are going to use these tips to create self-reminders on bookmarks.
- ▶ Give each student a 12" piece of decorative cord, scissors, and a glue stick.
- ▶ Then give the following instructions for making a bookmark.
    - Select one large rectangle (*Bookmark #1*) and two medium rectangles (*Bookmark #2*).
    - Use pinking shears to trim one long edge of the medium rectangles and all four edges of the large rectangle.

- Punch decorative holes along the side of the medium rectangles.
- Glue one medium rectangle to the center of each side of the large rectangle.
- Distribute two small white rectangles (*Bookmark #3*) to each student. Have the students write one of their favorite (or most important) reading tips on each rectangle. Glue one of these to the center of each side of the medium-colored rectangles.
- Punch a hole in the top of the bookmark.
- Thread both ends of the cord through the hole at the top of the bookmark. Tie a knot in the two cords about 1" from the bookmark.
- Separate the two ends of the cord and string four beads on each end. Tie knots in each cord against the last bead.

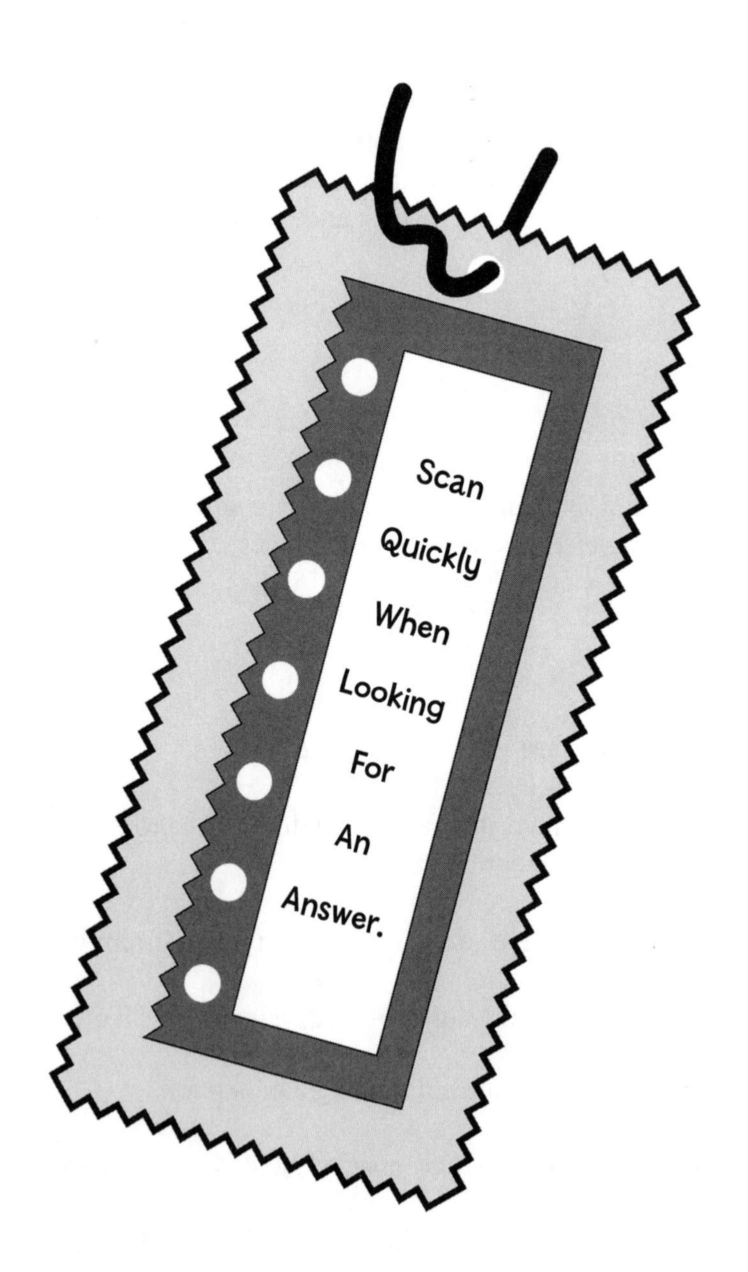

Candy Game

For every ◯, name a way to study your spelling words.

For every ◯, name a homework hint.

For every ◯, tell why you must pay attention in class.

For every ◯, name a hint for doing classwork.

For every ◯, name a tip for studying for a big test.

For every ◯, name a tip for remembering what you read.

Listening Poster

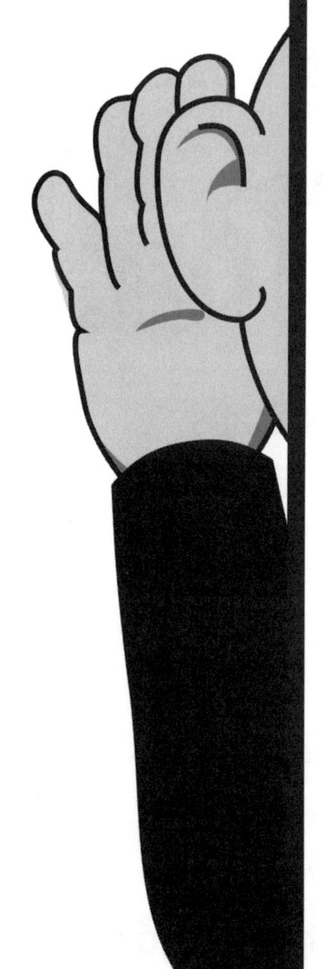

LISTENING

is a

learned skill

that requires

concentration

without

distraction.

GRID PATTERN

1	2	3
4	5	6
7	8	9
10	11	12

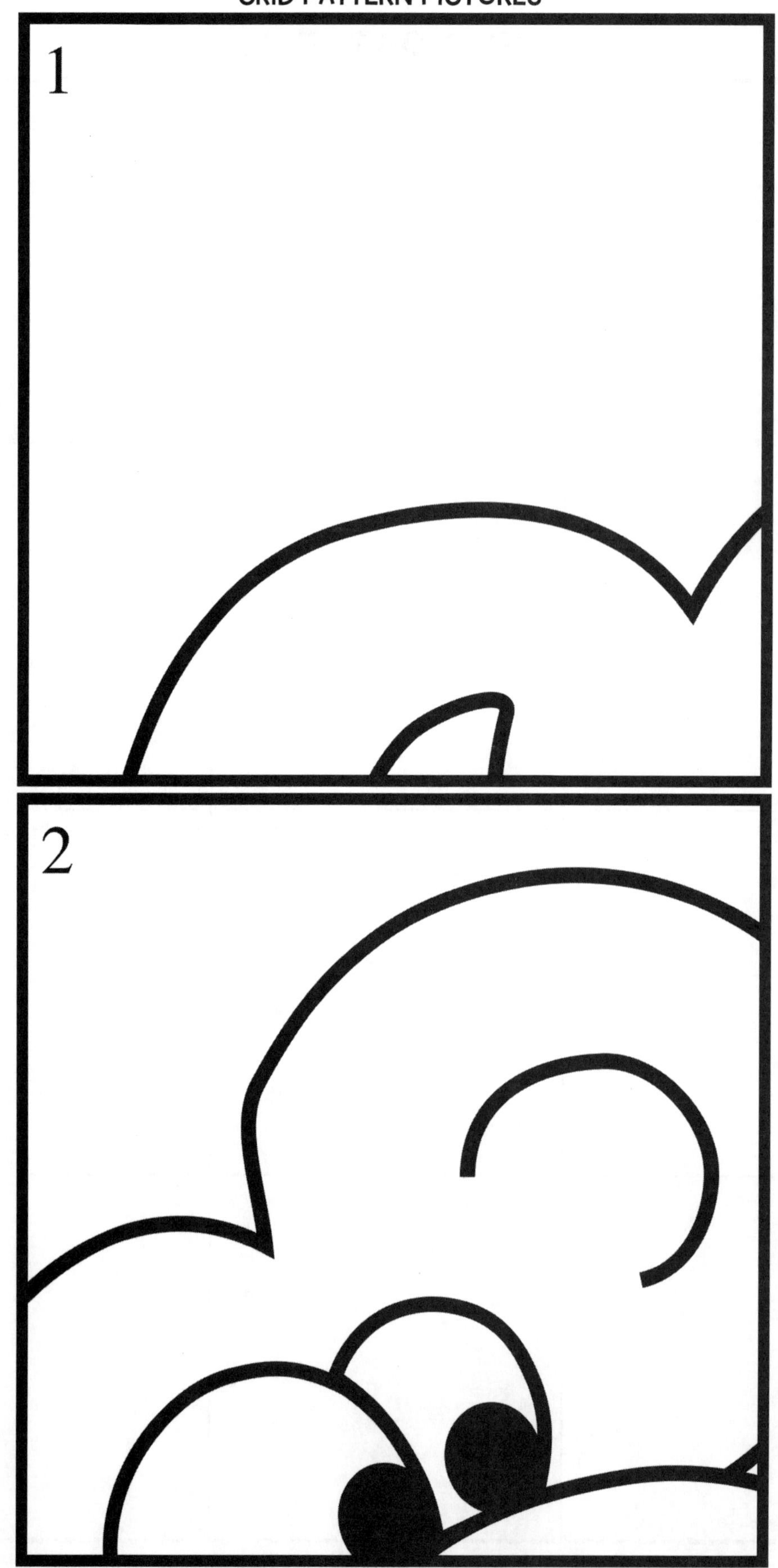
1
2

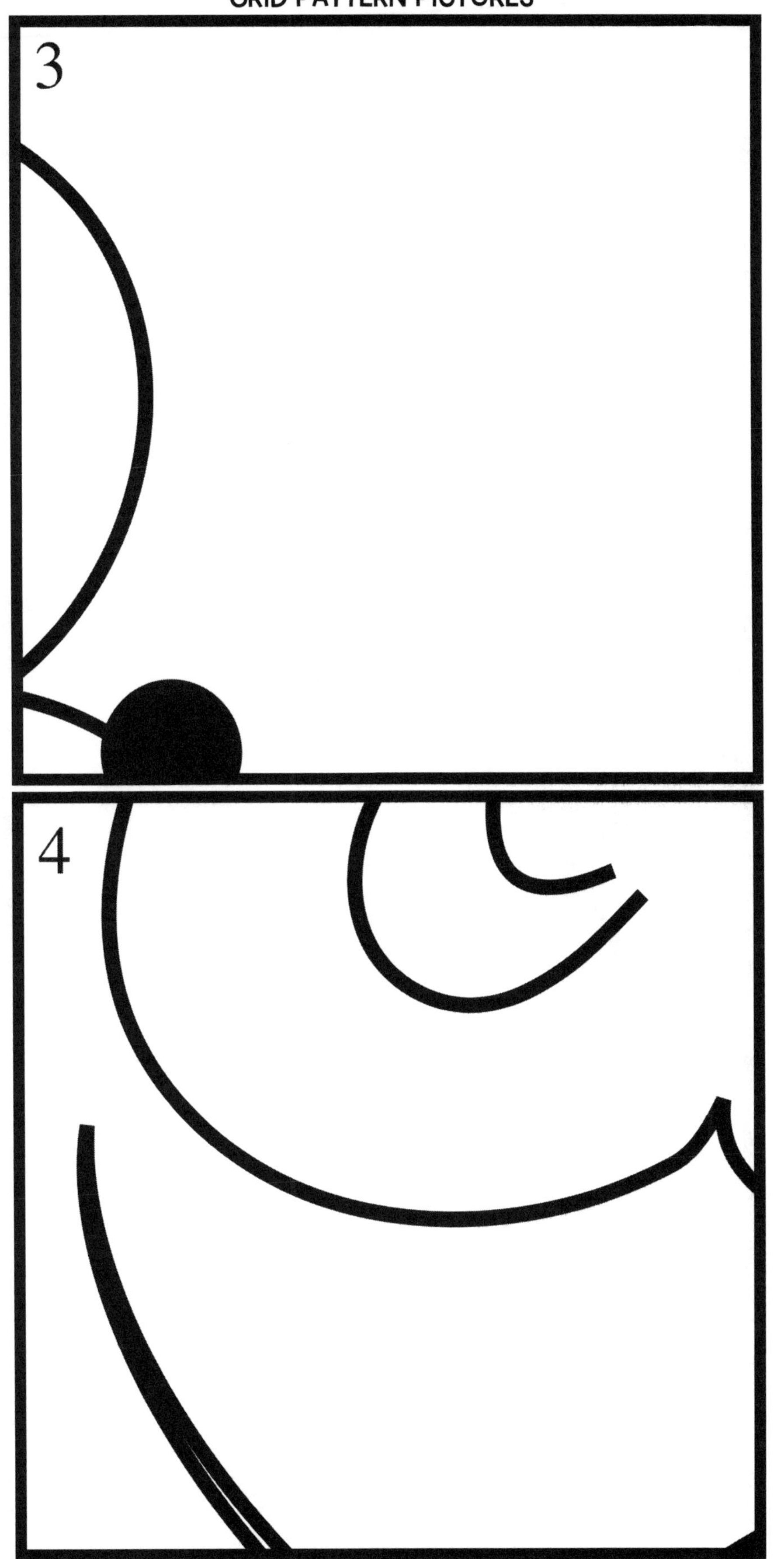
3
4

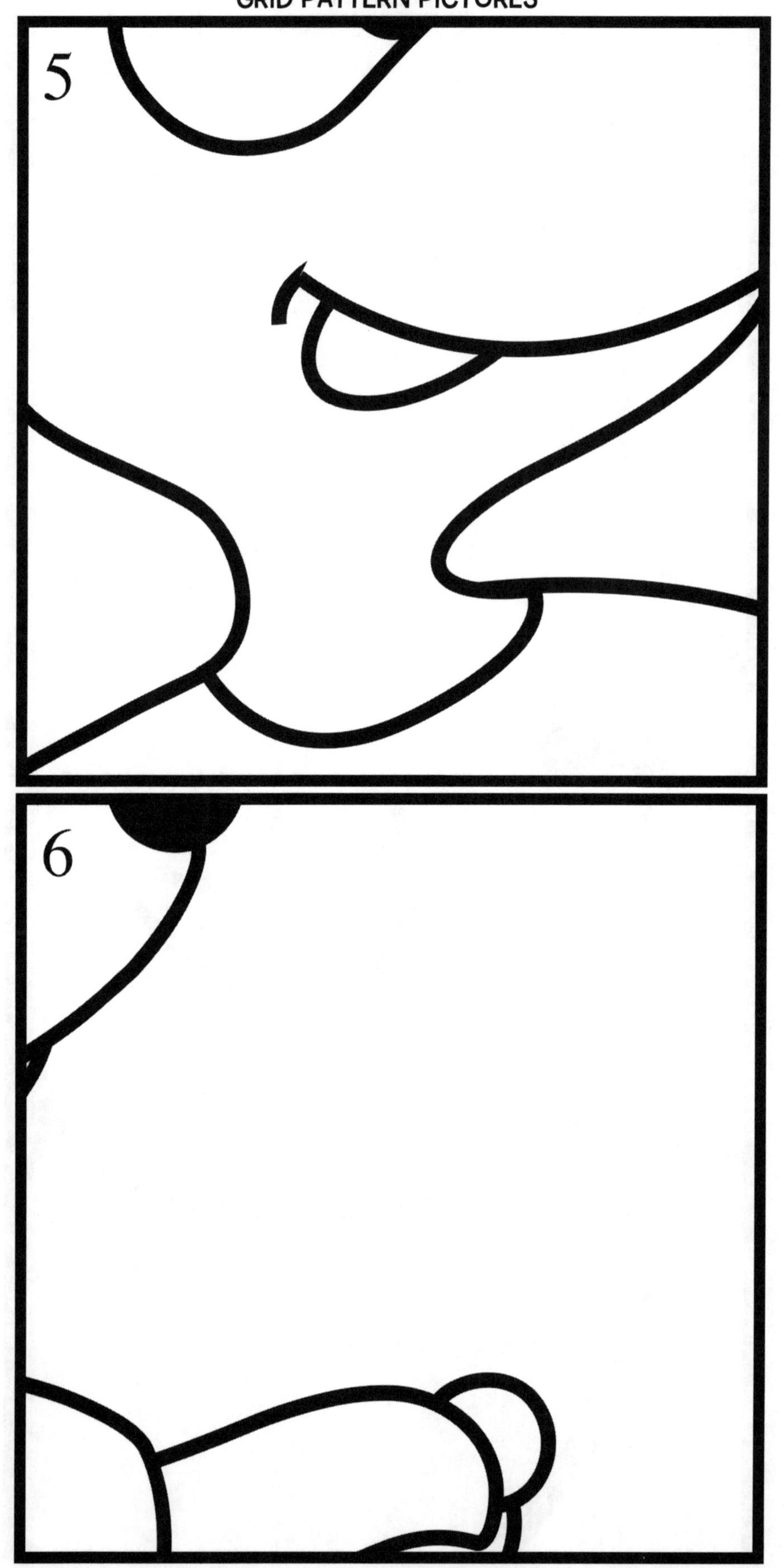
5
6

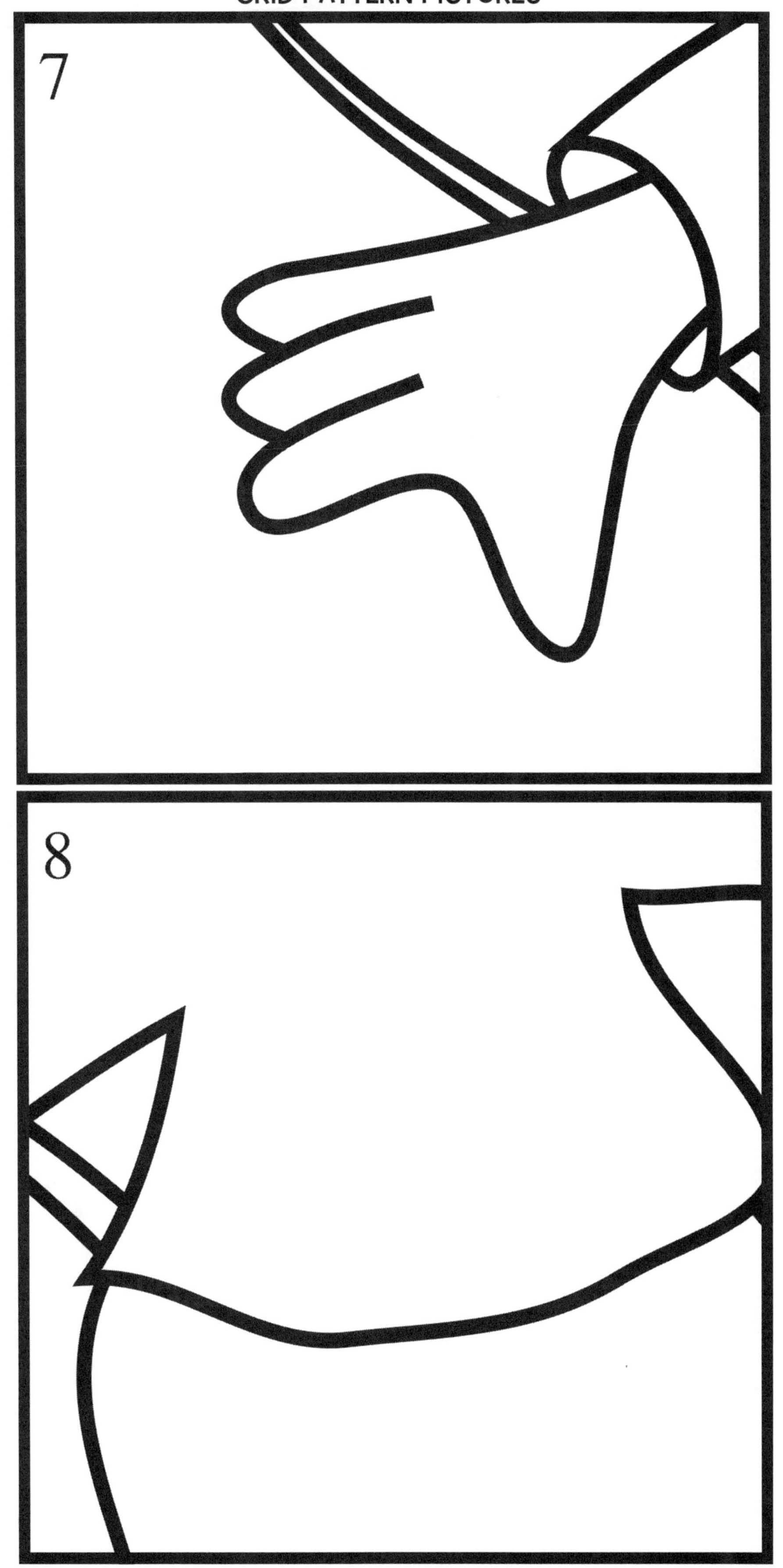
7
8

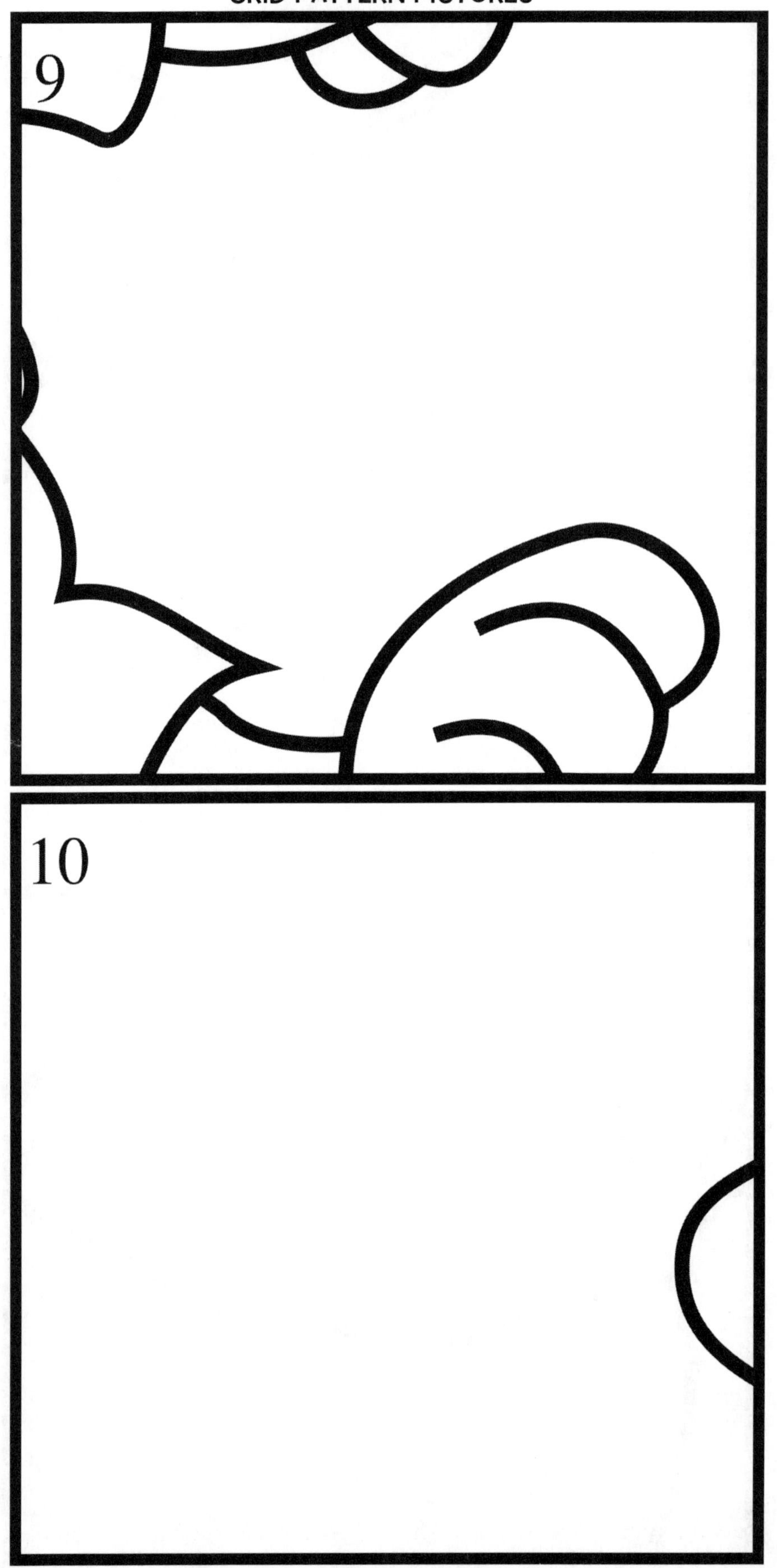
9
10

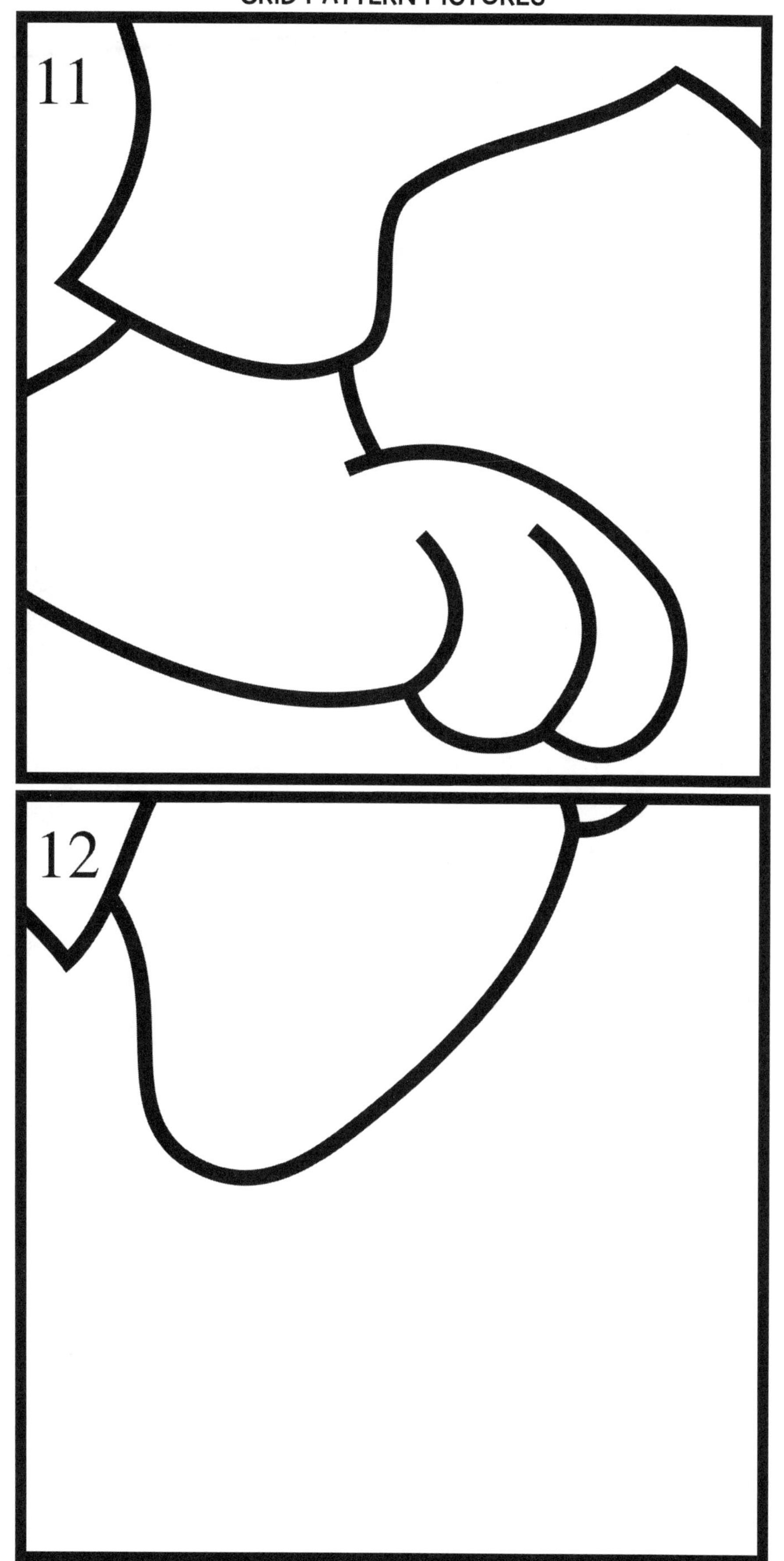
11
12

SCHOOL-RELATED SHAPES TEMPLATES

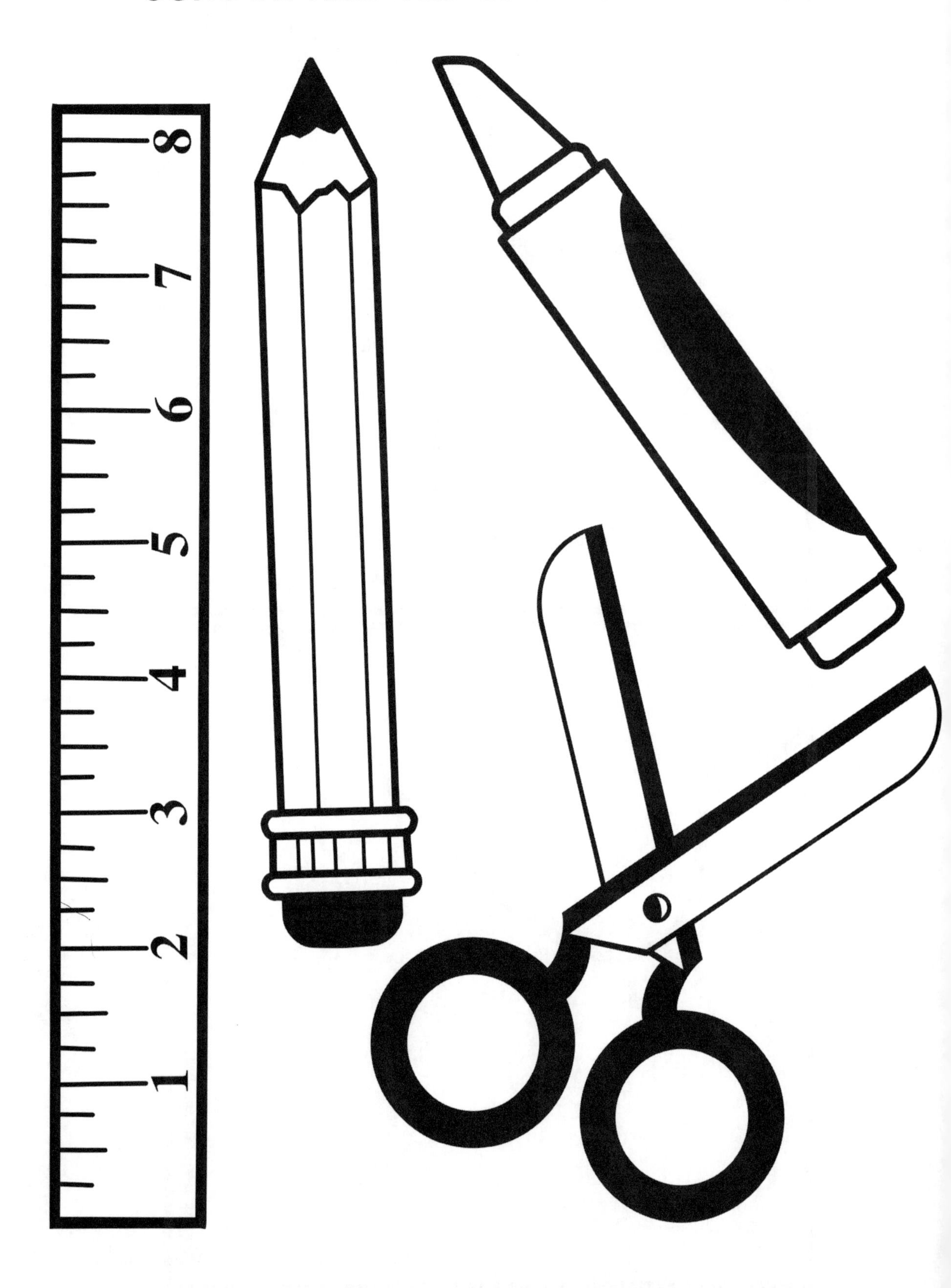

SCHOOL-RELATED SHAPES TEMPLATES

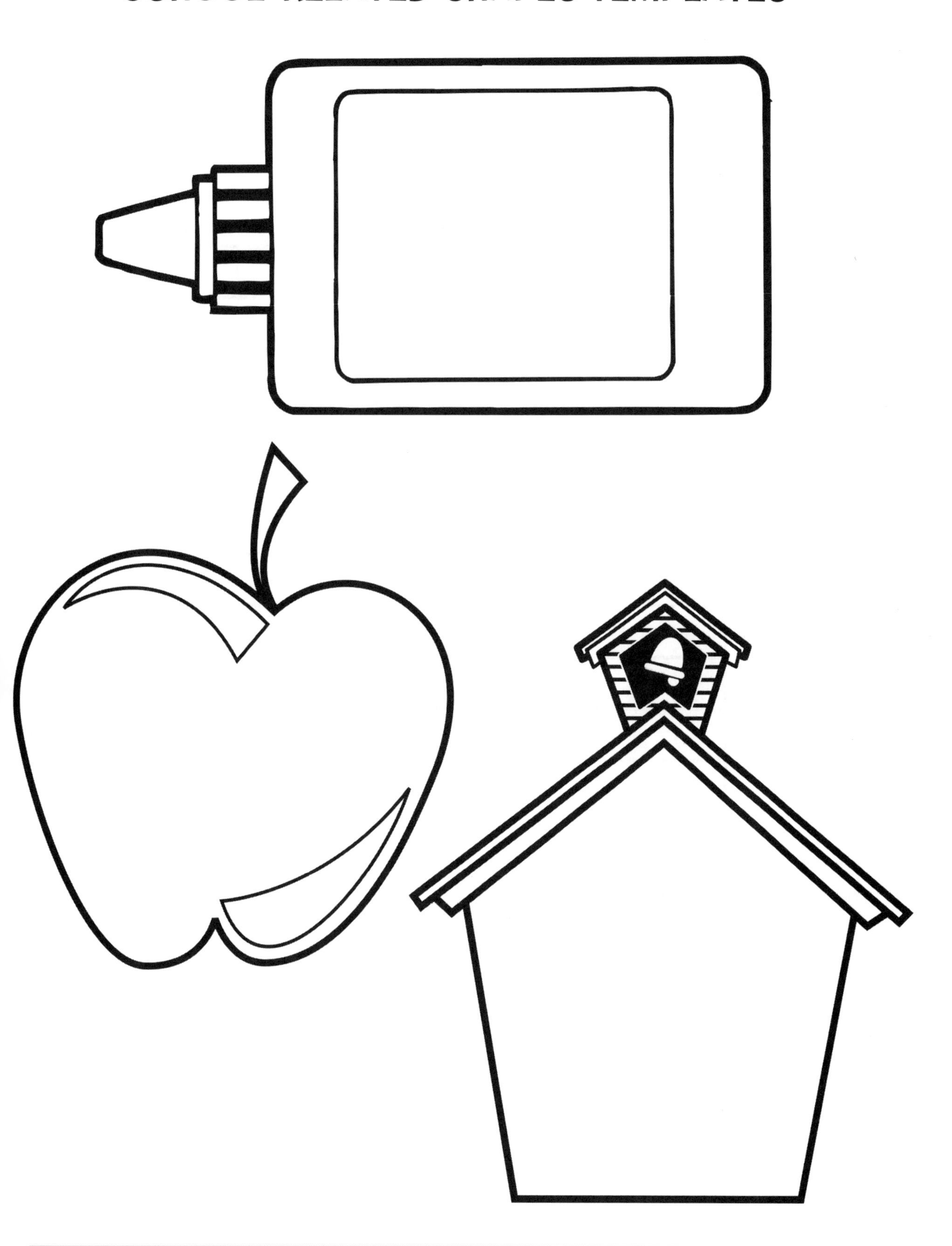

______________________'s Schedule Sheet

Day	What I Plan to Do	What I Actually Did
Monday		
Tuesday		
Wednesday		
Thursday		
Friday		
Saturday		
Sunday		

ARE YOU LISTENING?

ARE YOU LISTENING? LEADER'S DIRECTIONS

Read the following directions to the students. Read each direction only one time.

1. Color the dog brown.
2. Color the bushes green.
3. Color the sun orange.
4. Color the chimney bricks red.
5. Color the house yellow with a red door.
6. Color the curtains on the left pink and the curtains on the right purple.
7. Color the trunks of the trees brown. The leaves on the left tree should be yellow and orange. Color the leaves of the tree on the right orange and red.

SQ3R

Survey

Read only the chapter title, subtitles, italicized terms, and boldface type. Make predictions about what these imply the chapter will discuss.

Question

Go to the first major heading. Anticipate what will be in that section. Using the interrogatives *who, what, where, when,* and *why*, turn heading #1 into questions. Write the questions down.

Read

Read the chapter, section by section, for the purpose of answering the questions written in the previous step.

Recite

After you read a section, cover the page(s) and recite what you can remember.

Review

Look at the section and see if you missed any important information.

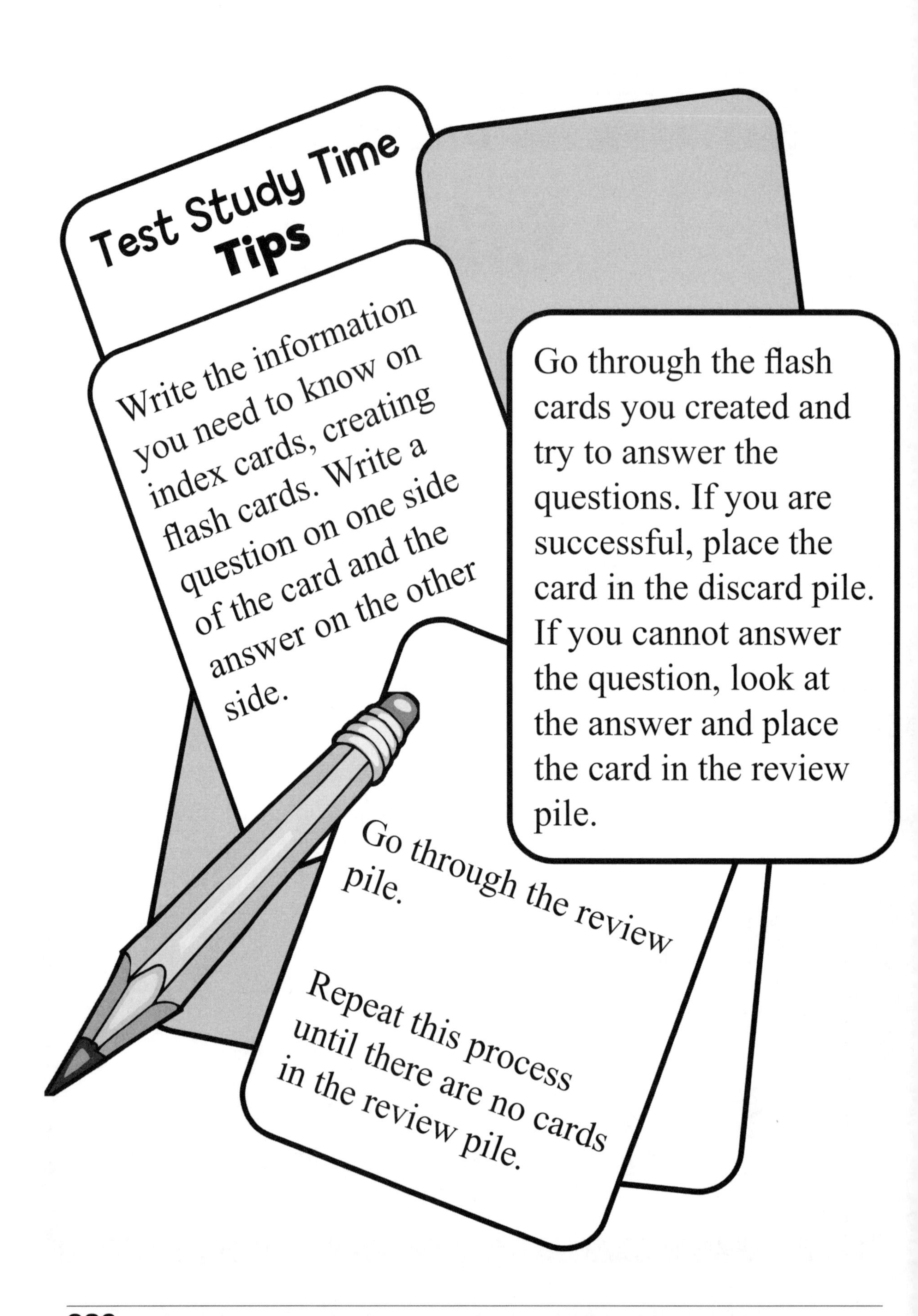
Test Study Time
Tips
Write the information you need to know on index cards, creating flash cards. Write a question on one side of the card and the answer on the other side.
Go through the flash cards you created and try to answer the questions. If you are successful, place the card in the discard pile. If you cannot answer the question, look at the answer and place the card in the review pile.
Go through the review pile.
Repeat this process until there are no cards in the review pile.

Concentration Tips

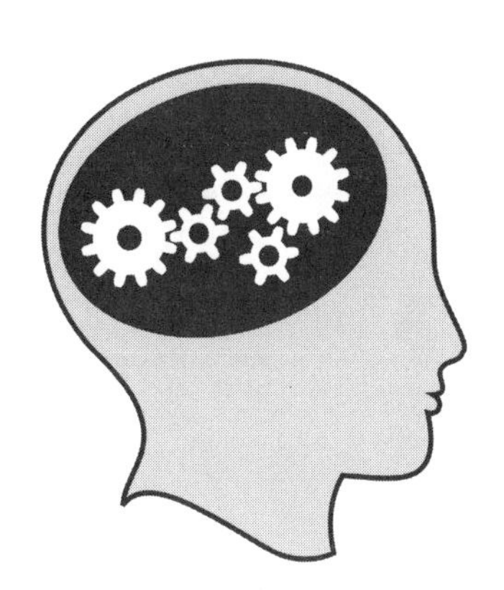

Breakfast is essential.

Be well rested.

Exercise makes you feel better and keeps your body chemistry in good condition.

Study with a pencil in your hand.

Keep a water bottle nearby.

A quiet place for study is best.

Control TV viewing—more than 10 hours/week may reduce the ability to study and concentrate.

Consider listening to quiet music on a headset—or "white noise" (oceans sound, surf, etc.).

Plan a small break between 20-minute study segments.

Bookmark #1

Bookmark #2

Bookmark #3

The Lunch Bunch

Lunch With The Counselor

Sometimes a lunch bunch is the only way to spend time with students without interrupting their academic schedules. A lunch bunch simply involves inviting several children to have lunch with the counselor in the counselor's office. Students get their lunches according to their normal routine, then bring them to the counselor's office. While the students have lunch, the counselor gently leads a discussion in this informal setting.

You can establish a lunch bunch as an on-going lunch date or as a single event. It can also be effective as a periodic check-in with specific students and is especially good for dealing with social skills and friendship issues. It quickly becomes a popular event with students, and you may discover that many students will ask to have a lunch bunch with their friends and you.

You may create the lunch bunch by identifying a group of students with a common interest or concern. You may also decide to invite only one or two students and a friend or two. Because the time is discussion-based, the same materials can be used with any age group. The age of the group will determine the depth and sophistication of the discussion.

Because of the need to actually eat lunch and the amount of discussion that occurs, only one or two discussion starters are necessary. The time goes very quickly.

The goals for this group are to:

- provide an informal guidance setting for students.
- examine friendship and other social issues.
- have contact with students who might not otherwise be available.

ASCA STANDARDS, COMPETENCIES, AND INDICATORS FOR THE LUNCH BUNCH

Participation in these group activities will address the following ASCA standards, competencies, and indicators:

Domain	**A/ACADEMIC DEVELOPMENT**
A/A:1.1	Articulate feelings of competence and confidence as a learner
A/A:1.5	Identify attitudes and behaviors which lead to successful learning
A/A:3.3	Develop a broad range of interests and abilities
A/A:3.5	Share knowledge
A/B:1.1	Demonstrate the motivation to achieve individual potential
A/B:1.2	Learn and apply critical thinking skills
A/B:2.4	Apply knowledge of aptitudes and interests to goal setting
A/B:2.5	Use problem-solving and decision-making skills to assess progress toward educational goals
A/B:2.6	Understand the relationship between classroom performance and success in school
A/C:1.2	Seek co-curricular and community experiences to enhance the school experience

Domain	**C/CAREER DEVELOPMENT**
C/A:1.4	Learn how to interact and work cooperatively in teams
C/A:1.5	Learn to make decisions
C/A:1.6	Learn how to set goals
C/B:1.2	Identify personal skills, interests, and abilities and relate them to current career choices
C/B:2.1	Demonstrate awareness of the education and training needed to achieve career goals
C/C:1.1	Understand the relationship between educational achievement and career success
C/C:1.2	Explain how work can help to achieve personal success and satisfaction
C/C:1.3	Identify personal preferences and interests which influence career choices and success
C/C:2.1	Demonstrate how interests, abilities, and achievement relate to achieving personal, social, educational and career goals.
C/C:2.3	Learn to work cooperatively with others as a team member

Domain	**PS/PERSONAL/SOCIAL DEVELOPMENT**
PS/A:1.1	Develop a positive attitude toward self as a unique and worthy person
PS/A:1.2	Identify values, attitudes and beliefs
PS/A:1.5	Identify and express feelings
PS/A:1.9	Demonstrate cooperative behavior in groups
PS/A:2.1	Recognize that everyone has rights and responsibilities
PS/A:2.2	Respect alternative points of view
PS/A:2.3	Recognize, accept, respect and appreciate individual differences
PS/A:2.4	Recognize, accept and appreciate ethnic and cultural diversity
PS/A:2.5	Recognize and respect differences in various family configurations
PS/A:2.6	Use effective communication skills
PS/A:2.7	Know that communication involves speaking, listening, and nonverbal behavior
PS/A:2.8	Learn how to make and keep friends
PS/B:1.7	Demonstrate a respect and appreciation for individual and cultural differences
PS/B:1.9	Identify long- and short-term goals

Master Supply List For The Lunch Bunch

Collect these supplies prior to presenting the group.
Place all the supplies in the same box as the lessons copied on cardstock.

(*Note:* Select one topic or activity for discussion for each session.)

GENERAL SUPPLIES:

- ☐ Pencil or pens
- ☐ Six-sided die with a different color on each side—red, yellow, blue, green, orange, and purple (Or make a die using a wooden block and markers.)
- ☐ Bean bag (optional)
- ☐ Craft sticks (optional)
- ☐ Red, yellow, blue, green, orange, and purple markers or paint (optional)
- ☐ Posterboard (optional)
- ☐ Container (optional)

COPY ON WHITE COPY PAPER:

- ☐ *Color-Coded Questions* (pages 330-338)
- ☐ *Treasure Hunt* (page 339)

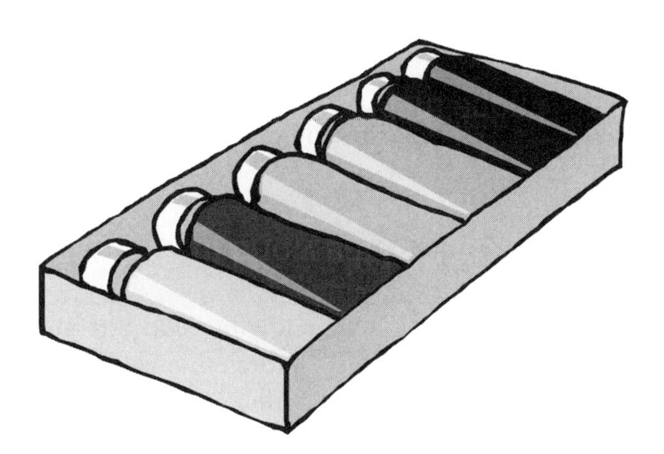

The Lunch Bunch

Materials:

TREASURE HUNT:
For The Leader:
- ☐ *Treasure Hunt* reproduced on white copy paper (page 338)
- ☐ Pencil or pen

COLOR-CODED QUESTIONS:
For The Leader:
- ☐ *Color-Coded Questions* reproduced on white copy paper (pages 330-337)
- ☐ Six-sided die with a different color on each side—red, yellow, blue, green, orange, and purple (Or make a die using a wooden block and markers.)

CRAFT STICKS:
For The Leader:
- ☐ *Color-Coded Questions* reproduced on white copy paper (pages 330-337)
- ☐ Craft sticks with red, yellow, blue, green, orange, and purple tips
- ☐ Container

BEAN BAG TOSS:
For The Leader:
- ☐ *Color-Coded Questions* reproduced on white copy paper (pages 330-337)
- ☐ Simple color wheel made with posterboard and colored markers. The wheel is divided into six sections colored red, yellow, blue, green, orange, and purple.
- ☐ Bean bag

For Each Session:

- ▶ Invite the students to have lunch with the counselor. Reproduce the invitation on page 339.
- ▶ Choose one of the following activities:
    - **Treasure Hunt:** Go around the circle, allowing each person to respond to the items on the inventory. Discuss each answer before moving on to the next student. Award points as indicated on the inventory, creating a game of the discussion. Emphasize that the points are only for fun.

- **Color-Coded Die and *Color-Coded Questions*:** Going around the circle, each person rolls the colored die. He/she answers the *Color-Coded Question* that matches the color on the top of the die when it comes to rest.

- Alternative to using a die with the *Color-Coded Questions:*

    - **Craft Sticks***:* Place the sticks upside-down in the container so the colored end cannot be seen. Have the player draw one stick from the container and answer its corresponding question. The stick should then be placed back in the container. This game is easy to play while eating lunch.

    - **Bean Bag Toss:** Students may toss a bean bag onto a color wheel or floor mat with the specific colors painted on it.

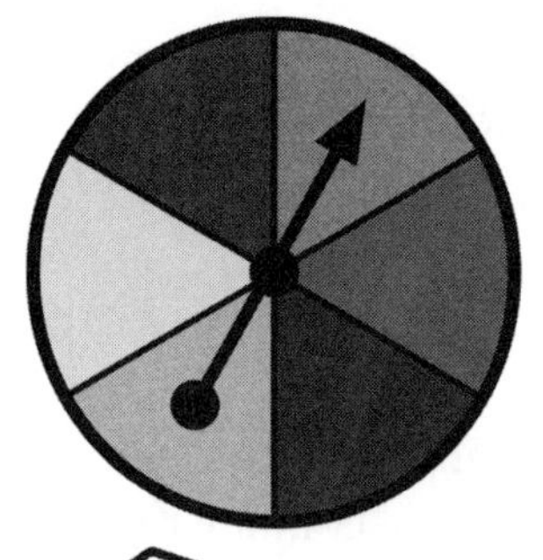
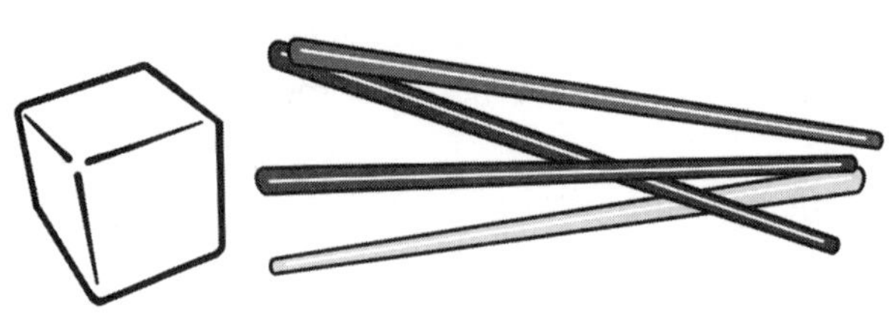
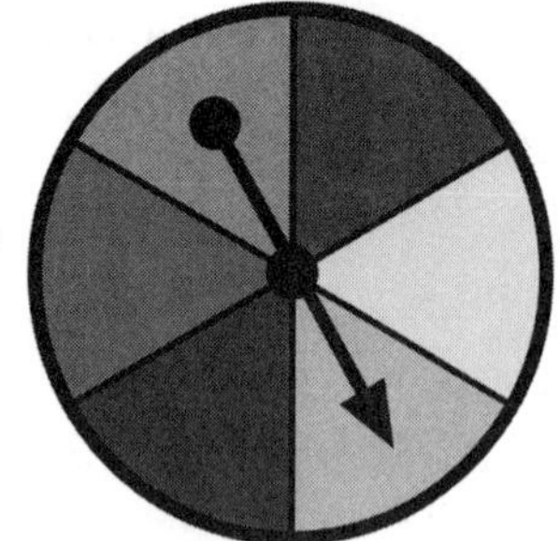

My Dreams

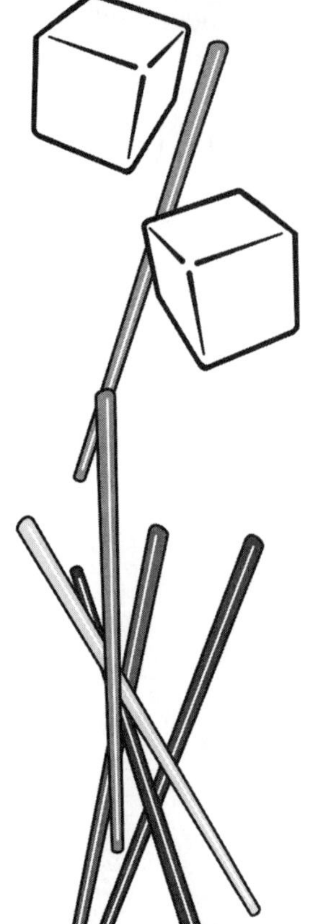

Complete this sentence:

Red	The part of the world that interests me most is...
Green	I hope that someday I will...
Blue	This year will be perfect if...
Yellow	When I grow up, I will...
Orange	When I am finished with school, I want to live...
Purple	The person I most want to be like is...

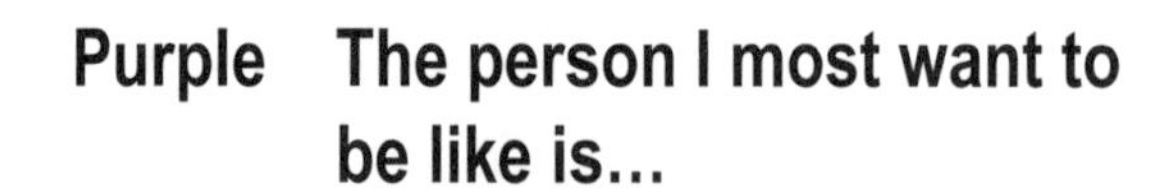
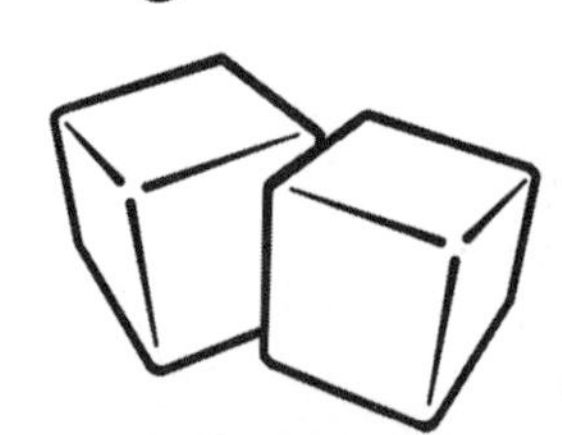
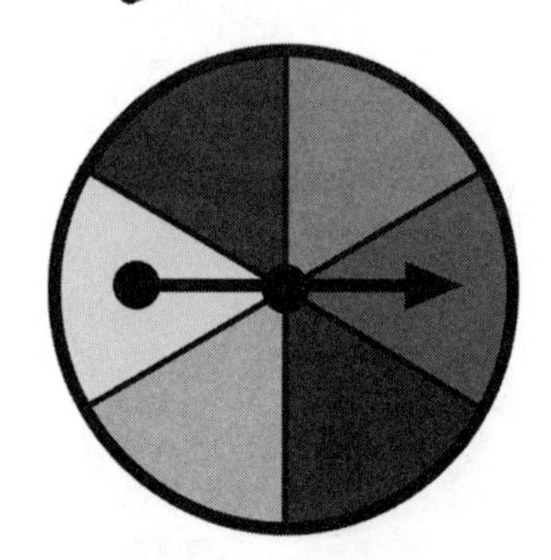
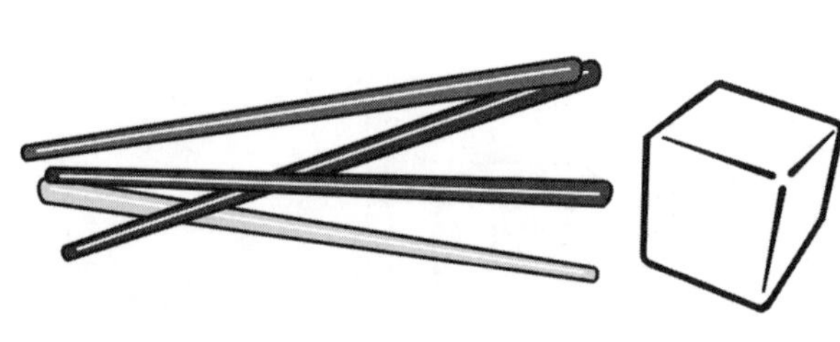
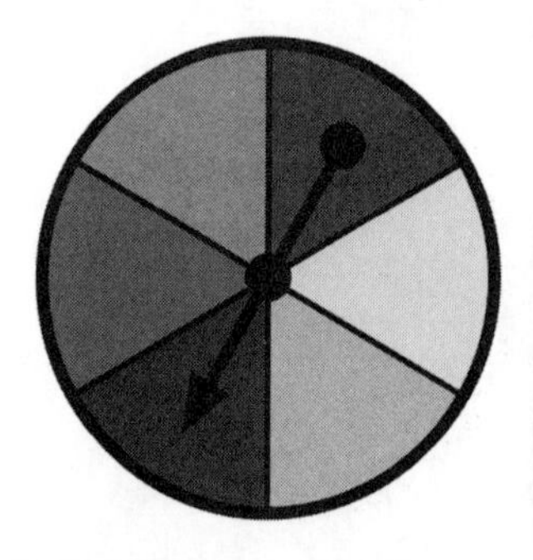

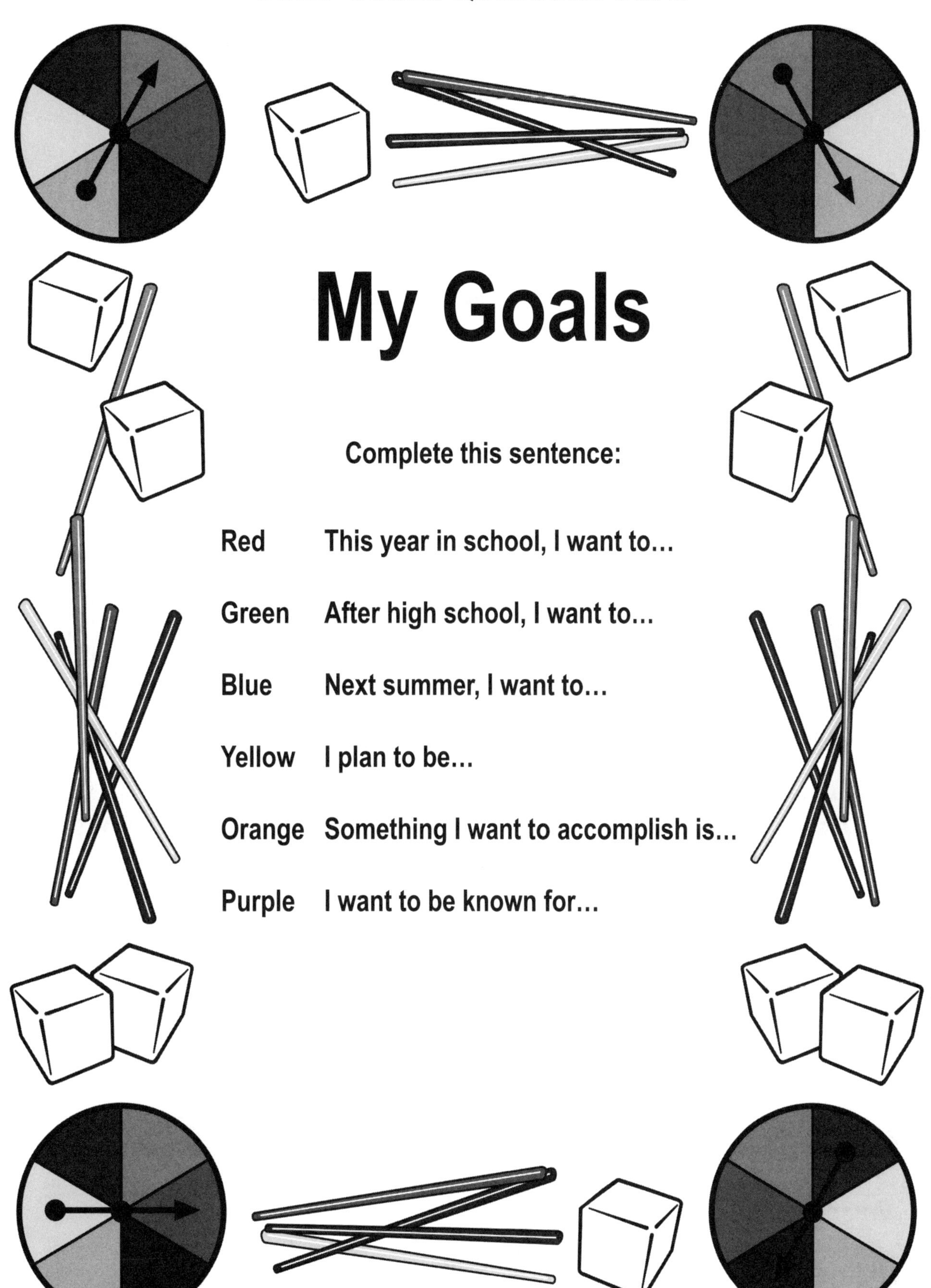

My Goals

Complete this sentence:

Red	This year in school, I want to...
Green	After high school, I want to...
Blue	Next summer, I want to...
Yellow	I plan to be...
Orange	Something I want to accomplish is...
Purple	I want to be known for...

Color-Coded Questions Set 3

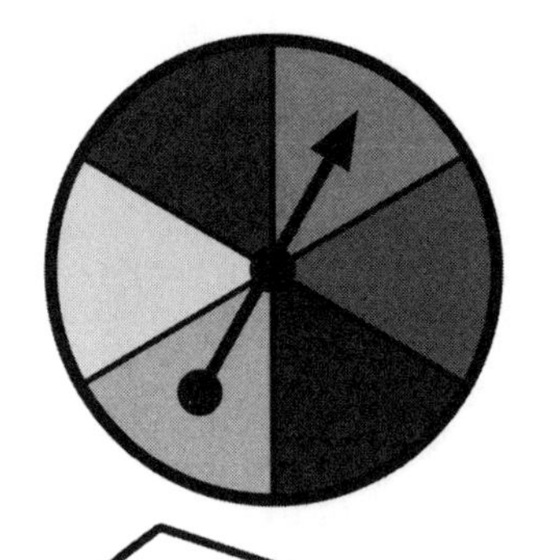
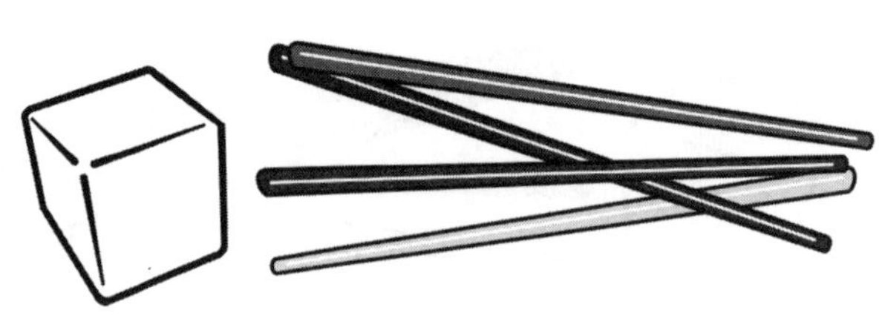
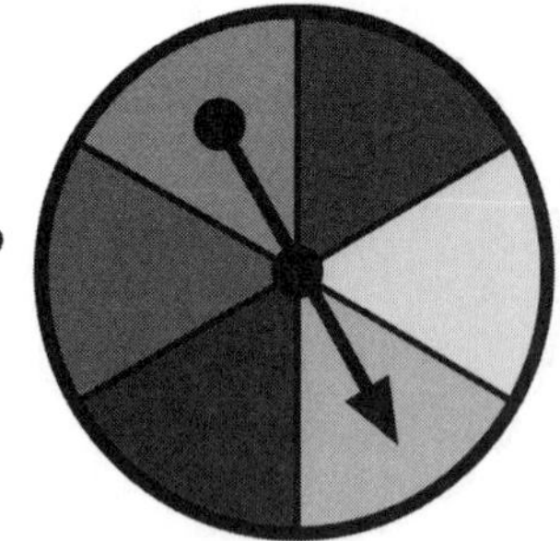

My Wishes

Complete this sentence:

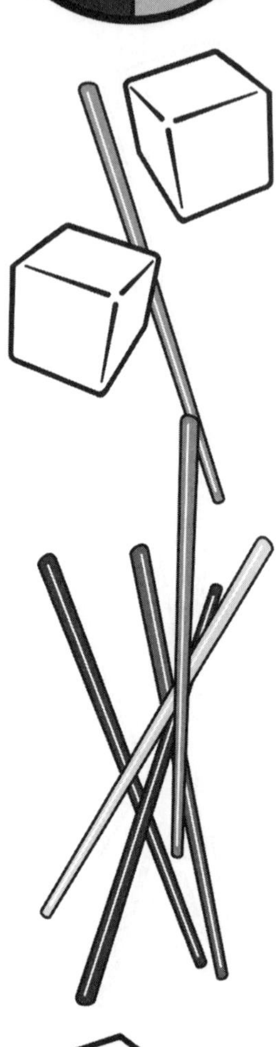

Red	If I had a magic wand, I would...
Green	If I waved a magic wand over my family, it would...
Blue	If I waved a magic wand over my friends, they would...
Yellow	If I waved a magic wand over the school, it would...
Orange	If I waved a magic wand over my classroom, it would...
Purple	If I had a million dollars, I would...

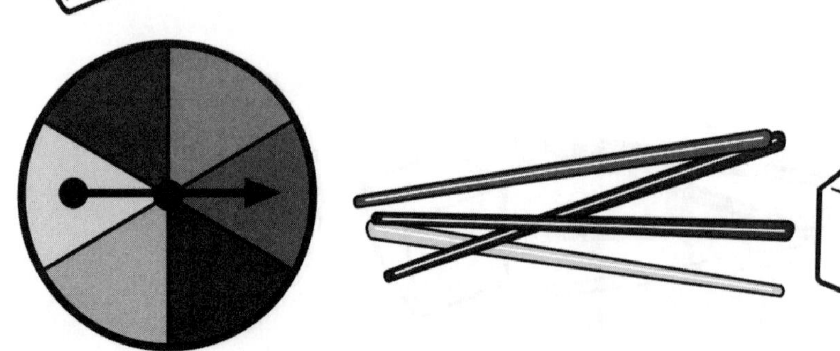
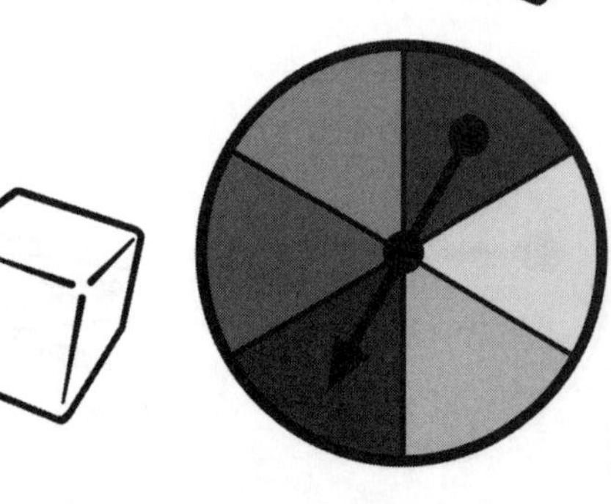

Color-Coded Questions Set 4

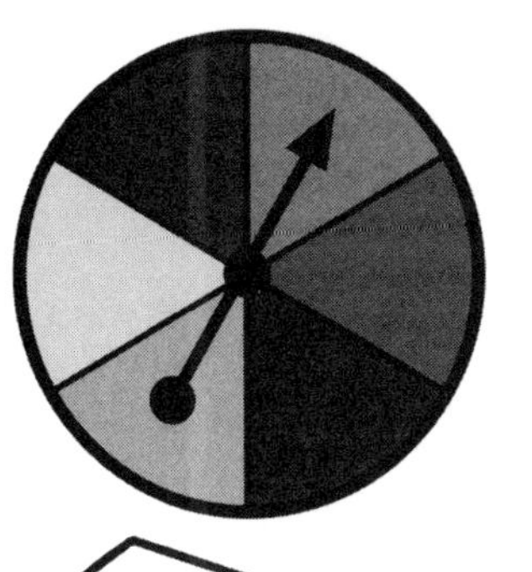

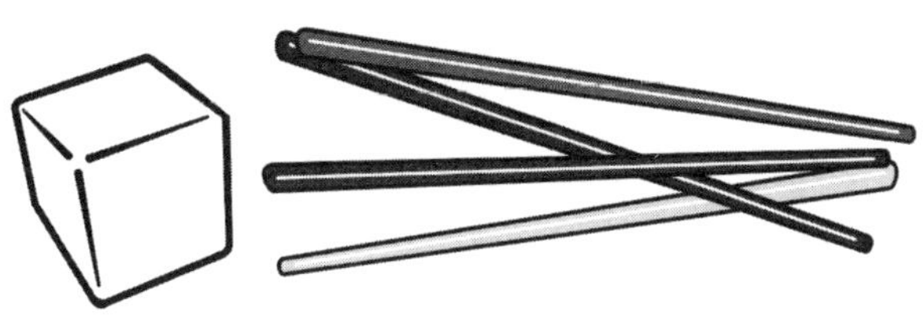

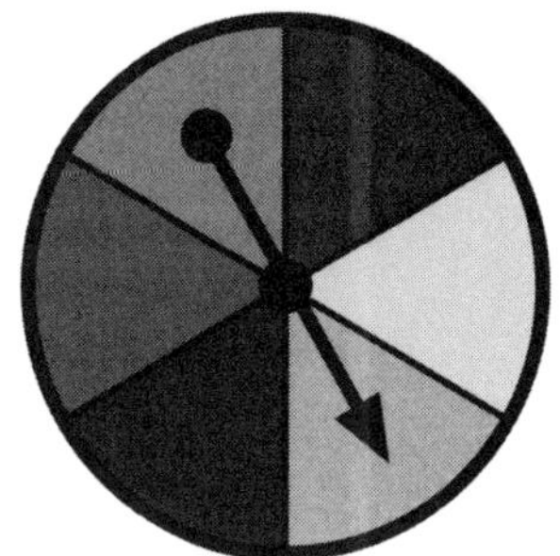

All About School

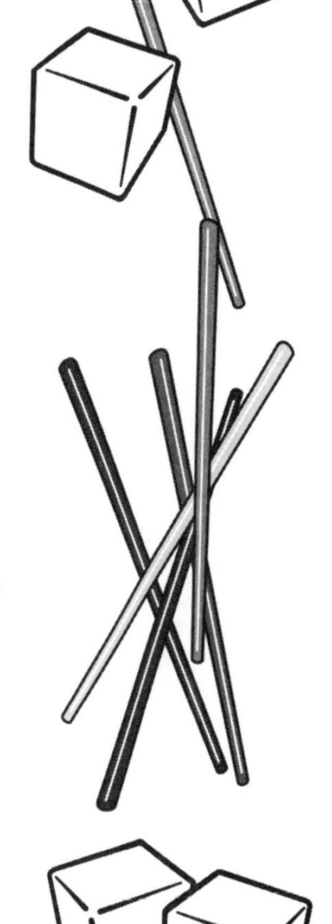

Complete this sentence:

Red	In school, the thing I like to do best is...
Green	I can make good grades if...
Blue	The best teacher I ever had was...
Yellow	The hardest thing for me to do in school is ...
Orange	The easiest thing for me to do in school is...
Purple	The problem I have in school is...

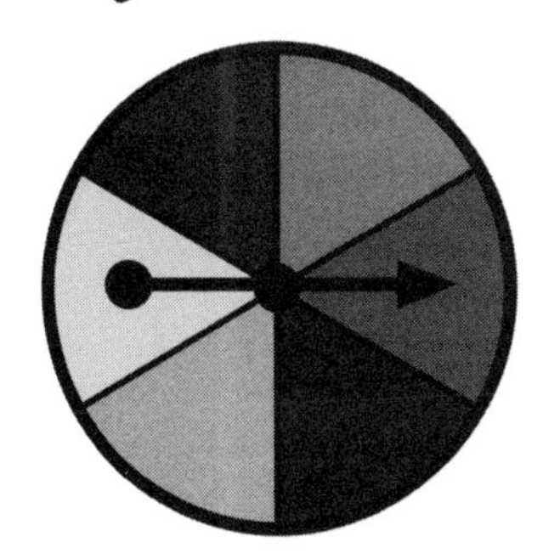

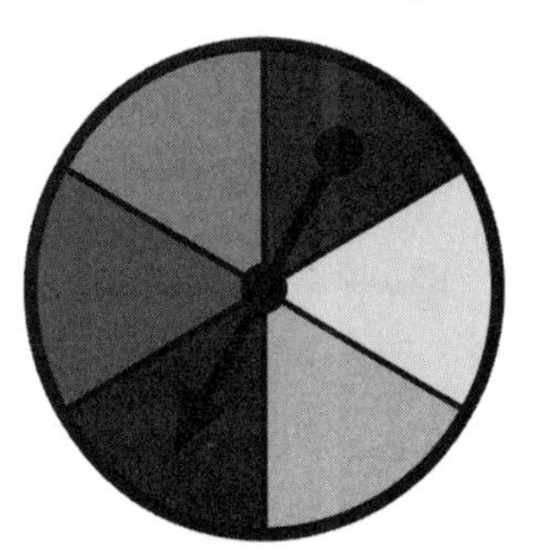

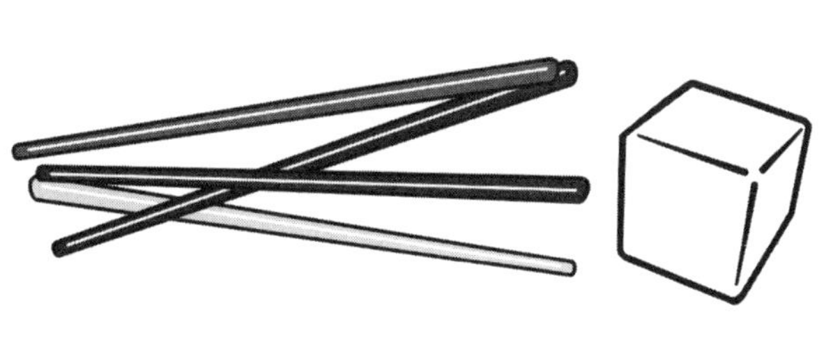

Color-Coded Questions Set 5

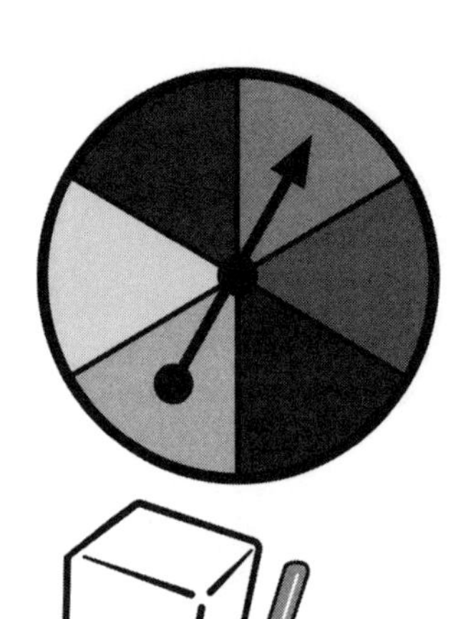
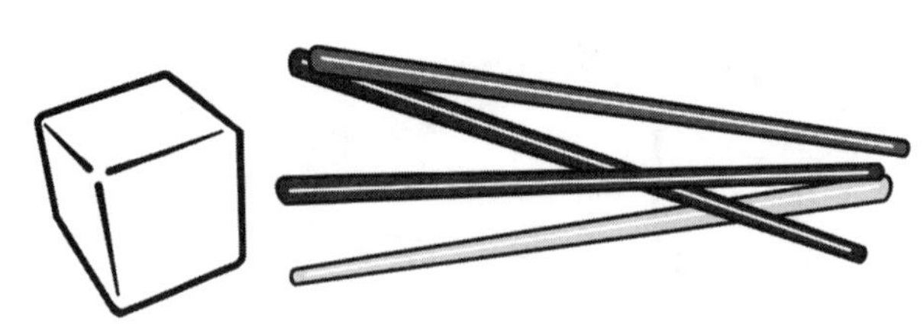
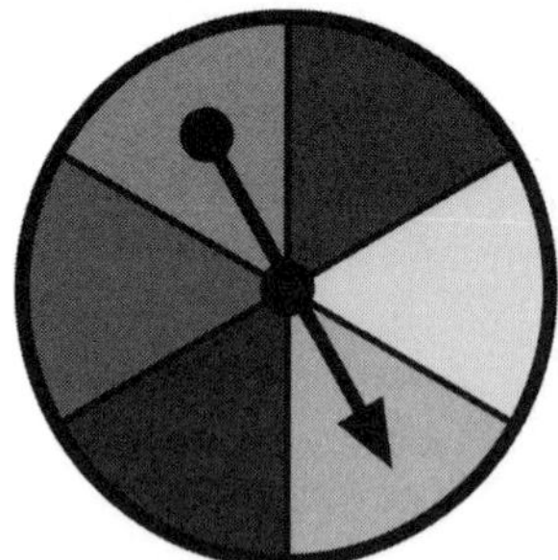

My Favorite Things

Complete this sentence:

Red	My favorite place to be is...
Green	My favorite animal is...
Blue	My favorite thing to do with friends is...
Yellow	My favorite thing to do outside is...
Orange	My favorite thing to do inside is...
Purple	My favorite holiday or time of year is...

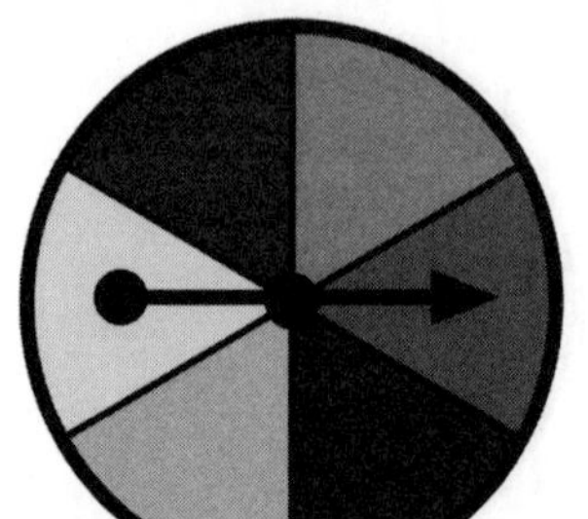
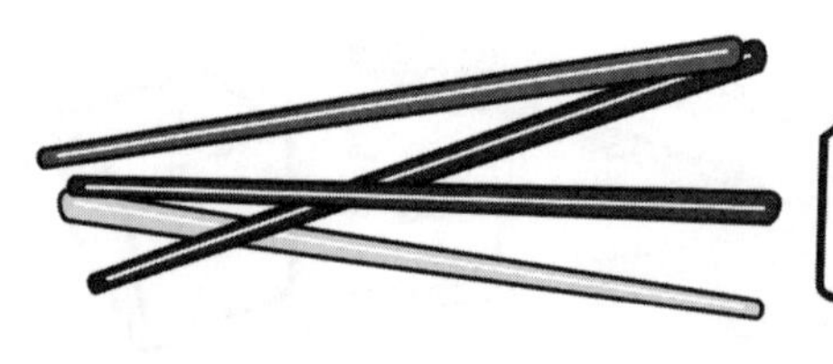
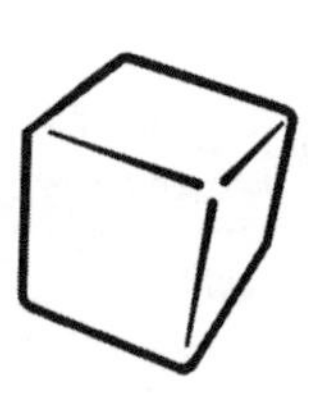
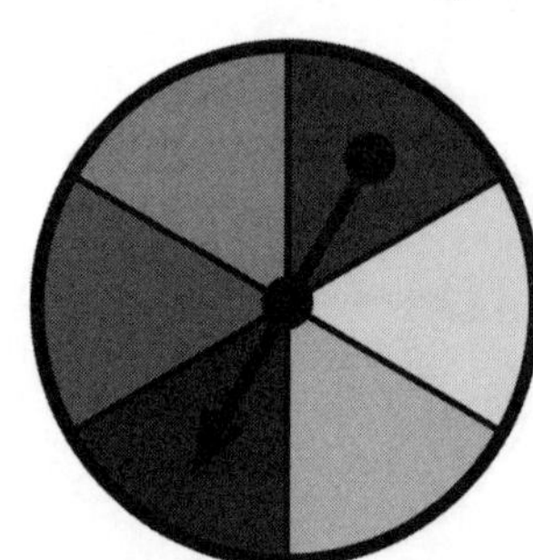

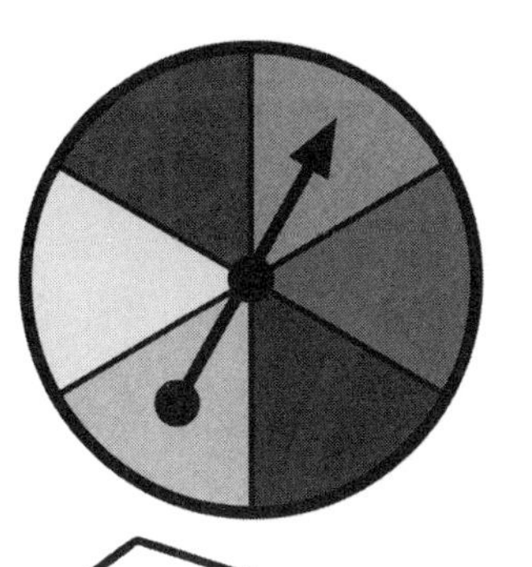
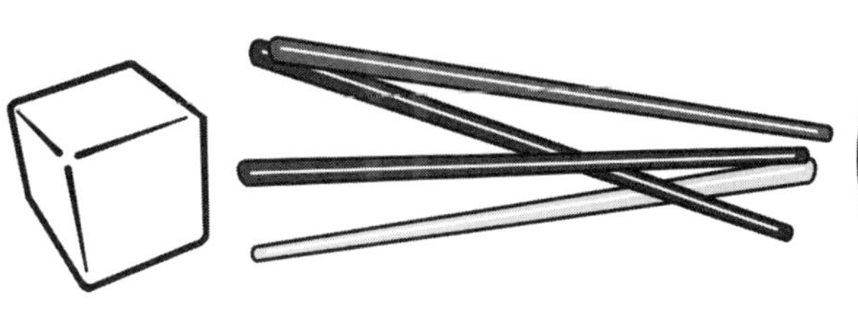
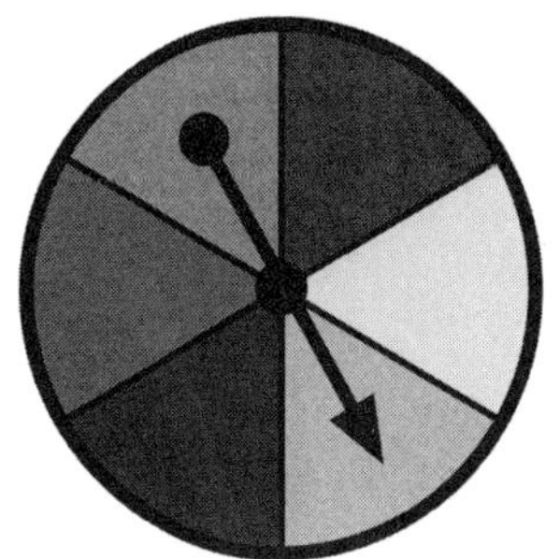

My Opinions

Complete this sentence:

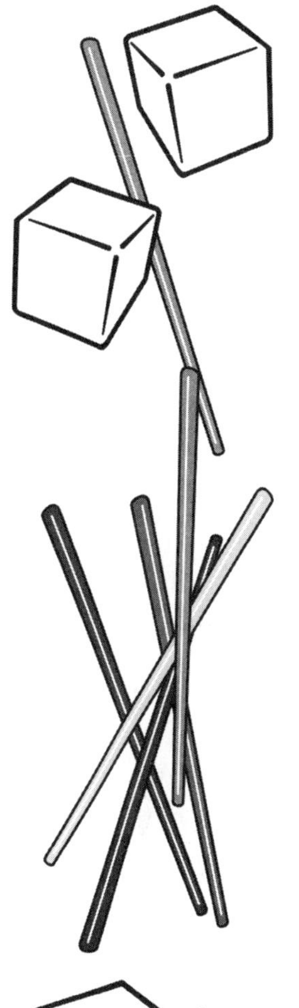

Red	The best sport is...
Green	The best television show is...
Blue	The best book I ever read is...
Yellow	The best video game is...
Orange	The best music is...
Purple	The best teacher is...

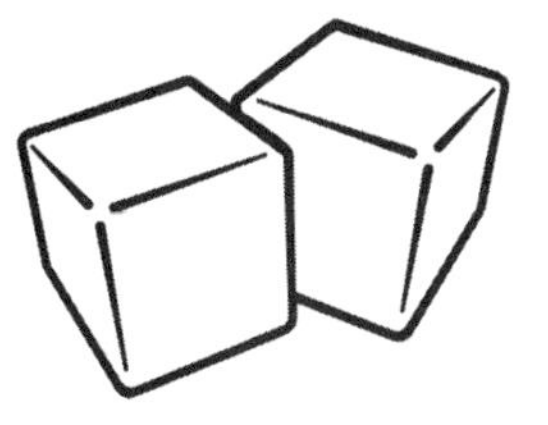
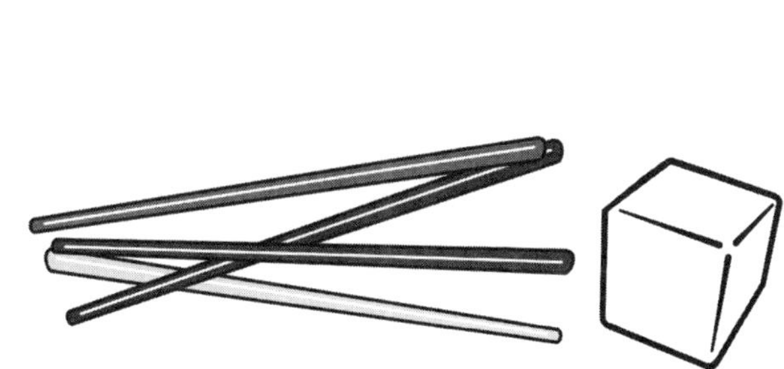
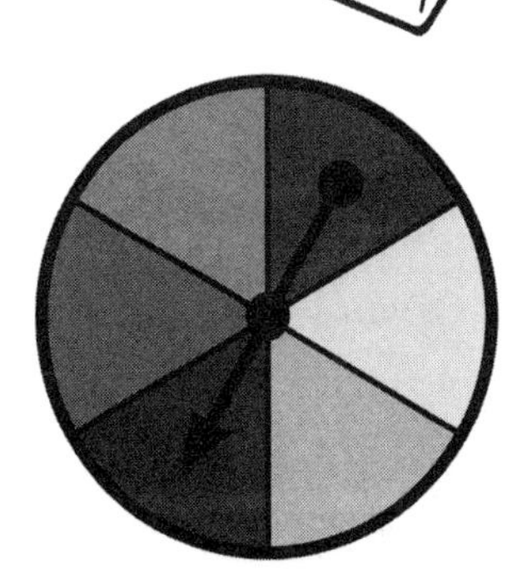

Color-Coded Questions Set 7

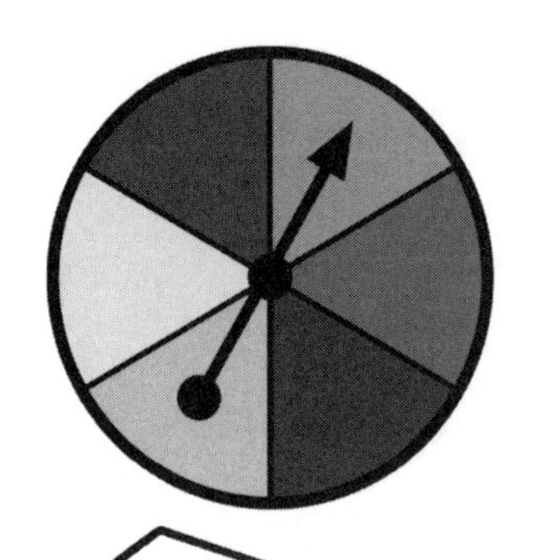
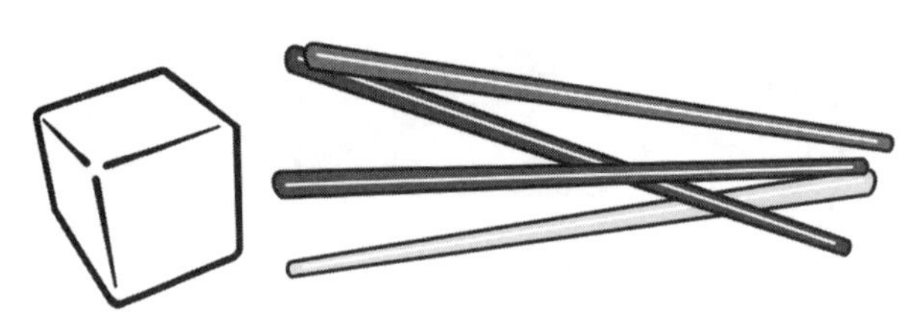
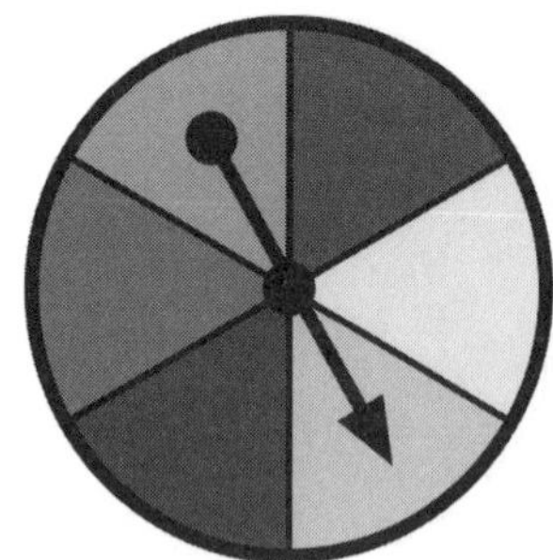

My Feelings

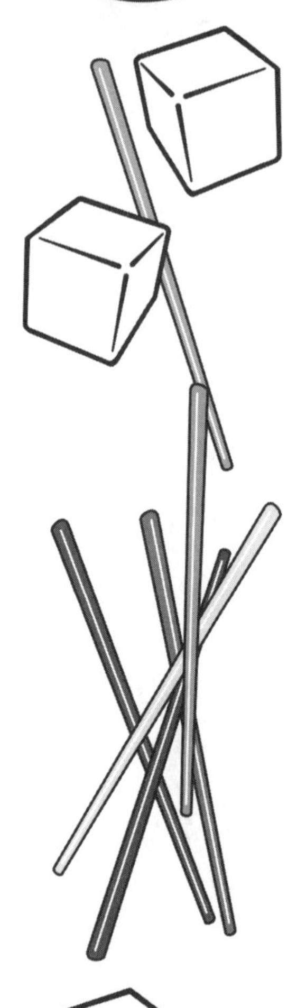

Complete this sentence:

Red	What I hate most is...
Green	I am afraid when...
Blue	I am angry when...
Yellow	I am sad when...
Orange	I am happy when...
Purple	I have a difficult time when...

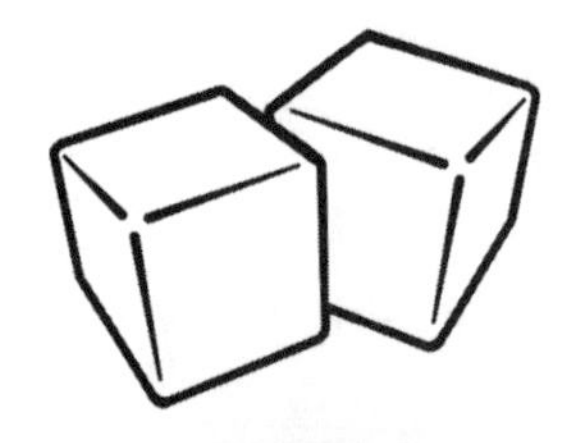

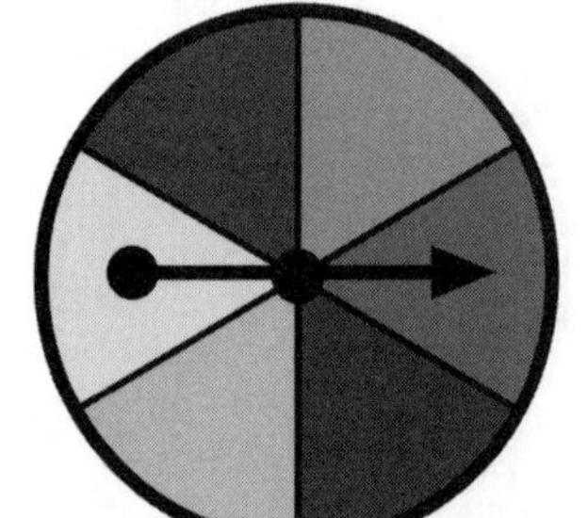
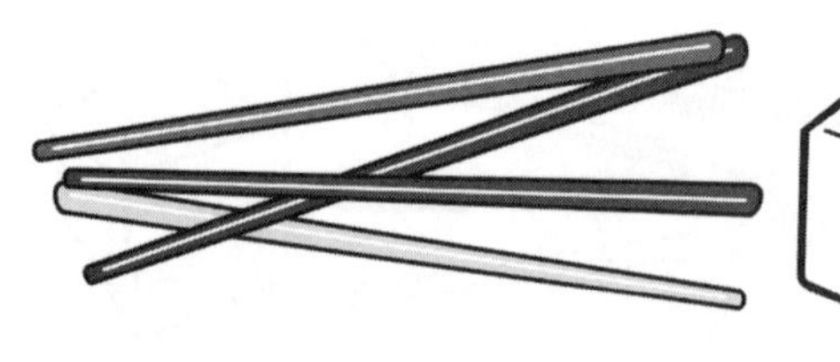
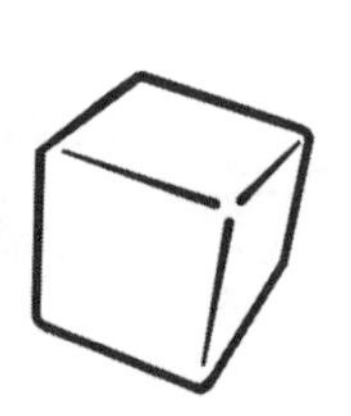
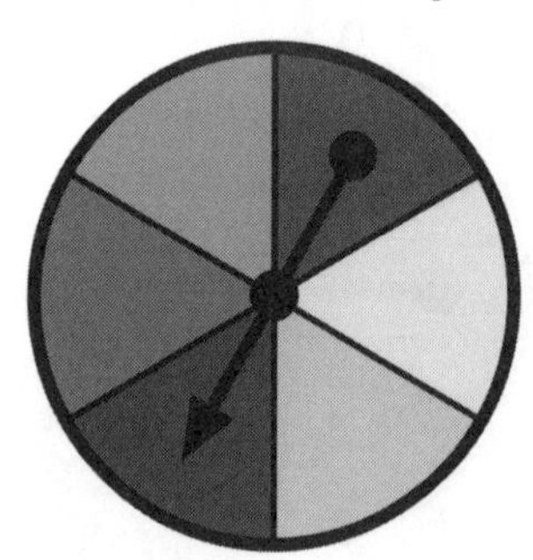

Color-Coded Questions Set 8

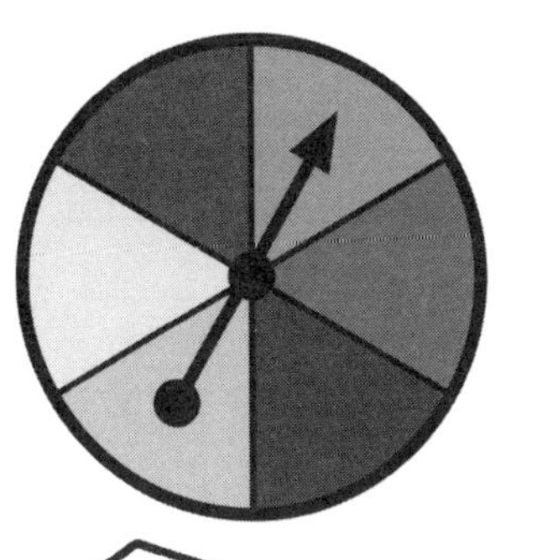
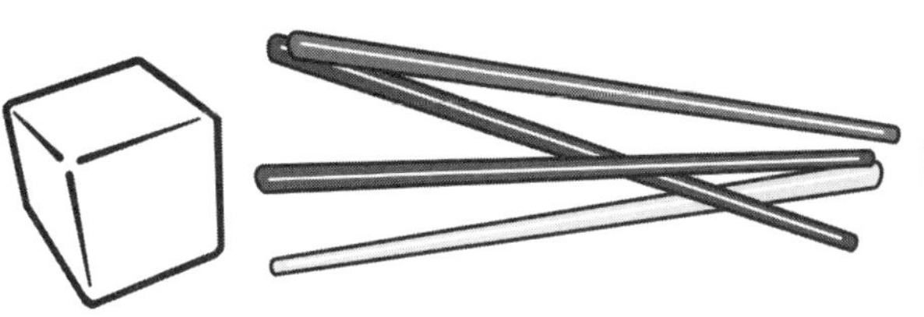
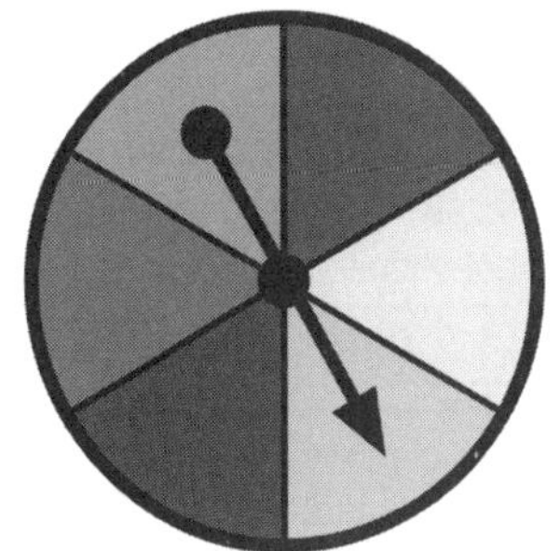

All About Sports

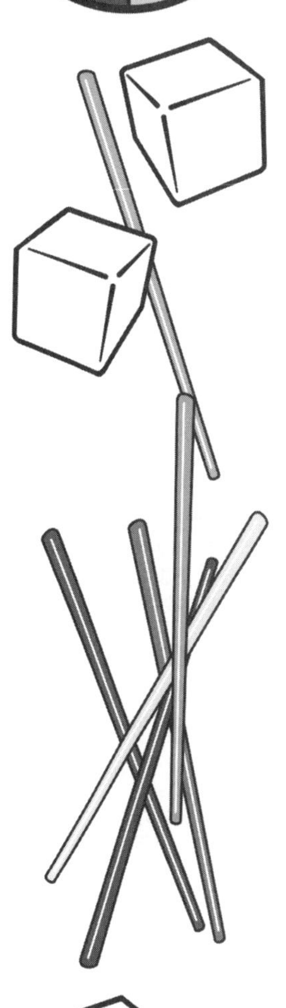

Complete this sentence:

Red	The sport I like to watch best is...
Green	The sport I like to play best is...
Blue	The most difficult sport is...
Yellow	The easiest sport is...
Orange	A sport I am good at is...
Purple	A sport I have never tried but would like to try is...

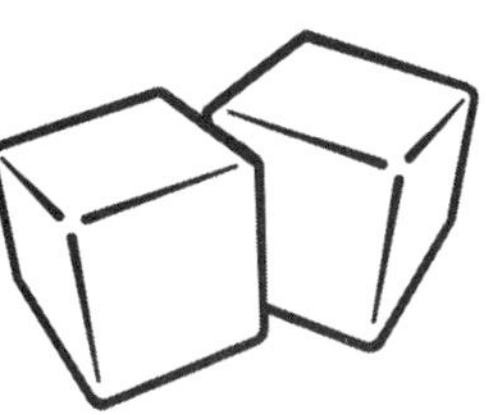
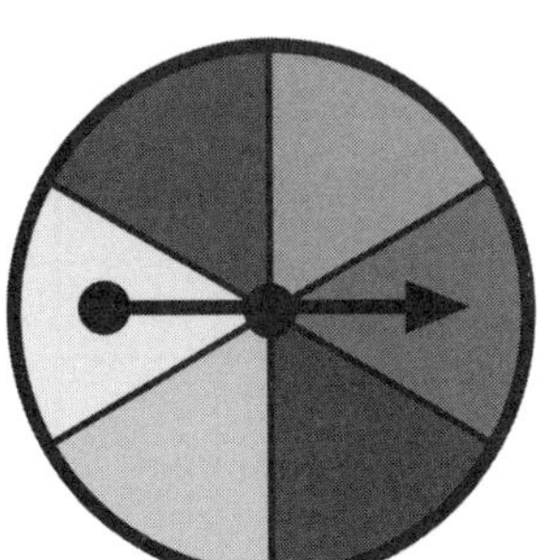
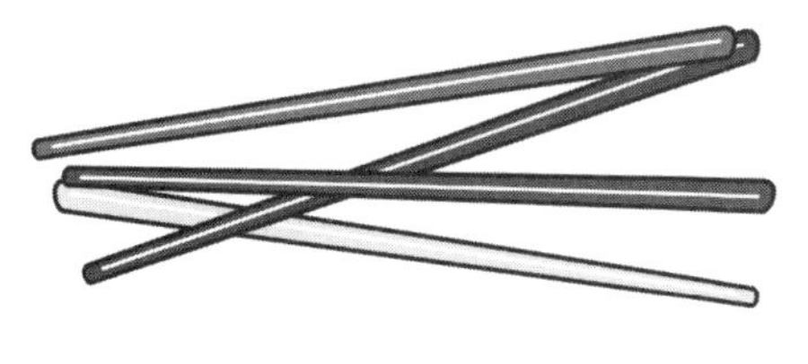
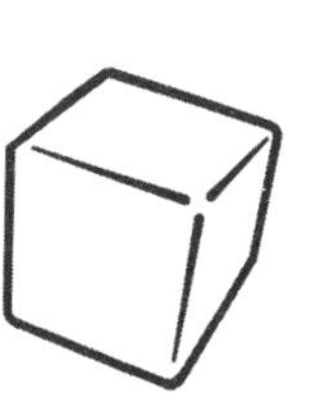
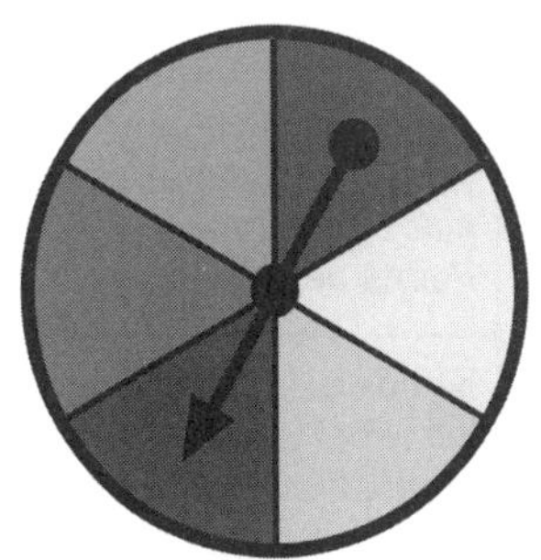

TREASURE HUNT

This can be a great activity for discovering more about lunch bunch members. Points are awarded based on answers to the following questions. The student with the most points "wins." Write students' names at the top of the columns. Ask the questions and award the points. Discuss the students' answers and make connections.

STUDENT'S NAME OR INITIALS									
How many people are in your immediate family? *1 point for each* *2 bonus points for twins*									
How many people live in your house? *1 point for each*									
Where do you live? *1 point for house* *2 points for apartment* *3 points for mobile home*									
Do you play an organized sport? *2 points for each individual sport* *3 points for each team sport*									
What regular activities are you involved in outside of school? *3 points for each activity*									
What can you do well? *5 points for each skill named*									
What is something you are learning to do? *5 points for each skill named*									
What do you like about school? *1 point for each idea* *2 points for each new idea*									
If you had 3 wishes, what would you wish for? *Points determined by counselor*									
If you were in charge of the school, what would you do to make it a better place for learning? *Points determined by counselor*									
If you could change one thing in your life, what would it be? *Points determined by counselor*									

A Special
Invitation For:
You are invited to a
Lunch Bunch
with the counselor.
Please get your lunch at your usual time
and bring it to the counselor's office.
Date:
Time:
LUNCH
LUNCH

APPENDIX

DOMAIN A: ACADEMIC DEVELOPMENT

Standard A: Students will acquire the attitudes, knowledge, and skills that contribute to effective learning in school and across the life span.		SMALL GROUP							
		Anger	**Behavior**	**Cancer**	**Friendship**	**Grief/Loss**	**Self Esteem**	**Study Skills**	**Lunch Bunch**
Competency A:1 Improve Academic Self-Concept									
Indicators	A/A:1.1 Articulate feelings of competence and confidence as a learner						X	X	X
	A/A:1.2 Display a positive interest in learning							X	
	A/A:1.3 Take pride in work and in achievement						X	X	
	A/A:1.4 Accept mistakes as essential to the learning process								
	A/A:1.5 Identify attitudes and behaviors which lead to successful learning		X		X		X	X	X
Competency A:2 Acquire Skills For Improving Learning									
Indicators	A/A:2.1 Apply time-and task-management skills							X	
	A/A:2.2 Demonstrate how effort and persistence positively affect learning							X	
	A/A:2.3 Use communication skills to know when and how to ask for help when needed	X		X	X	X		X	
	A/A:2.4 Apply knowledge of learning styles to positively influence school performance								
Competency A:3 Achieve School Success									
Indicators	A/A:3.1 Take responsibility for own actions	X	X	X	X			X	
	A/A:3.1 Demonstrate the ability to work independently, as well as the ability to work cooperatively with other students		X	X	X	X		X	
	A/A:3.3 Develop a broad range of interests and abilities				X		X	X	X
	A/A:3.4 Demonstrate dependability, productivity, and initiative							X	
	A/A:3.5 Share knowledge	X	X	X	X		X	X	X

DOMAIN A: ACADEMIC DEVELOPMENT

Standard B: Students will complete school with the academic preparation essential to choose from a wide range of substantial postsecondary options, including college.		SMALL GROUP							
		Anger	**Behavior**	**Cancer**	**Friendship**	**Grief/Loss**	**Self Esteem**	**Study Skills**	**Lunch Bunch**
Competency B:1 Improve Learning									
Indicators	A/B:1.1 Demonstrate the motivation to achieve individual potential						X	X	X
	A/B:1.2 Learn and apply critical-thinking skills	X	X					X	X
	A/B:1.3 Apply the study skills necessary for academic success at each level							X	
	A/B:1.4 Seek information and support from faculty, staff, family, and peers				X			X	
	A/B:1.5 Organize and apply academic information from a variety of sources								
	A/B:1.6 Use knowledge of learning styles to positively influence school performance								
	A/B:1.7 Become self-directed and independent learners							X	
Competency B:2 Plan To Achieve Goals									
Indicators	A/B:2.1 Establish challenging academic goals in elementary, middle/junior high, and high school								
	A/B:2.2 Use assessment results in educational planning								
	A/B:2.3 Develop and implement an annual plan of study to maximize academic ability and achievement								
	A/B:2.4 Apply knowledge of aptitudes and interests to goal setting								X
	A/B:2.5 Use problem-solving and decision-making skills to assess progress toward educational goals		X		X			X	X
	A/B:2.6 Understand the relationship between classroom performance and success in school		X					X	X
	A/B:2.7 Identify postsecondary options consistent with interests, achievement, aptitude, and abilities								

DOMAIN A: ACADEMIC DEVELOPMENT

Standard C: Students will understand the relationship of academics to the world of work and to life at home and in the community.	SMALL GROUP							
	Anger	**Behavior**	**Cancer**	**Friendship**	**Grief/Loss**	**Self Esteem**	**Study Skills**	**Lunch Bunch**
Competency C:1 Relate School To Life Experiences								
Indicators								
A/C:1.1 Demonstrate the ability to balance school, studies, extracurricular activities, leisure time, and family life			X					
A/C:1.2 Seek cocurricular and community experiences to enhance the school experience								X
A/C:1.3 Understand the relationship between learning and work								
A/C:1.4 Demonstrate an understanding of the value of lifelong learning as essential to seeking, obtaining, and maintaining life goals								
A/C:1.5 Understand that school success is the preparation to make the transition from student to community member								
A/C:1.6 Understand how school success and academic achievement enhance future career and avocational opportunities							X	

DOMAIN C: CAREER DEVELOPMENT

Standard A:
Students will acquire the skills to investigate the world of work in relation to knowledge of self and to make informed career decisions.

		SMALL GROUP							
		Anger	**Behavior**	**Cancer**	**Friendship**	**Grief/Loss**	**Self Esteem**	**Study Skills**	**Lunch Bunch**
Competency A:1 Develop Career Awareness									
Indicators	C/A:1.1 Develop skills to locate, evaluate, and interpret career information								
	C/A:1.2 Learn about a variety of traditional and non-traditional occupations								
	C/A:1.3 Develop an awareness of personal abilities, skills, interests, and motivations		X	X	X		X		
	C/A:1.4 Learn to interact and work cooperatively in teams	X	X	X	X	X	X	X	X
	C/A:1.5 Learn to make decisions	X	X	X	X		X	X	X
	C/A:1.6 Learn to set goals		X		X		X	X	X
	C/A:1.7 Understand the importance of planning							X	
	C/A:1.8 Pursue and develop competency in areas of interest			X	X		X		
	C/A:1.9 Develop hobbies and vocational interests			X					
	C/A:1.10 Balance work and leisure time				X				
Competency A:2 Develop Employment Readiness									
Indicators	C/A:2.1 Acquire skills such as working on a team, problem-solving, and organizational skills	X	X		X			X	
	C/A:2.2 Apply job-readiness skills to seek employment opportunities								
	C/A:2.3 Demonstrate knowledge about the changing workplace								
	C/A:2.4 Learn about the rights and responsibilities of employers and employees								
	C/A:2.5 Learn to respect individual uniqueness in the workplace				X				
	C/A:2.6 Learn to write a resume								
	C/A:2.3 Develop a positive attitude toward work and learning								
	C/A:2.8 Understand the importance of responsibility, dependability, punctuality, integrity, and effort in the workplace				X		X		
	C/A:2.9 Utilize time- and task-management skills							X	

DOMAIN C: CAREER DEVELOPMENT

Standard B: Students will employ strategies to achieve future career goals with success and satisfaction.	SMALL GROUP							
	Anger	Behavior	Cancer	Friendship	Grief/Loss	Self Esteem	Study Skills	Lunch Bunch
Competency B:1 Acquire Career Information								
Indicators								
C/B:1.1 Apply decision-making skills to career planning, course selection, and career transitions								
C/B:1.2 Identify personal skills, interests, and abilities and relate them to current career choices						X		X
C/B:1.3 Demonstrate knowledge of the career-planning process								
C/B:1.4 Know the various ways occupations can be classified								
C/B:1.5 Use research and information resources to obtain career information								
C/B:1.6 Learn to use the Internet to access career-planning information								
C/B:1.7 Describe traditional and non-traditional occupations and how these relate to career choice								
C/B:1.8 Understand how changing economic and societal needs influence employment trends and future training								
Competency B:2 Identify Career Goals								
Indicators								
C/B:2.1 Demonstrate awareness of the education and training needed to achieve career goals								X
C/B:2.2 Assess and modify educational plan to support career goals								
C/B:2.3 Use employability and job-readiness skills in internship, mentoring, shadowing, and/or other work experiences								
C/B:2.4 Select course work related to career interests								
C/B:2.5 Maintain a career -planning portfolio								

DOMAIN C: CAREER DEVELOPMENT

	Standard C: Students will understand the relationship between personal qualities, education, training, and the world of work.	SMALL GROUP							
		Anger	**Behavior**	**Cancer**	**Friendship**	**Grief/Loss**	**Self Esteem**	**Study Skills**	**Lunch Bunch**
Competency C:1 Acquire Knowledge To Achieve Career Goals									
Indicators	C/C:1.1 Understand the relationship between educational achievement and career success								X
Indicators	C/C:1.2 Explain how work can help one achieve personal success and satisfaction						X		X
Indicators	C/C:1.3 Identify personal preference and interests that influence career choices and success				X		X		X
Indicators	C/C:1.4 Understand that the changing workplace requires lifelong learning and acquiring new skills								
Indicators	C/C:1.5 Describe the effect of work on lifestyles								
Indicators	C/C:1.6 Understand the importance of equity and access in career choice								
Indicators	C/C:1.7 Understand that work is an important and satisfying means of personal expression								
Competency C:2 Apply Skills To Achieve Career Goals									
Indicators	C/C:2.1 Demonstrate how interests, abilities, and achievement relate to personal, social, educational, and career goals.		X		X		X		X
Indicators	C/C:2.2 Learn to use conflict-management skills with peers and adults	X	X	X	X				
Indicators	C/C:2.3 Learn to work cooperatively with others as a team member	X	X	X	X			X	X
Indicators	C/C:2.4 Apply academic and employment-readiness skills in work-based learning situations such as internships, shadowing, and/or mentoring experiences								

DOMAIN PS: PERSONAL/SOCIAL DEVELOPMENT

Standard A: Students will acquire knowledge, attitudes, and interpersonal skills to help them understand and respect self and others		SMALL GROUP							
		Anger	Behavior	Cancer	Friendship	Grief/Loss	Self Esteem	Study Skills	Lunch Bunch
Competency A:1 Acquire Self-Knowledge									
Indicators	PS/A:1.1 Develop a positive attitude toward self as a unique and worthy person	X	X	X	X	X	X		X
	PS/A:1.2 Identify values, attitudes, and beliefs	X	X	X	X	X	X		X
	PS/A:1.3 Learn the goal-setting process		X		X		X	X	
	PS/A:1.4 Understand change as a part of growth			X	X	X	X		
	PS/A:1.5 Identify and express feelings	X	X	X	X	X	X		X
	PS/A:1.6 Distinguish between appropriate and inappropriate behaviors	X	X	X	X			X	
	PS/A:1.7 Recognize personal boundaries, rights, and privacy needs	X	X		X	X	X		
	PS/A:1.8 Understand the need for self-control and how to practice it	X	X		X			X	
	PS/A:1.9 Demonstrate cooperative behavior in groups	X	X	X	X	X	X	X	X
	PS/A:1.10 Identify personal strengths and assets		X	X	X	X	X		
	PS/A:1.11 Identify and discuss changing personal and social roles			X	X	X	X		
	PS/A:1.12 Identify and recognize changing family roles			X		X			
Competency A:2 Acquire Interpersonal Skills									
Indicators	PS/A:2.1 Recognize that everyone has rights and responsibilities	X	X	X	X	X	X	X	X
	PS/A:2.2 Respect alternative points of view	X	X	X	X				X
	PS/A:2.3 Recognize, accept, respect, and appreciate individual differences	X	X		X		X		X
	PS/A:2.4 Recognize, accept, and appreciate ethnic and cultural diversity	X	X		X		X		X
	PS/A:2.5 Recognize and respect differences in various family configurations	X	X	X	X	X	X		X
	PS/A:2.6 Use effective communication skills	X	X	X	X	X	X	X	X
	PS/A:2.7 Know that communication involves speaking, listening, and nonverbal behavior	X	X	X	X	X	X	X	X
	PS/A:2.8 Learn to make and keep friends				X		X		X

DOMAIN PS: PERSONAL/SOCIAL DEVELOPMENT

Standard B: Students will make decisions, set goals, and take necessary action to achieve goals.	**SMALL GROUP**							
	Anger	**Behavior**	**Cancer**	**Friendship**	**Grief/Loss**	**Self Esteem**	**Study Skills**	**Lunch Bunch**
Competency B:1 Self-Knowledge Applications								
Indicators								
PS/B:1.1 Use a decision-making and problem-solving model	X	X				X	X	
PS/B:1.2 Understand consequences of decisions and choices	X	X		X			X	
PS/B:1.3 Identify alternative solutions to a problem	X	X		X			X	
PS/B:1.4 Develop effective coping skills for dealing with problems	X	X	X	X	X	X	X	
PS/B:1.5 Demonstrate when, where, and how to seek help for solving problems and making decisions	X	X	X	X	X		X	
PS/B:1.6 Know how to apply conflict-resolution skills	X	X		X				
PS/B:1.7 Demonstrate respect and appreciation for individual and cultural differences								X
PS/B:1.8 Know when peer pressure is influencing a decision								
PS/B:1.9 Identify long- and short-term goals	X	X					X	X
PS/B:1.10 Identify alternative ways of achieving goals	X	X					X	
PS/B:1.11 Use persistence and perseverance in acquiring knowledge and skills								
PS/B:1.12 Develop an action plan to set and achieve realistic goals								

DOMAIN PS: PERSONAL/SOCIAL DEVELOPMENT

Standard C: Students will understand safety and survival skills.		SMALL GROUP							
		Anger	**Behavior**	**Cancer**	**Friendship**	**Grief/Loss**	**Self Esteem**	**Study Skills**	**Lunch Bunch**
Competency C:1 Acquire Personal Safety Skills									
Indicators	PS/C:1.1 Demonstrate knowledge of personal information (i.e., telephone #, home address, emergency contact)								
	PS/C:1.2 Learn about the relationship between rules, laws, safety, and the protection of an individual's rights								
	PS/C:1.3 Learn the difference between appropriate and inappropriate physical contact	X	X						
	PS/C:1.4 Demonstrate the ability to assert boundaries, rights, and personal privacy	X	X	X	X	X	X		
	PS/C:1.5 Differentiate between situations requiring peer support and situations requiring adult or professional help	X	X		X	X			
	PS/C:1.6 Identify resource people in the school and community and know how to seek their help	X	X	X	X	X	X	X	
	PS/C:1.7 Apply effective problem-solving and decision-making skills to make safe and healthy choices								
	PS/C:1.8 Learn about the emotional and physical dangers of substance use and abuse								
	PS/C:1.9 Learn how to cope with peer pressure	X	X						
	PS/C:1.10 Learn techniques for managing stress and conflict	X	X	X		X			
	PS/C:1.11 Learn coping skills for managing life events	X	X	X	X	X			

Dear Parent,

I am inviting your child, ______________________________________,
to participate in a small group experience with me. This group will be an opportunity for your student to learn various skills and discuss shared concerns with other children. We will meet five to twelve times, depending on scheduling availability. Each meeting will last approximately 30 minutes and will occur during the regular school day. Groups are scheduled to avoid pulling a student from reading or math classes, lunch, or special programs.

Please sign below and indicate your preference for your student's participation. No student will be included without parental permission.

I am looking forward to working with your student. Please feel free to contact me if you have any questions or concerns.

Sincerely,

_______________________, Counselor

Group Title: ____

Student's Name: ________________________ Homeroom: _______

Please check one:

☐ **Yes**, my child may participate in the group with the counselor.

☐ **No**, my child may not participate in the group with the counselor.

Parent's signature: ______________________ Date: _____________

Due to Counselor by: ____________________

SUMMARY OF SMALL-GROUP ACTIVITIES
INFORMATION FROM THE COUNSELOR FOR PARENTS

STUDENT'S NAME: ______________________________

DATE: ______________________________

GROUP TOPIC: ______________________________

Your child's school counselor met_____ times with students for small-group sessions. The group was conducted as a discussion of a selected topic with one related activity. The activities and topics for discussion are identified below.

Session 1 **Date:** ____________________
Discussion Topic: Getting Acquainted, Purpose of Group, ____________________
Activity: ____________________

Session 2 **Date:** ____________________
Discussion Topic: ____________________
Activity: ____________________

Session 3 **Date:** ____________________
Discussion Topic: ____________________
Activity: ____________________

Session 4 **Date:** ____________________
Discussion Topic: ____________________
Activity: ____________________

Session 5 **Date:** ____________________
Discussion Topic: ____________________
Activity: ____________________

Session 6 **Date:** ____________________
Discussion Topic: ____________________
Activity: ____________________

Session 7 **Date:** ____________________
Discussion Topic: ____________________
Activity: ____________________

Session 8 **Date:** ____________________
Discussion Topic: ____________________
Activity: ____________________

Session 9 **Date:** ____________________
Discussion Topic: ____________________
Activity: ____________________

Session 10 **Date:** ____________________
Discussion Topic: ____________________
Activity: ____________________

Session 11 **Date:** ____________________
Discussion Topic: ____________________
Activity: ____________________

Session 12 **Date:** ____________________
Discussion Topic: ____________________
Activity: ____________________